SOUTH FROM TOULOUSE

South from Toulouse

ANDREW SHIRLEY

1960

CHATTO & WINDUS

LONDON

Published by
Chatto & Windus Ltd
42 William IV Street
London WC2

*

Clarke, Irwin & Co Ltd
Toronto

Printed in Great Britain by
Butler & Tanner Ltd
Frome and London

Contents

(There is a simple map on p. 8)

List of Illustrations

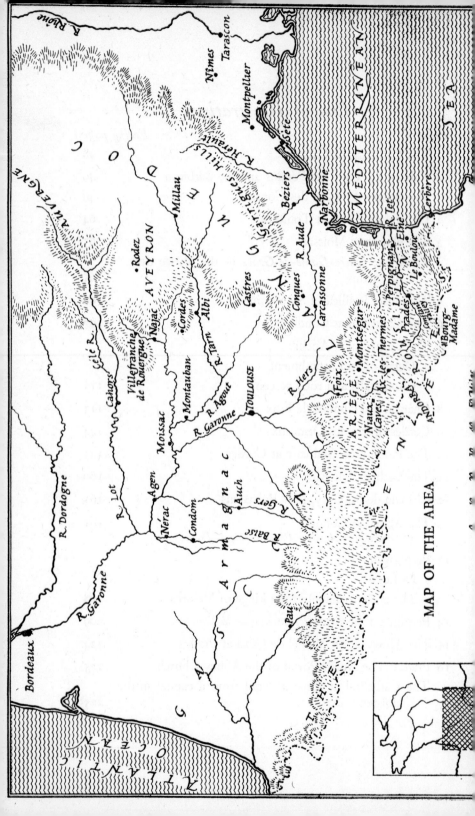

MAP OF THE AREA

Introductory—On Deviation

'ALITTLE off the road, over against the Silver Mine, stood Demas (gentlemanlike) to call to passengers to come and see; who said to Christian and his fellows, Ho, turn aside hither and I will show you a thing.'

I suppose it was the word 'gentlemanlike', with all its suggestion of glossy salesmanship, which stuck this phrase into my mind in very early years. It was the family practice for the children to lie down in the drawing room for half an hour after lunch, while my mother read to us, which she did very well. It was a lovely room, designed by my architect father. The light fell in from the south and east, diffused by the foliage or branches of a tall acacia, a varied light falling warmly or harshly according to season on to the walls, which I do not remember as anything but a mild olive green. Plain paint was a novelty in the early days of the century. It was a room with plenty of recession. In one corner to the right of the fireplace stood a regency table with a magic Turkish clock above, which told you the time by the signs of the Zodiac, when a rarely visiting cousin had persuaded it to go for a few weeks; an oriental and frequently timeless clock. Opposite were two tall windows with hard, William-Morrisy window-seats, which made better shelters than the table for a recumbent child, as you were protected from the heat of the fire by the central sofa. The width of them proves to me that I must have been quite small when I first graduated for these post-prandial sessions.

I was the youngest child, younger by nine years than the eldest; so what I listened to at first passed well over my head. But my mother's reading voice had a May sun quality to it—so light and fresh—that the sequence of the sounds captivated me and introduced me without my knowing it to a pleasure that has never left me, the sound of English words. As the words began to make sense, phrases began to settle into my mind:

'And he fell with a crash in the dust and his armour rattled upon him.'

'So Arthur killed Flollo, the Roman governor.'

'Pity it was to see such worthy knights go singing to their death': and also Demas, as we have seen, begging me to turn aside.

So I was launched upon the world with the slightly unpractical backgrounds of Homer, Renaud of Montauban, Bunyan, with a dewdrop of Malory thrown in. But all four encouraged me to travel. Renaud himself had vagrancy forced upon him by the changes and chances of his struggle against Charlemagne. I still have my copy of Robert Steele's abridgment of Caxton's translation, illustrated by Fred Mason in the manner of Walter Crane, to whom the book was dedicated. At long last I have been to the Montauban which may perhaps have been Renaud's home town, by accepting Demas's invitation to turn aside, an invitation for which I have a higher regard than Bunyan meant me to.

Indeed I make this same invitation (gentlemanlike) to those who drive down to the Costa Brava. Turn aside. You will have to spend a night or two on your way south, and it will cost you little in time and kilometres to see and eat at a few of the places with which this book is concerned. There are, after all, only three passes (except for the smugglers who seldom use cars) through the Eastern Pyrenees. On a single holiday you could use two of them and find a double choice of deviation. The pass of Bourg-Madame, the most westerly, has the best scenery of the three. Originally the place was called La Guingette, which means 'a place of refreshment (with music and dancing)', far more suitable to it than its present name, puffed up as fat as a pouter pigeon to commemorate the re-entry into France in 1815 of Louis XVIII's sister, the Duchesse d'Angoulême. Next to the east is the fastest of the three, Le Perthus, the pass which Hannibal used. I think the road must be of fairly recent construction, since older maps spit scorn on its quality as barely suitable for cars. The valley which leads you to it is full of smiles. Almost at the sea's edge is Perpignan, the ancient capital of the kings of Majorca, from which the oldest road for serious traffic, the Via Domitia, twists its way along the high-crest coast-line, dipping and rising unmercifully, without detouring the folded hills, until it comes steeply down to the frontier towns of Cerbère and Port Bou.

These three passes form the southern base of the triangle of France which this book describes. In choice of towns and monuments it is confessedly arbitrary. I have been to places because they sounded interesting or attractive. Naturally there were disappointments but—little Spartan that I am—I have kept them to myself; there is no point in describing what one has not enjoyed, which is quite a different thing from describing something one has hated.

I have been little more consistent about geography (in so far as it concerns the exact delimitations of old regime provinces) than about history. I can more or less justify my Eastern frontier, which stops at the Languedoc possessions of the old Comtes de Toulouse and carries down to the coast near Montpellier, where you enter the old Spanish domains of the kings of Aragon or Majorca. Montpellier was sold to France by the last king of Majorca, whose capital had been Perpignan. From Montpellier you travel one of the oldest invasion routes—east to west or west to east—in Europe to Perpignan and the key roads lead to Spain. But on the western side, you might almost say I couldn't read my maps. At least, I stuck mainly to the lands of the Comte of Toulouse and one of his major vassals, the Comte de Foix. I hope I shall not be unduly scolded for visiting the Armagnac country in Gascony, where they make the noblest liqueur after Cognac, or for peeping into a neighbouring château, Nérac, where Henri IV held his court.

Historically, I have found myself much more mediaeval than I had expected. The reason for this, I think, is that the aftermath of the sixteenth-century wars hit this mainly Huguenot part of France in an unexpected way. After the religious toleration promised by Henri IV, their own king of France and Navarre, in the Edict of Nantes, his son and grandson, Louis XIII and XIV, changed their policies to a physical suppression of the

Huguenots by the '*dragonnades*', the billeting of troops on Huguenot houses, fully licensed to use any means they chose—and not the tenderest—to change their victims' religion. This is a shameful episode in French history, which combined with the drift to Versailles destroyed the natural country culture of great houses. The lesser nobility stayed on, later hung on; today, I was told by the librarian of Auch, they are mostly ruined. 'The old Duke, who set them too high a standard in the nineteenth century, did it,' he added darkly; but I could not extract the Duke's name from him. So the architecture you see dating later than 1600 tends to take the form of civic and bourgeois buildings, rather than noble châteaux.

*   *   *

It is a highly individual part of France, and this is not surprising when one considers how it is placed and how the rivers run. The controlling feature is the volcanic central mass of France, the Puy de Dôme and Cantale, those mountains of Auvergne with the high spines of hills running off to the west. From early times the Auvergne has been a sparsely populated area, impenetrable if not hostile to the passage of the trade which by-passed these inhospitable hills to fertilise northern and western France. So on the east side the merchants followed the Rhone valley. On the west, our side, rivers tear their way down in flood from the high mountains in valleys running east to west. Some like the Tarn are caught into the long course of the Garonne, which flows north through most of our country till it sets the pattern for the rest, turning majestically westwards towards the Atlantic. Many of them sink their individualities in the great Dordogne, which in turn meets King Garonne in his westerly course.

The consequence of the mountain and river plan is that this part of France is boxed away by the *Massif Central* to its east and north-east, while its northern frontier is sealed off by the rivers and its southern front by the Pyrenees. Only the south-east corner is open to trade in goods and ideas from the Mediterranean, and this was truer of the past than the present. Perhaps because of this isolation this land is the home of most ancient dwellings—in caves—of mankind, who found for their days such provision of water above and below ground, of game for subsistence above that they, like the men of Les Eyzies and Lascaux, found leisure for the arts. These same caves have served refugees constantly throughout historical times, even down to our own day; for at any time in the Pyrenees we may be walking the courageous path of an escape route into Spain during the days of the last war.

For centuries the men of this area of France have lived to themselves. You could only call their mood secessionist, if you were convinced that they even recognised the existence of the rest of France; and this is doubtful. Their worst troubles always came to them from the south and east in early times. Over the passes from Spain or along the Mediterranean coast wandered in their season Visigoths, Saracens and Moors seeking the richer vines of the north. The Frenchmen to the east, towards Marseilles, already had their hands full dealing with the raiding ships which attacked their coasts, and had no time to spare for the relief of the men of the Garonne. So, too, the men to the north in Poitou heard no news, or preferred not to hear it, of invasions in the south, until they themselves were touched. Their horns withdrawn into their shell, they gave no help to the tribes south of the Dordogne, who in the dark ages lived no more than a pent-up martyrdom.

*　　*　　*

This ancient separatism is particularly well illustrated by the old Romance of Renaud of Montauban, the sort of thing that is well out of fashion today, though very much *à la mode* in Pre-Raphaelite times. People say that the story is corny. Well, how should it be otherwise, seeing that it was codified about six hundred years ago? True, you have your stock characters, which then no doubt were lively characters and still exist today. Charlemagne —grossly misrepresented from the historical point of view— appears in the story as a carpet-eating, table-gnawing Hitler or, if you prefer it, a tycoon, or even a feudal overlord. He has his councillors, the Twelve Peers of France, among whom one finds diversity of character. There is Duke Naymes of Bavaria, shrewd and smooth, the only one apart from his cousin Archbishop Turpin who could talk Charlemagne out of one of his hot fits; there was Ogier the Dane, as honest as Duke Naymes, but much blunter, cousin to Duke Naymes equally and to Duke Aymon of Dordonne, the father of Renaud and his three brothers, against whom Charlemagne was to wage war for fifteen years. Aymon is the weak man of the story, always backing a right fidelity at the wrong moment and passionately putting the blame on the other parties. Then, of course, there is the rival court faction, a totally different set of families, Ganelon, Fulkes de Morillon and others, who would stop at no low action to curry favour with Charlemagne and to finish Duke Aymon's sons by any treacherous method. And there is the angry man, Aymon's brother, Duke Beuves, who starts the tale off smartly by killing Charlemagne's son.

Even the Duke Aymon faction agrees that this is not etiquette, and supports the king against their kinsman—an important criterion of relationship value in feudal times, when the king could seldom be sure whether he or the cousin came first. Charlemagne knights Renaud and his three brothers and holds them high in favour—and then comes one of those little accidents, which are so hard to explain. For Renaud is our hero, a mighty man physically and of unimpugnable honour; and he is accused of cheating at the Charlemagne Court Chess Club.

It had been a long game against little Berthelot, the king's nephew, who had asked Renaud to play, when suddenly up starts the boy, 'calls Renaud a foul name' and smites him 'on the visage so that the blood falls to the ground'. There is no time to call the club secretary, so Renaud picks up the golden chessboard, slugs little Berthelot over the head with it and kills him.

After that the story gallops away past every kind of escape story known to the Middle Ages (and they knew many) and past many battle-pieces. Success depended as often as not on the immense virility of Renaud's horse, Bayard, who thought nothing of swimming the Loire or of leaping high obstacles with four knights in full armour on his back. So Renaud escaped, thanks to

Bayard, from Paris, built a castle, Montfort in the Ardennes, where he lived in happy rapine till Charlemagne found it and smoked him out of it. On his retreat, his father pursued him hotly and destroyed almost his whole force, and would have thought nothing of killing his four sons and his nephew Maugis in deference to his oath of fealty.

The tempo of the story drops as Renaud and his brothers run out of food, find no one worth plundering, and are reduced to eating roots and so forth. Without striking originality, they decide to go back to their mother at Dordonne, who sees to her sons and nephew, gives them a much needed bath 'perfumed with herbs' and has them nobly served with food.

Just then the Duke comes in from hawking.

'Wretches,' he cries (for this is his regular mode of address to his offspring). The ensuing dialogue between him and his wife is indeed corny, but at least he has the sense to spend the night at another castle for an alibi, while Mother fixes the boys up with a lot of coin and convertible jewellery and a thousand knights, ready to go off to serve King Yon of Gascony.

*   *   *

Of Gascony—where lies Montauban. Here we get back to history, or something near it. We must leave half-told the enchanting Renaud story, perhaps allowing ourselves a last glimpse of Bayard, relying on him, as Renaud continually did, to make a point clear. Actually it is the best racing story in the book, though its theme (dyeing the horse white with a magic herb and hobbling him) would not satisfy the Stewards of the Jockey Club. But what concerns us is a point of dialect. As cousin Maugis, accompanied by the disguised Bayard and the disguised Renaud, approached Paris for the great race (which naturally Bayard wins, Renaud up), he was challenged by the guards. And who was his retainer, they asked.

'My nephew cannot speak French,' was the reply.

Again, when Montauban is attacked by Charlemagne, the Gascons say 'The French are coming'. Even in Caxton's day Charles VII's men, like Charlemagne's men, were Franks, people who came from afar, claiming rights they did not possess, speaking a language one did not understand. And it is still true today that the further you travel south of the Dordogne, the more trouble you will have with the local dialect. It is not only a matter of accent, though that is matter enough. It is a matter of the very words in use, quite a number of which you would not find in a reasonably qualified French-English dictionary.

In fact the language apes French. No; it approaches French in much the same way as a vintage-character port approaches the genuine article which comes from the 'Factory' (as they still call it in the eighteenth-century Oporto) of, say, Cockburn, Taylor, Graham, Dow and other famous names. Though French is the background of the language, words from many other sources have crept in. Elements have been there perhaps from the time of the Phoenicians, long before Franks had poured west of the Urals. There may be undertones from the Greeks, who were operative along this coast from early times; certainly there are recollections of the Latin tongue and, nearer the Pyrenees, infusions of hot-throated Hispano-Moresque gutturals. But as far south as Toulouse the dialect, though already nasal and staccato, is relatively easy to follow.

All these linguistic puzzles, which I am not competent to unravel for you, are the expression of history. For, after Roman times this area kept its individuality for a long while. Indeed Rousillon, the part next to the Spanish frontier on the Mediterranean, was not incorporated with France until 1659, having been until then an outpost of Catalan Spain; artistically as in language it is not yet a really French province. One must remember, too, that until the thirteenth century the court of the Counts of Toulouse was richer and more brilliant than that of the kings of France, who for the greater part of the time only ruled effectively in the Ile de France. The Counts were reckoned as royalty; indeed cadets of their house ruled at one time and another in Palermo and the clan rated as a force in Europe. Almost as vigorous, though not as powerful, were the rulers of the Comté de Foix, the town which controls the road to the Bourg-Madame Pass, a falcon's nest of a place, set on an abrupt hill which rises sharp

as a spear from the valley floor. Their territories ran up to
the frontier and embraced the strange iron-mining valleys of the
Vicdessos, where mediaeval rules dominated the industry till
they brought it to destruction in the industrial age. Beyond it, to
the west, and beyond the limits of this book, lay the kingdom
of Navarre, England's ancient ally.

And in this distant, secluded corner of France, whose doors
opened only to the Mediterranean and Africa, was re-born an
African heresy. Perhaps it again typifies the separatism of this
region that it should have become a second western centre of
Origen's doctrine of dualism, so long maintained in the Balkans,
and three hundred years later should have been the second stronghold in France of the Huguenot heresy. What a welter of blood
flowed from these two wars of religion, which led at the end to
the complete submersion of this area in the French kingdom. The
men of the south-west had the satisfaction, at least across the
border in Navarre and Béarn, that it was their king who now
ruled France and who welcomed them to join in the games of the
older family. Scars of unrest still slash the political face of this
country. It is almost a necessary pride which leads them to think
to the left of the rest of France, and has made Toulouse with its
influx of anti-Franco Spaniards one of the strong centres of Com-
munism. As they can go no farther to the left, there is always the
chance, since Russia's shameful martyrdom of Hungary, that this
part of France will be the first to swing completely to the extreme
right.

*   *   *

As varied as the language is the landscape. The rivers have
separate characters, which their very names seem to express—
the Lot (which unreasonably is pronounced 'Lott') is middle-
aged, while the Ariège dances its way over boulders to the plain.
the Tarn is a husky fellow, who turns red with detritus after
heavy rain; the Garonne keeps up a purposeful speed. You are
seldom far removed from the sense of mountains. At the confines
of the vast, brickfield plain of Toulouse they seem as ethereal
as a far-off butterfly fanning its wings in the heat, a coloured

B

shimmer. Those between Castres and Carcassonne, to the east, are soft rock, relatively perishable, easily torn and wounded by rain and weather. Quite different are the Pyrenees, the most civilised and enjoyable mountains I have ever seen. Their valleys are no V-shaped depressions like those of the Swiss Alps. Wide and generous in soil and vines, they allow you space to see, to estimate and to admire the sharp or rounded outlines of rock serenity, which the peasant and his goat have for centuries denuded of tree life.

Lakes, caves, caverns, grottoes, rivers above and below ground, castles on high-sailing rocks, villages clinging to the hill-side—all decorate scenery which might otherwise be desolate below the high, rounded peaks and the long chines and spurs of mountain. And they preserve the humanity which seeps down with the rivers to the quieter land below as you get to the undulating country and the plains and more peaceful valleys of Gascony. There you are in oxen-country, where the ox replaces the horse as a farm instrument; and you see them like something from a Roman frieze, pulling, ploughing, straining, peaceable white or fawn-and-white beasts with their long horns and their ears shrouded from flies by reddish netting from which a tassel falls in a humble flourish.

They have neat ankles, and turn neatly at the end of each furrow. It is a special pleasure to watch them ploughing between the vines. At the end of each line the ploughman calls to his team in the sort of tone which would be gin-hoarse here but is wine-husky in Gascony and the south. And then the slow beasts turn with a deftness out of all proportion to their bulk, feel the drag of the plough ease as the man wheels it round the half-circle, and know instinctively when to take the strain once more against their deep chests. The farmers prefer them to horses in these parts and say that they are cheaper to feed, get as much done in the day, are less temperamental especially in the hot weather, and that their dung is every bit as good for the farm.

For indeed it can be hot, and the clay lands bake like bricks. At times the ground grows so hard that it needs a team of six oxen to the plough to break its surface. And then the rain, when it comes at all, comes in thunder-buckets and lies on the brick

surface in a temporary lake, breathing steam and vapour as the
sun returns to his dominion.

But this country north of the Pyrenees is by no means all plain.
It has many ideas in landscape, boastful escarpments and sharp
hills which set the roads twisting and turning to gain the summit.
And it has a fortunate geology. If you are to grow good wine
grapes, you must have plenty of lime in the soil; this has been
generously provided. As a result we find ourselves in the nectar
country of Armagnac. But if you do not believe that Demas has
something to offer other than a gold brick, you would not dream
of turning aside to a place with the cellar-dark name of Condom
to find out about it.

I

Cahors

IF you do one of the normal things and drive towards the Spanish frontier by the Limoges road (N.20), you are bound to pass through Cahors; and a very pleasant way it makes over the high waters of the Dordogne valley and the racing upland country that lies south of it. But it is also quite reasonable to slant in later from the Massif Central, turning west somewhere near Clermont Ferrand and hitting N.20 at that festive little town Brive, just north of the Dordogne crossing at Souillac. There is another choice for you at Clermont Ferrand; and if Bunyan's confidence man, Demas, were around, this is the deviation he would urge on you. Carry on a bit further south, he would say, and turn south-west over the Cantale mountains where that lovely cheese comes from. Then from N.126 you would switch to N.122 through Figeac, that semi-precious stone of picturesque antiquity, and, in no time, says Demas, 'in no time, you'll be down the Célé valley into Cahors. Scenically, it's the best approach.' And he hastily pockets his gold brick in case you should see any scratches on it.

The trouble about Demas is that there is always a good deal of truth in what he says. The approach from Figeac is beautiful, is impressive, yet it presents the calm beauty of a profile rather than the excitement of seeing your beauty from many different angles, half the art of being in love. Believe Demas at Clermont Ferrand rather than at St. Elour.

For coming into Cahors from N.20 is quite an experience. You have a moment of confusion, when two signposts point at right angles to one another, both stating 'Cahors 8'. The one pointing to the left adds, with an embarrassed cough, '*Route touristique*'. Know yourself for what you are at the moment. Turn left.

At first you may be a bit disappointed. For three or four kilo-metres the road is laced to the edge of the limestone plateau (which for reasons of dialect they call a '*Causse*' in this part of France); you see nothing of particular interest except the sort of hill-side you have been seeing for some way, and you conclude, if this is tourism, you would sooner have taken the main road. But every good plot has an introduction, and the producer of the Cahors drama has now got you tense enough to be allowed your first glimpse. Then you see the town and the reason for its existence: it is a sentinel against incursions into Gascony from the east.

Far below you, revealed by a turn in the road, still indistinct in detail, Cahors stands at the apex of a rich triangle of country, which is where the valley of the Célé joins the Lot as it makes its middle-aged way quietly and without fuss through a gap in the hills. It circles three sides of the high town in a gesture of affectionate protection. And all its valley is very green, very richly cultivated, dotted with farms and cheerful villages, bright in the sun. As the road twists down to the plain, the town's features show more definition; towers are springing above the roof landscape as you look at it—mediaeval towers. For the rest it looks a close-huddled ancient place, gashed here and there by self-assertive modern buildings like the Lycée.

You enter by a mediaeval gate, and soon on your right you come to a surprisingly large square, and as you pursue your way looking about for an hotel down the main street, you keep thinking 'I've been sold a pup after all; this place is just nineteenth century; whatever I saw from the distance will be nineteenth century, too.'

This nineteenth-century impression is emphasised by the jumble of little one storey shops on the left of the wide Boulevard Gambetta, which to tell the truth give it rather a mean air. There is, however, a decently antique explanation for them, which also introduces you to the constitution, so characteristic of this part of France, under which Cahors was governed.

By 1680, with Louis XIV making suitable epigrams, apothegms or obiter dicta on absolute monarchy, France seemed set fair for internal peace, and the present-day value of mediaeval walls was hotly questioned. In Cahors this led to a quarrel between the

bishop, to whom the town was subject, and the city council, con-
sisting of two Consuls as if Rome still ruled there and a body of
Capitouls,[1] or councillors. Behind this fringe of nineteenth-
century shops lie tall houses of the sixteenth and seventeenth century, which for purposes of defence had originally no windows
facing the open meadows within the town walls. These window-
less houses would be difficult to scale, after the main walls had
been rushed; but by 1680 they stood deprived of the amenity of
light for no practical reason. At last the civil and ecclesiastical
powers agreed that windows might be opened in the walls and
that gardens and terraces might be run out, and permission was
granted to build little garden pavilions on the allotted space, traces
of which can still be seen.

Everyone was happy, and pavilions sprouted in all shapes and
sizes of classical or of baroque design, until it was decided to
develop the rest of the old fortress meadowland. To dignify the
new town a Mairie was to be built. It is pleasantly proportioned,
neo-classical in style, and keeps politely to the alignment of the
old houses. A one-storey projection carries a terrace, and it was
this feature which dictated the present appearance of the Boulevard Gambetta and provoked a second row. In a mood like Tar-
quin's, Monsieur le Maire decapitated the taller pavilions by
ordinances of 1835, 1840 and 1843, dates, I presume, which record
stages of victory and defeat. The effect in an old lithograph is
certainly happy; but today the pleasant little garden houses have
turned shopkeeper, and a muddle of conflicting displays destroys
the planned harmony.

*   *   *

This battle of 1680 belongs not only to the pattern of old
Cahors, but is characteristic of local organisation throughout this
part of southern France. The development of the towns in France
follows quite a different line from ours, for they grew up, after the
defeat of the Romans, entirely under feudalism. With us feudalism was an import rather than a national conception; and our

---

[1] In fact these two names for magistrates and councillors have a Languedoc
and not a Latin derivation.

Norman conquerors had the sense to respect some of the Saxon customs and so to produce a legal amalgam less rigid than the French.

Each town would have one or more overlords, to whom the townsmen owed services in cash or kind; their only military obligation was the defence of their own walls. They had, of course, to pay with goods or money what amount they could compromise, but otherwise they were left relatively free to organise themselves. Whereas in England it was the king who granted a town its charter or right to hold fairs and markets, in France the central power was for centuries extremely weak. One has to think of the French king in, say, the eleventh or twelfth century as exercising no effective jurisdiction in the three principal regions to which this journey takes us—Gascony, Languedoc and Rousillon. It was the Counts of Toulouse and the Dukes of Aquitaine, the Viscomtes de Trencavelle and the Comtes de Foix who granted charters in their lands, and were paid for the grant.

Certainly in Languedoc a tradition of municipal self-government derived from Roman times, and in Cahors, Toulouse and Carcassonne the bourgeoisie maintained their rights with some success against their overlord, who never exercised so strong a control as his compeers in the north. But this did not prevent them being given away by their owners like a pint of beer, and it was by the gift of the Count of Toulouse that Cahors was made over to its bishop in 1090, when the cathedral was building. But the Count still kept an ecclesiastical control, since the bishopric itself was in his gift.

This duality of power was recognised in the ceremony of receiving a newly elected bishop. He was met at the town's bridgehead by the magistrates and leading citizens and by the local nobility as well. Within limits church and state worked in with one another and in public displayed respect for the other's dignity. And so the highest local noble, the Seigneur de Cessac, bareheaded and bare-legged, had the duty of leading the bishop's horse by its embroidered bridle from the bridge to the cathedral. After the lengthy and colourful investiture service was over (the bishop here was allowed to lay his armour and his satin slippers on the high altar) came the great feast. Here again the laity in the person of the Seigneur de Cessac abased itself before the new lord bishop, serving him with his food and wine, still in stark humility, recognising for a day the supremacy of the mitre over the sword.

But for a day only. Everyone knew the tradition, by which the bishop was expected to present to the Seigneur the richly embroidered bridle and the table service of silver-gilt in recompense for his submission. One parsimonious prelate tried to get away with it on the cheap. Feigning humility, he was served off simple pottery, and yet maintained the sweeping, episcopal gesture of the presentation. Public opinion was outraged. Everyone rose in his place, smashed his pottery plate, the adjacent jugs, any dishes that lay to hand, and off went the de Cessac to the law courts, where they estimated that the average value of the present was three thousand livres. The bishop's duties were as clearly defined in the popular mind as de Cessac's rights; and the bishop had to pay.

Then again one comes to the older story of the Bishop and the Bridge; and it must be said at once that Cahors had specialised in bridges from the earliest times. The first was Roman work, and when the water of the Lot is low you can still see the foundations in the river bed. But after about a thousand years of traffic the structure began to tire, and by 1250 the *Capitouls* decided to build a Pont Neuf—a new bridge, as it was still called when demolished without cause in 1906.

In no time there was a splendid storm in local politics. The bishop pointed out that the new bridge would ruin the revenue from his ferry, and that the project should be dropped. Who had the right to damage the revenue of Holy Church, he may well have asked, and may have added something unpleasant about interdicts, which the late Pope Innocent III had made so fashionable. Feelings ran high; no compromise could be found until one of the townsmen suggested that the Bishop of Tulle—the place whence came those silk-net scarves, so dear to Edwardian ladies —should be called to arbitrate. He lived far enough away, about eighty miles to the north, not to be dangerously biassed; and indeed this typically French case did not demand the wisdom of

Solomon for its solution. Very sensibly the Bishop of Tulle laid down that the city should levy a toll on the bridge (which, of course, had been intended all the time) and give their bishop a share as compensation for the lost returns from his pitiable ferry. This settlement was joyfully accepted by both sides as a stroke of genius. You had to go to Tulle for such Daniels as their bishop; and no doubt he and his retinue were richly feasted and nobly plied with the famous Cahors wine, before they went riding home with presents dangling from their saddle-bows.

So the 'new bridge' went forward, and a handsome thing it must have been. It carried five fortified towers, of which the central one was presented to the bishop for his garrison. One way and another it took forty years to build, and when the city's money began to dry up, the bishop saw them right financially. He was proud of the thing, and the city had it engraved on their seal. But one by one the towers must have fallen, for the photograph of 1906 shows no more than the long beautiful span of seven irregular arches. Local historians and archaeologists, the Horatii of their day, fought their battle to preserve their bridge as best they might; and they lost. But perhaps it is time I remembered that Horatius 'kept' his bridge so that it could be pulled down.

But Cahors still preserves another bridge which is worth motoring hundreds of miles to see, the Pont Valentré. You get to it from the nineteenth-century thoroughfare, Boulevard Gambetta, which I have described to you, by turning down a drab street to the right, suitably named Rue du President Wilson— the American who did so much to establish the nationalism which is finally destroying Europe—and there, suddenly, is the bridge before you. You forget all hatred for the sake of the three clamorous towers confronting you. The ground runs a little uphill to prove how strongly spring the arches of the bridge. Behind them rise high rocky hills as a backcloth; and at the foot of them there is just room for a railway, a road, and the middle-aged Lot, which must have had an impetuous youth to have channelled so deep a defile between this stiff range and the city's plateau.

'For what we have received . . .' The original conception survives, the central tower, the highest, was at once the watch tower and the garrison point, from which either end of the precious bridge could be reinforced. Drawbridge and portcullis protect the outer towers, which are slitted for archers and machicolated for the tough men in the top storey who poured down on to the attackers their unwelcome salutes of hot lime, stones, blazing or boiling oil, and an occasional liquid lead.

Nineteenth-century restorers have overlaid the proud rough stones with a slimy preservative, which fortunately is flaking off. They slipped in some bogus shelters for archers, which were not part of the original design since they did it in deference to legend. They introduced, however, one detail with which one need not quarrel overmuch. On the top of the central tower you may see the devil desperately trying to claw away the topmost stone.

When one thinks of all the things that go wrong in the world and are called in their season 'devil's work', we should consider our own character as well as his. Time and again he has been as stupid as we, as the story of the Devil of the Pont Valentré shows.

The devil was, of course, a trader in souls and to buy the soul of the architect due to start the Pont Valentré in June 1308 would have been a major coup. So the devil offered his services as a handyman in exchange for the architect's soul, and was taken on. The architect saw to it that the devil was kept really busy, and as the towers rose higher and higher, the devil's services were more and more in demand, since a winged hod-carrier clearly saved time, and there was a time-clause in the contract between the town and the architect just as there was between the architect and the devil. The tower must be finished by a certain date; if it were not, the architect's soul was forfeit.

Now the architect showed his quality. He had worked the devil to the bone—for the devil was bound to carry out his every instruction—and one stone only was left to be laid. If it were laid in time a soul would be preserved for heaven, otherwise lost to hell. Time and again the devil dislodged it, so that it fell crashing into the slow waters of the Lot; but the architect had good nerves. On the last day before contract date he gave the devil orders which he was bound to fulfil. More water was needed for mortar to lay the final stone. 'Go off and fetch it,' said the architect to the devil and, unkindly, gave him a sieve. The name of this architect who betted on a certainty has not been preserved.

*   *   *

To have built two large fortified bridges in a matter of seventy years argues a volume of traffic that spells prosperity. Now it is time to see what they did with the money they earned; and we will turn off to the left at the bottom of the Boulevard Gambetta. Here you start to work your way up from the river level through the old poorer quarter of the town, called the Badernes (the very sound of which seems to express contempt), slanting up the hill to the quarter of the Soubirous. Both these names have their origin in the old patois, Badernes deriving from the Romance word '*dernos*', meaning low quarters, and the other from the Languedoc word '*soubeiran*', used to indicate the higher ground in a town. In the centre, stands the ancient cathedral, with the old bishop's palace beside it, an oasis in a wrangle of narrow streets. As said the impeccable Arthur Young: 'Its streets are neither wide nor straight.' Nor were the money-making habits of the Cadurciens, as the men of Cahors are called. In the crusades against the heretics of Albi, a neighbouring town, Cahors took no part. But she took the financial opportunity of the devastation created by them, and lent money for usury on a large scale, a practice heavily condemned by the mediaeval church as against nature. Indeed Dante gives the citizens of Cahors a very bad notice in the *Inferno* (Canto XI), and brackets the place with Sodom, which in this picture of banking seems going too far. St. Louis drove them out of the town, out of the Place des Petites Boucheries where they conducted their nefarious practices, and they set up their money-changers tables in Westminster. Soon the English came to the experience of Languedoc. Not only the king but all the prelates were ensnared by them, until they became, says the chronicler, Matthew Paris, a scourge worse than the plague.

*   *   *

If you can allow the time, begin by wandering aimlessly through the antique ways. Let the flavour win your palate before you look at the colour of your wine. The place is full of good detail, and if you try to analyse it all at the first gulp, your judgment will be moidered. Let the congestion of antiquity take hold of you; realise how few open spaces there were, how few there are, how small are the eight *places*, how some of the streets are bridged over so that you move as it were along a pavement of black and white light. Odd, unexpected splashes of colour, pink, blue, orange, appear like exclamation marks on the houses. And all the time you are subconsciously absorbing the stuff the buildings are made of: stucco over brick, and where the stucco has flaked you see that the bricks are almost to the Roman pattern; that these narrow pink bricks are used also very prettily with timbering; that there is a lot of good timbering and many carved corbels; that stone also is abounding, great blocks of it, mostly with coarse ornament, but sometimes treated with refined skill.

As you wander aimlessly turning right or left as a perspective pleases your eye, the immense variety of style comes home to you. Here indeed is a long history of pent-up life, gradually sharpening into features.

In the Rue des Bas Fondues, in the low quarters, you will see finely carved Renaissance windows; nearby in the Rue du Tapis Vert, where once the council met, are arched mediaeval doorways. A little higher up, close to the river, is the miniature Place Ste. Urcisse and the spirited west front of its church, crowned with three small towers. In its dark interior lurk columns with strange capitals. If you turn down to the river, look out from the Quai Champollion over the little suburb of Cabessut, with its ancient grey tower partly screened by trees and its fields carpeted with the vines from which came the fierce-throated, great-hearted wines of Cahors. Vieux Cahors is not a great wine or a great type of wine in the sense that the Burgundies and Clarets can be. What they vaunt as their best, the Pelure d'Oignon (the Onion Skin), has no more real in quality than the old waiters at Stone's Chop House, dressed in their knee breeches. It is a *faux-bonhomme* of a wine, whereas the true Cahors has a certain passionate—'violence' I was going to say, but I think that brusqueness is the word. As it attacks your palate, it is completely genuine.

* * *

But what has come over this chapter? It was to deal with the old town of Cahors, but has lost its way in feudalism, in bishops, in bridges at the perimeter of the town, and finally in vineyards outside it. If we forget the wine for a moment and the alluring by-ways of history, we should now be looking to our right at one of the most remarkable buildings of the city. It is secular, and was a very grand private house indeed, said to have been (in a legendary mist) the place where Henri IV spent the night of his victory over Cahors after an eight-day siege and fighting of unparalleled ferocity. It is the Hôtel Roaldès, the palace of a local legal dynasty. Three sides are exposed to public view, a circumstance of which the architects took full advantage in making their plan. The eastern side is no great thing to boast about, beyond a pleasant arrangement of mullioned windows; it is the northern and southern aspect that are the more encouraging, for there one sees the true Renaissance instinct blossoming from the Gothic. The south front rises from a stone base to a warm brick, half-timbered wall, the half timbering taking the form of St. Andrew's crosses—a sparkling effect. Above their general level, the designer placed with a flourish a top-storey loggia, a delicious place in which to read, to make small talk, to open the first passes towards a love affair after the heat of a southern summer's day, which the river below was just beginning to cool. And beyond the river, you would be looking at the well cultivated height of Mont St. Cyr. It is a covered loggia; once the sun was westering, you would be reasonably cool. And under the stars . . .?

No half-timbering but stone, dressed and carved, is reserved for the northern front. The decoration has still the scattered generosity of Gothic, a balance by light and colour rather than by line; and yet the conception of this front is progressive. Although you get the traditional ornaments of the region—the carved roses, suns in their glory, and pleached trees—there are moments when a moulding or a low door looks forward to the Renaissance. From the architectural point of view this countryside lies away

from the main current of French taste in the early sixteenth century; and so this house which on the Loire would have been
designed about 1480, was probably built around 1510. Both Spain
and France learnt their classical idioms in Italy; and at this time
Cahors was past its age of international banking, and lay only on
the pilgrimage route to St. James of Compostella in Spain. As yet
there was no architectural news of this kind to come out of Spain.
Cahors was not entirely up-to-date.

Disengage yourself from the river and turn into the town
again, into the old square of Jacques Chapou, and there you will
find the cathedral, a surprising place. As you look to the right,
you see the massive tower, a masonry tower for refuge, only
broken high up by two Gothic windows with a frowning set of
three more above them. To the right of this is a strange tri-lobed
doorway which makes you think of Moslems, a brick vault over
it with a lovely statue and, smoothing the whole thing out, a low
dome or cupola. You have instinctively the feeling that you are
up against something pretty old, and out of sheer curiosity go
round the corner to the right to find the official entrance in the
west front.

Here the effect is totally different, and you get to wondering
who this old lady was, who had so much interest in her appearance that she was always having a new hair-style or face-lift. She
started on the job of changing her look from her 1100-ish ideas
some time in the thirteenth century, and she didn't stop there.
There should be a prize for anyone who gets the date of her rose-
window correctly: in fact it is seventeenth-century, an astonishing
anachronism. This front is not, for me, beautiful, but ugly, massive, forceful. What should have been in all conscience two
independent towers have been grafted into the main block of the
structure. It is a matriarch of a place.

Pursue your way round the outside of the cathedral, and you
will come upon the north door, a triumphant thing. The arched
entrance is set in an almost square frame, its outer flanks decorated
with pilasters between which are stripes of carved rosettes. In hot
sunlight they have the effect of jewellery, for the carving is at once
deep and broad, producing a fine dazzle of light and shade. The

doorway itself is recessed, and over it, in a shaded light, is sculptured the Ascension. One hand wide open in blessing, the other clasping a closed book, Christ rises, framed in an oval glory. Angels support his upward flight at the lower sides, while from above two others fly down in a rush of welcome from Heaven— one of the most marvellous renderings of movement I have seen from the thirteenth century. Below him are ranged the Apostles, grouped in pairs beneath tri-lobed arcades. Some have said that the upper pair of angels are bearing the message of the Ascension to the Apostles; but it seems to me still that their flight—for they seem ascending from a dive to an upward curve—is not that of purposeful messengers but one of salutation.

The outside of the choir makes better sense after one has seen the interior, so let us take ourselves back to the west door and go in. If you come directly across the Place Jacques Chapou and enter as I did on my first visit, you will be totally unprepared for what you see inside, as the two domes are concealed from you. First of all you must descend seventeen steps to reach the level of the nave floor, but you are arrested at the top step by two pools of light below you. You look up, and see two flat domes which might have come out of the Middle East; for they are constructed in the Byzantine manner. The wide, long nave endorses this impression.

And somehow it is at this moment that one begins to analyse the feeling of strangeness of which one has inwardly been conscious all this time. This cathedral is Eastern in conception. Some say that its architect must have been to Cyprus; and this could well be so, though I do not myself recall anything there which would serve directly as an archetype. The men of Cahors were traders; their city lay on one of the great spice routes through France. Travellers and pilgrims to the Holy Places of Jerusalem would pass and re-pass their way and tell the tales of what they had seen. Yet my personal feeling, which I cannot back with scholarship, is that this place, so individual among the Romanesque churches of this region, represents the direct experience of a single architect. Whoever built it had been to the Middle East, perhaps to Jerusalem.

Recovering from this architectural shock, you begin to look about, to find that the twin lights from the domes (one of which was frescoed in the fourteenth century with the Martyrdom of St. Stephen) throw the Gothic choir into shadow, so that for once the High Altar is not as dominant as one would expect. Before its reconstruction in the fourteenth century, the chancel would have been apsidal, and indeed two of the minor apses remain, treated as chapels; and very delightful they are. There is a good deal of detail interest around you in monuments, heraldry, iron-work, and a remarkable fourteenth-century Virgin of the Litanies. I wanted to see the treasury as well, of which I had read some-where long before; and this involved chasing the sacristan, who I was told might be in the cloister. He was not there, but I found instead a most alarming old dame, dealing with a nice young man and his wife.

'I am looking for a priest,' I heard him say, 'to give my friend the Sacrament. He's dangerously ill in the hospital.'

'There's no one,' said the four-square woman.

'What? No one in the cathedral?'

'No one.'

'Anyone at the seminary?'

'Don't know.'

'Well, might there be?'

'Don't know.'

'You would perhaps be kind enough to tell me where is the seminary?' said the young man, by now getting tensely agitated and emphasising by his good manners the degree of his friend's illness.

To use words to describe the route would have been a sense-less waste of such treasurable things; so she did it in mime. It required both her hands to illustrate the turnings, and involved the use of a version of the breast stroke, which I took to indicate a long stretch of straight road. By the time she had repeated her mime three times, I believe I could have found the way there myself.

Then it was my turn, and I did not rate my chances of finding the sacristan with her help very high. I was right.

'The cathedral,' she said. Not even '*In* the cathedral'—
that would have wasted a word, and one must 'practise the
economies'.

So back I went on another, equally frustrating search for the
sacristan, and returned to find Old Four-square deep in conversation with a thin, fresh-faced type, who wore a merry eye, a beret
and a drooping cigarette. Now, after her economies, she could
spend. It was a technical conversation, too; all about funerals,
baptisms and first communions. He was disturbed not to have
seen her at Monsieur X's funeral. A splendid affair that had been;
eight carriages. There were quite a surprising number of obstacles
which had prevented her attending, each of which was described
with loving care.

'The sacristan is not in the cathedral,' I slipped in at last. 'Is this
gentleman he?'

'No.' And she turned to first communions forthcoming.

I fidgeted quite blatantly, until I succeeded in gaining the
attention of the merry eye. He found me the sacristan and so
enabled me to tell you about the treasury. It took him a minute
and a quarter.

Led by the sacristan, I advanced upon the vaulted chapter house
which alone is worth seeing. The treasure was small but mediaeval, a bishop's ring or two, a little enamel and so on. The prize
of the group is the Crosier of Bishop Pons d'Antejac (1235–6).
Made of gilt bronze and set with turquoise and other semi-
precious stones, the crook contains two beautiful plaques, one of
the Annunciation, the other of the Incontro, which is singularly
moving. The staff is plated with silver, on which are chased
serpents devouring one another; again almost an oriental
effect.

Then I returned to the cloister, the quality of which had
impressed me while I was awaiting the good pleasure of Old
Four-square. It is a flamboyant thing both in the ordinary and in
the architectural sense, for the vaulting follows broken lines and
is almost too clever. There is a great deal of rich ornament over
the two ogee doors which lead from the cathedral, and much subsidiary sculpture on the inner side of the northern arcade. Samson

c

and Delilah, bears, lions and other less plausible beasts are displayed for your pleasure. In time you pass from this animal kingdom, and the ornament changes to elaborate canopies designed
to hold saints and martyrs. The statues were never completed; but
even so the splendour of the canopies contrasts well with a certain
severity in the buttresses, which in turn blend finely with the style
of the main building. For it is from here you get the best view
of the stark west tower and the finest impression of the choir with
its tall windows and double tiers of traceried balconies. The
flying buttresses, which farther north would prop this great
height, are treated here as stabilising projections of solid stone,
a method common in this area.

A third door leads off from the cloister, again with lavish carving over it, and takes you into the courtyard of the Archdeacon's
House. This is a dazzling, early Renaissance house, all gaiety, all
wit without self-conscious polish. I can't put my finger on the
essence of its welcoming charm, nor by what feature it is created.
I did go up to the first floor unobserved; but it is not a worthwhile
enterprise, apart from the fact that it is private and I had been
guilty of illegal entry. I came down, however, still with the feeling
that the creator of the place must have been a wonderful host,
who put everyone at his ease and made them talk their best. And
yet, when you detect its façade in the street, simple to the point
of austerity, you almost feel you have caught out someone leading
a double life.

You are thinking, perhaps, of re-joining the Rue Nationale, the
principal north and south street of the old town, just as the Gambetta is for the new: but as you look vaguely to the right coming
out of the cathedral you see a tremendous seventeenth-century
building. A central mass two storeys high, crowned by a rounded
pediment and flanked by recessed blocks, lies at the end of a deep
courtyard, which is defined by other buildings projecting and
receding in such due order that you have the impression of a
complicated military manœuvre frozen. The troops were so
beautifully trained that each man stopped at the word of command in his exact position; and so fine was their array that the
general left them there forever.

The 'general' was, of course, the bishop or the architect who designed his palace. I have heard people quarrel over the state in which bishops used to live; but I never found one who would tell me where else the episcopal offices were to be for dealing with rents from town and country, the ecclesiastical and civil legal departments, the accountancy department, and all the other necessary trimmings of administration. 'Couldn't a bishop have a room for his stationery?' one might almost ask in the tone of the third Duke of Buckingham, who, when requested to econ-omise on a pastry chef, replied: 'Can't a gentleman have a biscuit with his wine?' Besides all this, hospitality was still a duty of the Church in those days. Nowadays in England, and no doubt in France too, some of these mundane problems have been central-ised by such bodies as ecclesiastical commissioners; the same extent of bishop-space is no longer necessary, and in anti-clerical France the government has snapped up their buildings. The old palace, well-ordered, well-proportioned, dignified, is now the Préfecture. It still looks efficient.

Beside it runs the Rue de la Daurade, an ancient street with windows dating from the thirteenth century, which leads you to a space you can hardly dignify with the word square, though it is now the Place de la Libération, having once been the 'Petites Boucheries', the usurers' den. On one corner is a lovely mediaeval and Renaissance house, where once the poet of a slim eclogue talent, Olivier de Magny, lived. While Gambetta, escaping from the siege of Paris in his 1870 balloon, is typical of the fighting Cadurcien, de Magny, Fénélon the quietist, and Clément Marot, poet and literary critic, seem rather to have contemplated the pace of their river Lot. But we will continue our way northwards through the Soubirous towards the only relic of the University which taught them all.

*   *   *

But no! This is France and we have neither eaten nor slept since we arrived and started looking for a hotel in the Boulevard Gambetta. I cannot pretend to be completely informative on this subject, but I have been very lucky in food twice and have returned to the same hotel, the Eskualduna. This is a very un-French-sounding name, you may think. In fact it is not a French word at all, but Basque; and it is the Basque word for 'Basque'. For that is Monsieur's nationality, while Madame is *de la région*. Their joint knowledge provides you with some remarkable food for 450–600 francs. Madame's *coupe d'oie*, her private paté, gets you off to a very good start; if you have a lucky day, you may have *poulet aux girolles* as well. And '*girolles*' are according to the unexcitable dictionary 'a kind of edible yellow fungus'. It is accurate on 'edible' and, no doubt, on 'kind' but surely there is some word omitted which might otherwise encourage you to ask for, to seek for this delicious flavour, as precious as the Alpine mushroom, *morille*.

Madame will tell you about the tobacco trade in these parts, too; and tobacco-growing is one of the things I never think much about in France. One should do so, says Madame, since it is the most profitable thing to do. It only takes three months to mature as a crop from the time you put it into the ground; but it requires a great deal of fertiliser and plenty of cultivation. You should not leave more than nine, preferably seven leaves on a plant, and you take your gamble on a September harvest. The cold September dews will drill holes in the leaves and lower their quality, so the cautious farmer harvests early. He sells them by the 'manoc' to the government factory, a practical, old-fashioned measure. You have cut the leaves and dried them in your barn, and you put twenty-four together, twisting a twenty-fifth round them for packaging. That is your manoc. If you are a farmer's daughter, as Madame was, you then work the winter through in the snuff factory at pleasant wages as a pleasant change. It makes a profitable life.

If you don't like these ideas, then you could try for food at La Taverne, whose owner is Monsieur Escorbiac. I do not think he would ever fail you. And let me say that when I am writing about food, I am writing about the sort of thing the average tourist (which is all I am) can afford now and again. If by having picnic lunch, bought in the market, you have saved up for something special here is a man who will not cook you dishonest food with a lot of long names.

He is a member of the 'Docte Collège des Frères en Gueule'— the learned 'College of Brothers by Palate', is the nearest translation I can think of. And this is not something like our Wine and Food Society, to which one can belong by payment; you have to be approved and elected by your professional competitors. This must be a stiff test. Apart from any other risk, each elected member gives a dinner in rotation; and no professional chef would care to have his dinner provided by an indifferent cook.

There is an element of what Stevenson used to call 'mediaeval tushery' about the organisation, which came to me as a surprise in France. For example, the Fraternity wear mediaeval hats and cloaks and have devised a coat of arms. I cannot blazon it adequately, since occasionally, I am sorry to say, you find metal on metal, an insidious heraldic disease. But one could call it something like this:

On a field *vert*, within a bordier of chain, *or*, between two hanaps of the same a knife and fork in saltire, *argent*, manched *azure* and surcharged three fleur-de-lis of the second. In chief, a chef's hat proper; in base, a dinner bell of the third, langued of the first.

Motto: Frères en Gueule.

The fraternity has the sound idea of making even council meetings an excuse for a banquet. If the master of the feast is wise, he will tell his mayor and council that in giving it he will make known the choice products of the district; there is always a good chance of a grant in aid, since the French believe in this form of publicity. Monsieur Escorbiac told me that he was successful. This is the feast he laid on for his brethren, which he called 'the marriage feast of the trufle to the wine of Cahors'.

Les Délices de foie gras aux diamants noirs
Le Blanc de Blanc 'Chantrerie'

Les Grives de Limogne au genièvre
Le Rosé de Quercy

La fricassée de cèpes Thédirac
Le Cahors nouveau

Le Porcelet farci à la Quercynoise
rôti devant la braise de sarments
accompagné de Marrons
Le Château de Camy 1947 en magnum

Les Cœurs de laitue à l'huile de noix

Les petits Rocamadours

Le Parfait aux perles noires pralinées
Les Mignardises cadurciennes
Le Corbeille de fruits de la vallée du Lot
Champagne Deutz 1949 au magnum

Le Café Valentré
Armagnac Réserve due Domaine Latapie 1914
La Vieille Prune
La Crême de Noix
La Fine Champagne Salignac

I think I should have died well before the end of this divine
sequence of flavours. It is one of the consequences of war-time
rationing that my stomach has expanded outwardly but not
inwardly, and I cannot (I believe this goes for other Englishmen)
eat as I did in the days when peace was peace. Grives de Limogne
are thrushes; I don't know them cooked in juniper berries; but I
have met them locally in other forms twice as we shall see.
Neither have I personally experienced this special dish of suck-
ing-pig, cooked over vine-twigs; but I have since tried pork with
chestnuts at home, and the two flavours combine like Castor and
Pollux. Then, imagine an ice flavoured with truffles—'black
pearls', how tender a name for them—and almonds burnt in
sugar. The walnut ice and the brown-bread ice we used to have
at Winchester gave perhaps the same brisk contrast of texture.
Otherwise in this happy part of France, where they are native,
I met the beautiful things I have listed for you. Only the unadven-
turous, the sadly ulcerated, or those to whom food has only calory
content would not make a day's journey for a part of this
experience.

*   *   *

The northern part of the old town, the Soubirous, specialises, one might almost say, in towers. There are ancient fortified towers along the cliff where the walls used to run above the river; there are church towers; the tower of the Barbican by which you entered the town, with the sinister-named *Tour des Pendus*, the Tower of the Hanged, beside it; the Tour Pélegri, sole survivor from the ancient university of Cahors.

Pope John XXII never forgot that Cahors was his native city; nor indeed is he forgotten there, for one of the most splendid towers is christened after him, though it was built by his brother to whom he had given the bishopric. It is dramatic; below the fierce battlements (nineteenth-century) are four great windows, while in the floors below the windows are placed in pairs diagonally from left to right; in bright sun this dark stripe of windows is quite astonishing. But even if he did not build the tower, he did found the university which specialised in civil and canon law as well as medicine, and at one time was among the best in Europe. It was suppressed in 1751; and now the tower of the hostel for poor students founded by this Canon Pélegri in 1368, who became a papal nuncio and negotiated a truce between England and France, is the sole memorial to the ages of learning. Its twisting staircase is a lesson in intelligence.

Here it was that Clément Marot, a poet unjustly forgotten by us, received his first steps in education; and it is odd to be reminded in this way that to a Cadurcien in the sixteenth century true French was still a foreign language, which had to be learnt. Indeed some critics attribute Marot's most delicate sense of language to this very fact—he never lost the wonder at the flexibility and jewelled clarity of this foreign language he had mastered. It was not always second nature to him, but remained as it were a treasure brought from afar which had to be carefully considered before it was expended.

This was about all the consideration he gave to the world or to the consequences which might flow from his words or actions. His father had been *valet-de-chambre* to the king, and when he died in 1526, the post passed on to Clément, already too well known for his epigrams. Not for nothing was Martial one of his favourite Latin authors, from whom he made some translations, as he did from Horace, Ovid and Virgil. He was all of a scholar, too, not only in the classics. He indulged his critical sense, for instance, by emending badly printed texts of Villon's poems with an extreme of sympathy, although he considered Villon dated and provincial—the sort of poet you can only read with explanatory notes. This is a most perceptive point to have made so early, and it is true today as it was within seventy years of Villon's death.

Marot could wield the sword as well as the pen, and was among those of the king's household captured at the fatal battle of Pavis in 1524—'*oultre rudement blessé*'—with a really nasty wound in his arm. From then onwards he was seldom out of trouble. He produced an innocent-seeming lampoon at the expense of the Doctors of the Sorbonne. François I was rebuilding the Louvre and, à propos, Clément wrote:

> *Le roi aimait la decoration*
> *De son Paris, entre autres biens ordonne*
> *Qu'on y bâtisse avec proportion*
> *Et pour ce faire argent et conseil donne.*
> *Maison de ville y construit belle et bonne,*
> *Les lieux publics devise tout nouveaux,*
> *Entre lesquels, au milieu de Sorbonne,*
> *Doit, ce dit-on, faire place aux veaux.*

A cattle-market in the centre of the Sorbonne! The angry doctors bided their time, and then clapped him into the Châtelet prison, when all his patrons were out of Paris, on a charge of heresy. Eventually he was freed by the Bishop of Chartres, just in time to gain the reversion of his father's post as the king's *valet-de-chambre*. A year later he is in gaol again, this time for rescuing a prisoner on his way to the Châtelet. François I bails him out, but really cannot keep so unbalanced a character as a member of his household; and poor Clément loses his post.

Yet his talent to amuse never seems to have deserted him. By now in very reduced circumstances, he writes a long and enter-

taining letter in verse, after the current practice, explaining to the
king how his purse had been stolen by his valet, a miserable
Gascon, and suggesting that the poor poet might meet with
justice from the generous François. His verses won him their
reward; a heavy purse of gold came his way.

But he felt insecure. Perhaps those doctors of the Sorbonne
were still watching for a slip from his impetuous tongue, for he
took a step which must have confirmed their worst suspicions
and went off to the court of the Protestant Queen Margaret of
Navarre at Nérac. In a poem, a gesture of farewell to Paris, are
these lines. A caress, a sigh rather than a kiss they seem to be, with
all their quiet consonants, with all their varied assonance.

> . . . *Adieu les dames*
> *Adieu les filles et les femmes,*
> *Adieu vous dy pour quelcque temps.*
> *Adieu vos plaisants passetemps:*
> *Adieu le bal, adieu la danse . . .*
> *Adieu les regards gracieux*
> *Messagers des coeurs soucieux.*

The last couplet with its changed beat runs off in a rustle of
silk. No wonder La Fontaine paid him the compliment, among
others, that he was a goldsmith in language.

On the way to Nérac, which we too shall visit, he had staged
a state entry for the queen at his home town of Cahors. A good
deal of correspondence in verse had passed with the Consuls and
the *Capitouls* (whose replies are not recorded for their poetic
value); everything was arranged, the right speeches were made,
and let us hope that the Monsieur Pierre Escorbiac of the day was
up to the job. And the cavalcade would have ridden away under
the five towers of the Pont Neuf on the road to the Huguenot
stronghold of Montauban where they would turn to the right
down the valley of the Garonne, through Agen, to their miniature
palace at Nérac, with its gardens running down to the banks of
the Baïse.

Here, far away from the strife of tongues, in the bosom of
France, he wrote a poem about his youth, *Adolescence Clémentine*,

which gives him the right to criticise Villon for dependence on scenes which no longer exist. There are still shepherds on the hillsides of the Limogne; there is still the landscape; the portrait of his father teaching him the arts of literature is vivid like all great writing, well drawn as all great paintings.

From this reflective mood, he was called back to the king's favour, only to lose his place again for suspicion of heresy. What long memories had those old doctors of the Sorbonne. But either Marot was a heretic or a fool. A fool, in whose rooms heretical books have been found, would fly in succession to the two French-connected courts hall-marked as Huguenot; which is just what Marot did; a heretic would have had just the books which Marot had. So there is the choice for us, judges of history. But the charm that Marot must have had! In a year or so he was back again at court, fully recognised by François I as the greatest poet of the day.

And then again disaster fell. It has been suggested that the king put to him the idea of a metrical version of the psalms. This is interesting, if true, in the light of the close Franco-Scottish alliance. Marot set to work on them, and his religious poetry achieved an immense popularity. The trouble was that the Protestants liked them too and (which is funny when one comes to think of it) sung them to popular tunes, just as Moody and Sankey did three hundred years later. This, of course, was easy money to the Sorbonne. The poet is censured by the doctors once more; the king, whatever his previous part, forbids him to continue, and poor Clément takes the road once more.

This time to Geneva and Calvin, which surely must confirm the doctors' verdict. But not even in this Protestant paradise could Marot keep his head, and soon he was in trouble and requested to leave for a very odd couple of sins. Adultery one can understand—but why backgammon? There was not much left for him now, and he moved to Turin, which then was French soil by a technicality. And there he died in obscurity, 'permanently in trouble, but consoled by hope', the man whom the French poets held in reverence for two hundred years, a man with all the gifts but judgment, a man of Cahors.

Puisque de vous je n'ai autre visage,
Je m'en vais rendre hermite en un désert,
Pour prier Dieu, si un autre vous sert,
Qu' ainsi que moi en votre honneur soit sage.
Adieu amour, adieu gentil corsage.
Adieu ce teint, adieu ces friands yeux.
Je n'ai pas eu de vous grand avantage:
Un moins aimant aura peutêtre mieux.

CLEMENT MAROT

II

Montauban to Moissac

IT seems for the moment the most sensible thing to continue
on our road towards Toulouse and Perpignan, the gateway to
our three passes into Spain. So from Cahors you keep along
N.20, an unexciting stretch of road from which I retain only two
vivid impressions—the scent from bushes of wild honeysuckle,
and the sudden entrance under a mediaeval arch to the covered,
pillared market of a village on a hill-side. I remember, too, the
extreme flatness, the extreme dreariness of the last twenty-two
kilometres from Caussade to Montauban, which is our next port
of call. For some sin which despite a reasonable choice I have not
yet identified, it has been my lot twice to picnic by the side of this
unloveliest road in the district.

Montauban is a town with a most extraordinary atmosphere.
You may not like it. I think that the clue to the place is hidden in
dust and ashes below the fact that it has once been a capital in
France, but a defeated one, of a religious faith. Somewhere deep
down in the subconscious life of the city are 'the tender tongues
of the little snakes that eat my heart'. As you walk the pavements
you will notice that many of them are decorated with geometrical
patterns of coloured pebbles. Are they a distraction from or a
monument to the buried Huguenot conscience? For Montauban
dried her tears faster than her sister city, La Rochelle.

Both cities had their moments of triumph for their faith. While
for La Rochelle the grand hour was the repulse of the armies of
Henri III in 1573, Montauban (equally a city with special privileges for Huguenot worshippers) was able to beat off the best
forces of Louis XIII in 1621. There was an element of irony in
this. The king, whose father, Henri IV, though he lapsed from
the reformed religion still protected it by the celebrated Edict of
Nantes, was inclined by Richelieu to create a centralised and
uniform state, in which the Huguenots were a dissident element.

To survey his first military triumph, Louis XIII lodged at a neighbouring castle, Piquecos, from which he would be able to witness the successful assault on the town. The affair was to be laid on in customary formal style and, naturally, to prevent undue agitation, quite a reasonable lunch was prepared. The Bourbons always had an appetite. I am not clear whether all this was eaten in strict order or whether the menu includes a great many dishes which our great grandparents would have called 'removes', set on the table for your choice but later taken away.

> Purslane salad ('a low edible succulent') with sugar
>   and vinegar dressing.
> Both breasts and one leg of boiled capon.
> Boiled knuckle of veal garnished with taillerons.[1]
> Two covers of paté.
> Four mutton cutlets in carbonade.
> Two legs of hazel-hen, yellow sauce.
> The breasts of two partridges with verjuice (a sauce
>   of sour fruit or grapes).
> Slice of turtle-dove: the trail of a ring-dove in pastry
>   with verjuice sauce, eight small slices of lemon.

Then follow various fruits and sweets which, frankly, I do not understand, though I wonder whether or not I should like sugared almonds flavoured lightly with fennel. They drank light wine ('*clairet*').

And with all this before them, within them, behind them they did not see the capture of Montauban. It was an heroic spirit which animated the town. Old Marquis de la Force had entered it shortly before the royal attack, bringing with him the thin support of a few sons, a wife (over-age for fighting, technically) and

---

[1] '*Taillerons*' does not appear in any dictionary of cuisine known even to so high an authority as M. André Simon, who was kind enough to help me and judges it to be a kind of garnish like a *croute mitonnée*. It might be, he thinks, a version of the *Taillis* for which this is the recipe in *Le Viandier de Guillaume Tirel dit Taillevent* (1326–95).

'*Prennes fygues et raysins, lai d'almendes et eschaudes, et galetes, crouste de pain blanc coup menu, et faites bouillir le lai; prennez saffran pour lui donner couleur, et sucre, et puis mettes bouillir tout ensemble tant qu'il soit bien liant pour tailler.*'

some scant troops. He had fought as a Huguenot with the King's
father, Henri IV, and his party undertook the defence of the most
vulnerable and decayed part of the fortifications, using the weak-
est part of the walls as a decoy to induce an attack, against which
they had built another but screened rampart. Even the poets,
apart from the cuisiniers, got busy over the contest, confident of
victory. Wrote the king's poetaster:

> *Parpaillots, vous êtes tous morts,*
> *Quelques grands que soient les efforts*
> *De votre folle résistance.*

(Heretics, you're dead already, however great may be the efforts
of your insane resistance.)

Which reminds me of the lines prepared for the victory dinner
by the poetaster of the Blackburn Rovers when they met the Old
Etonians in the final of the F.A. Cup in 1882:

> *All hail ye gallant Rover lads.*
> *Etonians thought ye were but cads.*

Whatever Blackburn Rovers, whatever Louis XIII ate on the day
destined for victory, there were no laurel leaves in the salad.

Then with the full rigour of siege warfare royal cannon thun-
dered against the rotting walls of Montauban, cannons of all
calibres; nothing so practical as 25-pounders, but guns called by
romantic and almost mythical French names—'*coulverines,*
bâtardes, moyènnes, faucons, fauconnaux'. Yet, despite the ruin
by bombardment that this constant gunfire caused the city, there
were moments of gentility. The artillery was commanded by a
lapsed Huguenot, an old friend of Henri IV and like him a *coureur
de femmes*, de Bassompierre. To a general of his temperament and
breeding it was natural to grant the townswomen's request that
they should still do their washing where it had always been done,
at the foot of the old bridge, without being fired on. I suppose the
men and women of Montauban had not had such clean linen for
centuries, since a small posse of washerwomen was sufficient to
cause a cease-fire. In dank, remorseless November, its forces
depleted by disease, the royal army raised the siege after eight

months. The king and Richelieu confirmed the privileges of open Huguenot worship to the town.

A short eight years after this proud moment came the fall. The Huguenots were again in unwise revolt, this time with La Rochelle, their other capital city, in alliance with England, an ineffective England. While La Rochelle struggled through to capitulate with full military honours, Montauban had not a brave Rochellaise Duchesse de Rohan to lead them, nor their Mayor, Guiton; their own Marquis de la Force of the last siege was not with them now. They gave in. Suddenly they dwindled into bourgeoisie, which La Rochelle, still a smart town, has never done.

Richelieu transferred to both towns an episcopal see; and here is the contrasted manner in which they accepted this salt in the wound. By 1659 the bishop's palace was built at Montauban, enshrining parts of a castle which had acknowledged the domination of the Black Prince. Where a bishop has a palace he has a see, even if the cathedral lags. Next, the men of Montauban went for their own dignity, building a civic square with a double series of arcades in brick of lovely quality: not a true square, since the corners are cut off to allow arched entrances, which again are generous in the perspective they grant you of the run of arches. Licking their new bishop's boots and blacking their own, they were still ready to start a cathedral in the new classical manner and to complete it by 1739 (not an age of faith) after only forty years of building.

Observe the Rochellais by contrast. For the design of the cathedral, virtually imposed on them as a fine, the city employed an architectural family, Breton by origin, and as well known to them as to Paris, the Gabriels, who later built the Palais Royal. One can be sure that the Gabriel family understood and co-operated with all the delays over the cathedral of La Rochelle. The City and architect delayed the complete acceptance of this ecclesiastical insult over a full hundred and forty years.

* *

The most attractive approach to Montauban is made from the Toulouse side, where it introduces us to a striking panorama. In the centre, beyond the mediaeval bridge, stands the bishop's palace, brightly dressed in seventeenth-century brick and stone, emphatic with its high slate roofs and the projecting wings, a place of sharp shadows. Over its left shoulder is the tall tower and spire of the old church, St. Jacques, designed to the pattern of which Toulouse's St. Sernin is the prototype. The major defect of its western façade is concealed from the angle at which we are looking. On to it has been plastered, gummed, grouted, agglutinated, inhered, united inseparably the ghastly copy of one of the 'world's great pictures' executed in nineteenth-century encaustic tiles. Time itself will not suffice to efface this horribly durable 'Don de L'Etat', made at the instance of Armand Cambon, whose importance otherwise escapes me. I looked him up in the easy books and found him not. His name, of course, is the same as that of France's great ambassadorial family. But I simply will not spend more time in tracing the identity of the man who had this beastly thing done, and got the government to pay for it. His name is imperishably part of it—and serve him right.

On either side of the palace, flanking a line of pleasant enough houses, lie belts of greenery. On the left are the trees of the Cour Foucault, seven avenues of chestnut. It was an eighteenth-century gift to the city; according to the old prints under their shade the élite of Montauban paraded. Inevitably the trees have been renewed but they still shed a peaceful coolness. To the right, trees mask deteriorating Victorian balustrades which lead down to the Jardin des Plantes. Here the memories are military, and illuminate a happy facet of active men in repose. Lord Alanbrooke, we know, is a bird-watcher. I have known brigadiers who specialised in, for instance, Napoleonic prints or in Van Dyck's etchings, tracking down their last decayed impressions, discovering with enthusiasm yet another stage of repair to a plate which no one had ever noticed before. And so there is also the Marshal of France who dedicated to Montauban its Jardin des Plantes. Niel had done well in the Crimea, and was creating the *Garde Mobile* against the threats from Prussia. He never lived to use it in action, since he died in 1869. But his name endures for

The Cathedral at Cahors: North Portal

Cahors: La Tour des Pendus and the Barbican

Montauban: Le Pont des Consuls

a greater success: he acclimatised a rose noisette from South Carolina. In my young days Marshal Niel still was fashionable along with others like Madame Abel Chatenay, so pink, so large, so perfumed that you started day-dreaming about the original lady. So it does not seem unreal that the Marshal's rose should have been yellow tinged with pink, nor that in any decent garden of, say, 1908 it was still worth its lead label as a horticultural substitute for a military decoration.

* * *

One cannot hope to like everything in an old town, and if you want a rest from enthusiasm you can drift off to the square with the cafés by which we entered, and contemplate anew a revolting fountain, which splashes water over the city's arms, executed in blue tubular neon lights. Somewhat revived you may like to set out again in search of domestic architecture; for the place is full of good courtyards and façades. And of stories, too. Bishops, for instance.

Before the days of the discreet and innocuous Jardin des Plantes a bishop had installed his mistress outside the city's precincts and had constructed a tunnel by which he might gain her house unobserved. Could this true story have been the base of old A. E. W. Mason's story, *The House of the Arrow*, where a similar situation is used? An essential factor in the same thriller is a matter of timing a motor-cycle by different routes, which Mason once told me he had tried out on a route in the Wye Valley. I wish that twenty-five years ago I had known enough to fill the gap by asking him if he knew Montauban, and so could have elucidated part at least of his construction of that remarkable thriller. He was a man with a singularly retentive mind, as his good biography of Drake shows, with its interpretation of the tides in relation to the famous game of bowls.

There are a lot of strange tales connected with Montauban, even if you have not taken my original story about Renaud and Montauban too seriously. Let us step from the bishop and the novelist—up or down, according to the snobbery you practise—to an eighteenth-century count, the Comte de Guibert, who was

D

born in the place. I know his face only from an engraved portrait
—the hard, close eyes, the selfish nose, the cleft chin: the sort of
face over which men and women will always disagree, the face of
an outstanding cad.

He would regale his friends with gallant tales of his military
victories, real or imagined, until he came to find those of the
blanket less exacting. How did this dog come to touch the heart of
Julie de L'Espinasse, one of the most delightful *salonnières* of
eighteenth-century Paris? All the men with the new ideas, the
Encyclopaedists—Diderot, Marmontel, the notable d'Alembert—
came to meet within her door. But to her the day was lost if
among the forty cleverest men in Paris she did not find her
military bore. The romantic woman who aims at intellectuality is
mince-meat for the de Guiberts of this world. She burnt out her
heart at his altar, after she discovered that during the period of
their intimacy he had married and had children. Poor Julie, who
died! Yet she would have condemned as jealous any man who out
of affection had dared to tell her the manifest character of her
lover.

* * *

I am sorry to say that I have not yet learnt to sleep comfortably
or eat well at Montauban; but it may be possible. We did at one
hotel, a noticeable one, commit the indiscretion of leaving behind
a change coat and a summer frock of my wife's and wrote for their
return, enclosing some form of payment for the return postage.
With promptitude the hotel replied that, yes, they had the garments, but they were too heavy to go through the post in one
parcel. With the brilliant practicality of the English, I suggested
that perhaps two parcels would solve the problem. Then silence
fell and deep oblivion. It took in the long run intervention by the
French Tourist Bureau in London (most willingly given) and our
own consular offices to recover the clothes, which travelled in-
nocently in one parcel. They had clearly helped out the hotel staff
during the summer months.

So it is wiser to stay at some neighbouring place in the last
resort if you have not found time for the museum on your first

day. Even if your passion for museums is not fully developed, you
might still like to visit this one—of course, it is in this uniquitous
bishop's palace—for the sake of the painted decoration in the
smaller rooms or for the Gothic vaulting attributed to the fierce
times of the Black Prince. For this was a violent corner of France
in the early stages of the Hundred Years War. When after our first
victories, France acknowledged defeat in the Treaty of Bretigny
(1360), Cahors, Montauban and Albi were handed over to us
without a struggle. This was more than the citizens would take;
and within ten years the inhabitants of each town had expelled our
garrisons. Such memories are evoked by the Black Prince's
arches.

Very different characters inhabit the other storeys; and it is
important to remember that the place is not always open after
noon. But if you write ahead to the delightful curator, Monsieur
Ternois, he will show you anything you wish to see if you specify

The place is sacred to the memories of the two native artists of
marked importance; indeed it was founded as the result of the
bequest to the city of the contents of his studio by the painter,
Ingres. But you see first, primarily because it is on the ground
floor, just on the right as you go in, the work of the other great
son of Montauban, Antoine Bourdelle; sculpture, drawings, watercolours. They gave me a shock.

When I was young, which seems some time ago, people were
always talking up Bourdelle. My clever sister, who spent three
years in Paris after the first war, had the name on her tongue. I
read articles about him in the *Gazette des Beaux Arts*, listened to
Clive Bell, and generally behaved like the average young prig of
my date. I just couldn't see the point of Bourdelle, and dismissed
him as 'academic'.

What is so depressing is that, as the examiners used to say, I
could not answer Part II of the paper. I was quite right in Part I.
Bourdelle is academic, but of the very highest class. At Montauban
that single room, filled with the full vigour of his light and shadow,
with the dash of his drawing and the warm intimacy of the
watercolours, swept away the cobwebs of my imperception, and

left me too with a strange sense that I had lost something irretrievably which I had never had. You can experience something like it as you look at photographs or drawings of places that have been destroyed, or from reading such a description as that in Antony à Wood of the Quad of All Souls in the Reformers' day of the 1550's, a litter of illuminated manuscripts, of smashed reliquaries, statues and stained glass. The loss that you can cause yourself through inattention or through lack of appreciation, though unimportant to anyone else, is also shocking once you notice it. And I grasped the sad fact that I had lost thirty odd years of Bourdelle, that rich and brilliant artist, through no fault but my own.

Suitably chastened, I went upstairs, soon smugly saying to myself that at least I had looked at an Ingres or two in the past so that I shouldn't have *that* experience again. Nor, of course, did I, because you don't think much about yourself when you enter the mausoleum of another man, however great or little he may have been. You look round a mausoleum; it has a single, personal imprint; and before or after your visit if the personality has impressed you at all, you begin to strike a balance. This one I found imposing but peculiar in a pre-Freudian way.

It was not, after all, usual in the mid-nineteenth century for people to have their tombs designed and paid for during their lifetime, as if they could not trust their relations, which certainly they could not in the sixteenth century when the practice was common. Had Ingres, perhaps, learnt of our Turner's fantastic legacy to our nation of all his unsold works and had Ingres studied the will before he decided to leave the contents of his studio to his native town, Montauban, of which he remembered little beyond the consistent cruelty of his painter father to his mother?

Probably not; at least I have seen no evidence for the idea. Yet it is odd to find two major painters in their countries doing the same thing within fifteen years of one another; and the difference between them is informative. Turner, the youngest man I think ever to be elected an R.A.—at least below the legal age for his diploma—bequeathed to the *nation* a purely personal collection of his work. Ingres, on the other hand, left to a *provincial* town some-thing with a much wider conception, less egocentric. The con-tents of his studio included far more than his own work. It in-cluded Greek vases, for instance; Roman sculpture; Etruscan ware; work by Flaxman who with the German classicists exercised a considerable influence on him, the last of the line in France—a pure academic draughtsman basing himself on Raphael and Pous-sin. In contrast with Turner, his bequest to a humbler city than London, is the less conceited on the face of it. But the Greek vases and the rest are there only as the nurse-maids who brought up 'the giant talent', Ingres.

I can't say that as a man I like him any more than I like Turner; but there are two features of his art, as shown in this collection, which one cannot neglect. Its extreme classicism has already been noticed. In addition the enormous group of detailed studies is a monument to his conscience as an artist and a declaration of his artistic faith, the equivalent of the *'testament politique'* which monarchs like Louis XIV or Frederick the Great left for their despised successors. There is one curious comment on Ingres as director of the French School at Rome. He had been industrious; with the help of M. Le Gos he had put the finances into order; he took personal trouble about every student both as an artist and as an individual. When he came to leave for Paris, everyone was genuinely devastated. How would they all get on without the help, so ready and friendly, of *'Le Maître'?* Then they found three months after his departure, that all the tension unconsciously created by his personality had relaxed.

The man was a tyrant. You have only to look at the portraits, unchanging through the years, of the tight mouth, of the low forehead, whether painted by him or one of his pupils. He was a tyrant to himself as well as to his first wife and to his pupils, who made something like a *cortège* for him when he walked abroad. For a major composition like, say, *The Martyrdom of St. Sym-phorien*, no fewer than four hundred preliminary drawings exist at Montauban; drawings of every position of every limb of every character in the picture, and of all the possible variations which might give the best harmony to the whole. He was a masochist of a painter. Or was he on the other hand an endless improviser like Chopin or especially Schubert?

Raphael was his god, and he tried to substitute him for the flat conceptions of his master David, to bring the tradition of French back to the Italian seed bed of academicism, where it had germinated, from which it had blown away. Delacroix, his contemporary, so much more intelligent and as highly gifted in a different way, touched the spot in his Journal.

> Ingres, who has never understood how to paint a subject naturally, believes himself the equal of Raphael by aping certain of his gestures, certain of his ordinary attitudes and Ingres gives them a grace which reminds you of Raphael. But with Raphael one is conscious all the time that these features derive from him himself and that he has not had to look for them.

*   *   *

What I had asked Monsieur Ternois to show me, when I called, were the landscape drawings by Ingres, which are exceedingly scarce outside Montauban. When he was at Rome, both as a student and as director of the French School, Ingres was always making these landscape notes, which he used for backgrounds to his enchanting portraits, whether in pen, pencil or oil, of visitors to Rome. I had seen only one or two before; but Monsieur Ternois could have shown me two hundred. There, English families were good customers, and Ingres would show them his sketch books all the time with still the same clear observing eye, the same energetic pen, so that they could choose a view suitable to their sentiments, light and firm as Raphael's or Bonington's; broad as Claude, if he washed a drawing. How did this classicist do these things, I asked myself and why had he not done more.

I fear the answer must be given in one of Constable's generalisations; for he is a philosopher of landscape. 'A man must walk the fields with an humble mind. To no arrogant man is it given to see nature in all its beauty.' Of this Jean Auguste Dominique Ingres was incapable.

You get a full look at Ingres as a man from the terms of his bequest. Though he realised that not all the five thousand drawings could be simultaneously exhibited (apart from the Greek vases and so on)—indeed they have not yet been completely catalogued in extenso ninety years after his death—he insisted on his personal importance. To be kept on permanent exhibition in a vitrine were, he ordained, his orders and decorations; the medals struck in his honour; the gold crown presented to him by the citizens of Montauban; the gilt crown with the green ribbons borne at his funeral by members of the Institut; the gilt crown borne at his funeral by his pupils; the casts of his hand and the cast of Madame Ingres's arm; Barry's statuette of the actress Rachel; his desk; his chair on which was to be posed his violin upon an open copy of Mozart's Don Juan. And finally, inescapably, his palette, with this slightly emetic inscription.

'Palette, Adieu vieux serviteur, qui avez peint *Oedippe L'Odalisque, Philippe V, Le Voeu de Louis XIII, St. Pierre, Homere,* et tant d'autres. Ce n'est pas ta faute si tous ces ouvrages ne sont pas meilleurs.'

('Palette, Farewell old servant, who has painted *the Oedipus, the Odalisque, Philippe V, the Vow of Louis XIII* . . . and so many others. It is no fault of yours if they are no better painted.')

Well really. After the minimum of bogus formality, he finishes with a contemptuous '*tutoyer*', '*Vieux serviteur*' indeed! He treats his palette as if it were 'the boots'.

Conceited, pompous, touchy and vindictive, Ingres could utter without the slightest change in the tone of his soft voice the cruellest phrase. His arrows had pierced before his enemies were warned by the twang of the bowstring. It was reported of him that he could recite, with complete accuracy, any adverse criticism levelled at him over a period of fifty years. A candidate for the Academy in 1825, he arranged to stand not for the first but for the second of the two vacancies, since its late occupant had been Vivant-Denon, the Director of Museums, from whom he fancied he had received a slight. How strange, how twisted a nature to extract pleasure from a triumph over ashes. He hated Delacroix— and it was mutual—who was the force behind the new school, the school with a future, and hated him for the colourist's gift which he himself never had; he hated Delacroix's brilliant management of yellow. At an exhibition Ingres saw him, and left. They heard him say: 'This place smells of sulphur.' 'Ça sent du souffre.' To him and his cold blues yellow was devil's breath.

*   *   *

In *Renaud of Montauban* the chronicler uses a convenient literary device. When he is at a loss for a transition, he writes quite frankly: 'now leave we to speak of Renaud thus wounded and tell of . . .' In short, let us drive to Moissac, a much smaller town than Montauban but one which contains what is left of one of the greatest and most powerful romanesque abbeys in France.

If you decide (wisely in my experience, but don't let that prejudice you for a moment) against staying in Montauban, you might instead choose Moissac. It is not far away and if you take N.127 you will do well to branch off the main road for a kilometre or two to the small town of Lafrançaise—the name alone tells you something of frontier warfare in the Hundred Years War —from which you get a wonderful, expansive prospect up the valley of the Tarn, by which stands Moissac.

As we drove in, we stopped to consult a group of people as to the merits of the two principal hotels, the Poste and the Chapon Fin—rather a pretentious name in a place thimble-size compared with Bordeaux. At the question, they went immediately into a huddled committee.

'Well, really, there was so little to choose between them; it made judgment a difficult matter. Both were good. Yes, the accommodation in both was good, and the food too.'

Their eyes wandered in quiet speculation over my little car, which by chance had been washed overnight and looked a little better class than usual. They advised the Poste on the whole; it was a little the more *soigné* of the two, we gathered, though the gap was so fine that only a fly could find its way through. As it turned out, we came first upon the Chapon Fin in the wide, main square. It looked out upon a hideous, nineteenth century covered market and upon a nineteenth-century theatre with formidable cracks and flaking playbills. But there were plenty of cars outside the Chapon Fin; and in judging a French restaurant or hotel by car standards, you should make variety your rood-stick. A good testimonial consists in a lorry or two, an old Ford, two passable Renaults and perhaps one car that looks expensive. Then you know that the place has something for everyone and is probably reliable, if not actively good. This was the foreground to the Chapon Fin; so we decided to take our post-picnic brandy on their terrasse and make a further reconnaissance. We observed that the place was full of locals; a hall-mark. And for that reason, and because of a certain simplicity in their welcome, we plumped for the Chapon Fin and never regretted it.

They did not scruple to say that the Poste was ahead of them in matters of decoration; but they were modernising too and for that reason they could not give us a room with a bath. On the other hand they could offer us 'this room'—and showed us something large enough to have accommodated at least six guests in the eighteenth century. The curtains met in the middle of the windows; the beds were good; Madame had the sort of eye which might mind what happened to anyone in her house. There was a family atmosphere about the place. One day the son, perhaps eight or ten, with the pale, slim-boned look of French boys, came in to the bar from the hairdressers, where he had had one of those severe crew-cuts, which the French believe strengthens the hair.

'*Ah, que c'est mignon,*' said his mother, a dark *belle-laide*, stroking what was left of his hair.

'*Ah, que c'est mignon,*' echoed with affection an amusing, pug-faced waitress, not stroking his hair because it was not her place.

'*Ah, que c'est mignon,*' said his beautiful half-sister of fifteen, stroking his hair with an immaturely maternal gesture.

All this while service went on at the bar.

*   *   *

But we should be thinking of higher things than crew-cuts. Moissac is one of many places in France (or England) which has once been grand and has not kept the pace. In this case it was no fault of the town but of 'circumstances outside our control'. It lies in the broad fertile valley of the Tarn, deep in cornlands and vine-yards. In its great days before the sixteenth century, it was a country of corn mills; and you can still see a stunning example of a fortified mill and bridge at Barbaste-sur-la-Baise a little higher up the valley, which once belonged to the abbey of Moissac.

The abbey held land in eleven dioceses in France and beyond the frontiers in Italy. Founded in the seventh century as a Benedictine monastery, it was affiliated with Cluny, the great reforming abbey, by St. Odilon in 1047, who installed as abbot Durand de Bredon his principal assistant as we should call him. Here was a great administrator, and a great builder, whose features we still know from a sculptured portrait which corresponds with the verbal description of him in a roughly contemporary chronicle. The slightly malicious mouth is common to both.

Since its foundation the monastery had been through the changes and chances which were common to the mortal life of its age. It had been burnt by the Saracens in 732 and then restored by Pepin the Short and Louis le Debonnaire. In the ninth century the Normans, landing at Bordeaux, sacked it anew; but this time the restoration, undertaken without royal support, was too hasty, too shoddy. The roof collapsed in 1030, and twelve years later there was a disastrous fire. What Durand de Bredon took over was a monastic salvage dump. He undertook the rebuilding of the abbey church and the addition of the cloisters, which, though not wholly completed in his life-time, are one of the great achievements of French architecture. In addition he reformed the manners and customs of the monks so that they rated for piety, knowledge and discipline among the greatest houses of their time.

Although they are not the first thing you would naturally see, perhaps we should visit the cloisters first, making a detour from the Chapon Fin. You come in from the Boulevard de Brienne, a name which commemorates with scorn the last of the lay abbots, Loménie de Brienne, a writer of slim memoirs, who at the age of nine had also been made lay abbot of the great Jumièges in Normandy. This was the sort of practice which left the church without popular support. Forgetting these cross-patch recollections of the irremediable, you find yourself confronted with uncompromising architecture, the west front of the church, a fortified door. What had been no more than a peaceable entrance to a church, was made a defensive point in the thirteenth century; and so the old entrance is arched over and flanked by sheer military work, wordless work but for the battlements, since there is no window anywhere. In short all this end was firmly blanked off to the attackers, unscalable, impenetrable.

You cannot enter the church that way. So, seeing a small door to the left you enter it to discover a peaceful kingdom of columns, of arches, of carving: the cloister. Confronting you is a square angle-pillar, on two sides of which the figures of St. Bartholomew and St. Matthew are framed within a low-relief, round-headed arch. To the right and the left lie the walks of the cloister, and beyond you see these walks return at right angles, the whole thing forming a perspective of tiled roofs and pointed arches interspersed with diamonds. Somewhere about the centre is a fine cedar; if you are at Moissac in spring, the pinkish fruit looks well against the red-brown stone.

All the capitals of the columns are carved; and the columns are set alternately in pairs and singly. Everything seems to be on the move and alive without being hasty; any chance over-effect of movement is controlled by the occasional dominating figure carved in low relief on a square pillar. The side walls are inlaid with old effigies and inscriptions. Along their flanks lie early Christian sarcophagi, used a second time for the tombs of holy or seigneurially distinguished men. This cloister, besides its ordinary purpose, is a sort of Campo Santo as well, and a reminder of early beliefs and rites, of the better chance of salvation you had if you were buried as near Holy Church as possible.

The detail of the capitals naturally attract the visitor, be he lay or skilled in this type of art. And the lay instinct is absolutely correct since this series is unique, apart from its own beauty, in the sense that it is the prototype for a wide area. In contrast with its successors it shows an individual attitude. Yet, since the cloister was an essential part of monastic life, if the place is to have a meaning, we must pierce the intention of the designed sequence of the narrative carvings, interspersed as it is with what one might call 'rest passages' of decorative pieces—flowers, curvilinear designs, or travellers-tale beasts. At such moments as the monk was at leisure from his offices, from his work in the arts, the garden, the cellar or the kitchen and from the struggle against the temptations of the world, it was to the cloister he repaired for repose. Here, too, he found messages on the capitals to direct his thoughts, messages sometimes underlined with an inscription. Some echoed the theology of his day, some like the patterned beasts could rest the eye and still the mind to the calm of meditation; others would remind him of the saints and martyrs of his neighbourhood, whose exemplary lives had been lived within air's breath of him, an encouragement to constancy.

Myself, I could see no sequence of idea at all when I first surveyed the cloister, and concluded—which was a partly accurate guess—that at some time their arrangement had been disturbed. Indeed it had been, but no later than the thirteenth century. So I was back at the problem—why was there this apparent confusion of sequence in which the Old and the New Testament themes were intermingled? Why, for instance, did I find Samson and the Lion quickly followed by the martyrdom of St. Peter and St. Paul? What on earth are the Triumph of the Cross and the Message to the Shepherds doing just after Abraham's sacrifice? Cain and Abel flanked by the Beatitudes and the Elect? Why is the Apocalypse suddenly thrown in as a trump card?

There had been, however, an underlying system, and a manner of thought so remote from our own, yet so implicit in the art of this time that with the help of the great scholars of the period, Emile Mâle, Ernest Rubin, Raymond Rey, I must try to distil a tenth of it for you.

The church at this time was still preoccupied with the reconciliation of the Old and the New Testaments, which had been a problem back as far as the fourth century. The theories were of course written down, transcribed for other monasteries, illuminated to illustrate the text which drew parallels between events in the two stories. Thus Samson and his defeated lion forecasts the triumph of Christ over the devil. Adam and Eve come close in order to the Baptism of Christ in Jordan, since it is baptism which delivers man from his fall. The Baptism of Christ was considered as the start of his mission, and in the liturgy of those days it was placed between Christmas and Easter. In this sequence, its representation comes between the Samson and the Transfiguration—with the deliverance of St. Peter (rather a friend of the abbey's) thrown in for good measure. And the whole builds up into the culminating scenes from the Apocalypse, which we shall see later in a different place.

All this may seem very like an indifferent sermon; but it is one which it is necessary to write if the point of Moissac Cloister is to be grasped. Here for the first time in this part of France (and I think anywhere) was elaborate theology carved in stone. An intellectual conception of interpreting the two Testaments is here portrayed. And, if on a particular day as a monk you did not wish to consider it, there were always the saints and martyrs and their lives to fix your mind. This was indeed a place for quiet meditation. And as we go elsewhere, we shall find other cloisters or their remaining capitals preserved in museums from previous destructions, telling the story of doctrinal thought as it changed generation by generation. For even in the Middle Ages thought changed.

An admirable and well illustrated guide-book with an English précis at the end gives you most of what you need to know. It is particularly useful since in the flurry of the French Revolution many of the figures on the capitals were decapitated, which makes the aid of a skilled interpreter all the more necessary.

Your first impression may be governed by the general pattern, before you come down to the detail. The arches are high-pitched with a slightly oriental smack to them. This is hardly surprising when one considers the regularity of the pilgrimages to the Holy Sepulchre in Jerusalem, which were shortly to provoke the first crusade. The capitals on which the arches rest are in form something of a truncated pyramid set upside down, and filled with carving which softens and at the same time excites what would have been a harsh outline. A diamond shaped opening divides each spandrel, making an emphatic dark point like an embellishment in jet on the red-brown stone. Above all this the sunlight dances on the drainpipe tiles, proper to this region beloved of the Romans. At the corners and in the centre of each side the rhythm of the arcade is interrupted by an uncompromising square pillar,

on one or more faces of which you find these low-relief sculptures
of saints or abbots which have the air of portraits. Indeed French
scholars claim that here is the cradle of their school of portraiture.
Here again the choice of subject has purpose. St. Peter and St.
Paul were intimate indications of the papal interest in the ministry
of Cluny. Moissac was one of the recognised stopping places for
anyone making the pilgrimage to St. James of Compostella in
Spain—hence the figure of St. James the Great. And so on. In the
same way the stories sculptured on the capitals depict the life of
the favourite saints of the order; St. Benedict, naturally, the
founder; St. Laurence and St. Saturnin (St. Sernin in the Toulouse
dialect) who were the earliest missionaries to France; and martyrs
from Spain—rather obscure to us today—St. Fructueux, St.
Augure and St. Euloge. Such were the themes for contemplation
set out to the monks as they repaired their minds for work and
worship.

There are two other considerations: the inspiration and method
of these sculptured stories. For these carvings reveal a new spirit.
No longer do they depend entirely upon the illustrations in the
Syrian or Coptic manuscripts to tell the detail of their story.
Almost for the first time, angels play their part. The Annunciation
to the shepherds is not conveyed here by a star, as it would be in
an early Syrian manuscript: an angel brings the heavenly message.
An angel blesses David before his combat with Goliath. This conception occurs earlier in literature in a favourite book of Gregory
the Great, but had never previously been expressed in this form.
There is modernism too. Babylon and Jerusalem are contemporary
fortified cities, attacked and defended by troops 'in modern dress'.
The sculptured kings are men of the sculptor's generation
costumed as he would expect to see them. Here we are on the
threshold of a new age. As Raymond Rey rightly says, this carved
Bible of the monks clears the way for the Bible of the poor.
Sermons in stone indeed.

*   *   *

If we had approached the abbey another way—say from the
main square or along the road from Montauban—we should have

seen something very different. The entrance to the cloister is, fittingly, unpretentious. But the tympanum over the flickering, oriental South door within its great porch is startling. Indeed it took my eye straight off the traffic and we nearly had a collision. The whole south flank is memorable, partly for the embattled fortifications which surround and surmount the porch, partly for the short, combative tower crowned with a beehive hat, slitted with romanesque windows, which crouches watchfully in the highest place. For on the tympanum is carved the message of the Apocalypse: Christ enthroned in glory, the climax to the Bible history and theology of the cloister. As is reasonable for a climax, it is over a generation later in date than the cloister.

The whole doorway is like a sheet of flame. The outer supports of the lintel which normally would be columns partly engaged, are in fact shaped into four cusps. The central support, which one could expect to be a pillar, is rectangular in section, and on its surface are carved six lionesses, crossing over one another in such a ripple and dazzle as one could never have thought the form of an X—for that is the essence of the design—could have produced. You are dimly aware of arcadings and statuary on the sides of the porch, without being ready as yet to give them your attention, riveted as the eye is to what is directly before it, so splendid as to admit of no distraction.

The lintel is almost Roman in its richly simple way. It consists as decoration of no more than eight carved roundels, blown on to this white marble beam by some kind of dragon at either end. And you see that this roundel is in fact a flower; and if you are a botanist you get down to the fact that it is not the common thistle stylised here, but the mountain variety, which the country people hereabouts still deferentially call a Charlemagne, since in those far-distant days it was considered sovereign against the plague. So you enter the abbey beneath an emblem of protection.

Over all is Christ in glory, a gigantic figure with his nimbus of the crucifixion. His right hand is raised in blessing while his left holds the book of the New Testament. Archangels and the symbols of the evangelists surround him; the twenty-four elders of the church attend him, arrayed as kings, wrapt in devotion. A purely intellectual appraisal must judge this to be one of the most finely ordered compositions in the world, through the proportion of the emphasis on the major parts and the rhythm which the minor details contribute to the whole. To those who will take it in conjunction with the stories in the cloisters as the declaration of faith which it is, it is a source of re-animation. Neither the hart desiring the waterbrook nor the owl that was in the desert ever found such solace. Not even the revolutionaries dared to swing a destructive hammer against its majesty.

When a little later the porch was built to support the defensive works above and to keep the weather from the original paint which ornamented the sculpture, its walls were enriched with bas-reliefs: reminders of the papal saints, St. Peter and St. Paul; something about the Virgin—the Annunciation, the Adoration of the Magi and the Flight into Egypt; moral stories about the wickedness of the world, Dives and Lazarus, and minatory figures of Luxury and Lust. My goodness! The shape you took on if you went in for those vices! But in all this a master hand is still at work on the long sinuous figures, freed now from the rigidity of the Byzantine tradition to achieve a singular grace and a quality of movement which had long been lost to the Western world.

It would in short be a pitiable thing to be in Moissac's country-side without pausing even for an hour to see these stupendous sculptures. And we have not done with the place yet. For there is still the church itself to penetrate, which you do through a sort of narthex, a little cramped in arrangement through being on the south rather than the west side. It is off centre from the entrance, which again gives it a slight and undeserved awkwardness. Moissac always had something new and inventive; and the virtue of this narthex is that its designer employed a device, now so old that one forgets it was once new, a very early type of rib-vaulting. The capitals are charmingly decorative, even if they tend to display nature red in tooth and claw.

The interior has suffered too much in the course of its history to give one comparable satisfaction. But after all, one cannot expect a perfect dinner every day; and I have often wondered how long one's critical sense could survive even six months of perfec-

L'Hôtel de Pierre at Toulouse: 'All the effulgent, restless energy of the south'

Moissac:
'Calm, emaciated, still,
the figure of Christ
is all forgiveness'
(12th-Century Crucifixion)

Toulouse:
Notre-Dame-de-Grace in
the Musée des Augustins

tion. The exterior, of course, has already given us the clue to
what we may see, since above the low round-arched windows of
the stone-walled aisles rise later additions in brick with tall
narrow-pointed windows, divided into two and filled at the top
with a rosette. Inside one recognises that the low windows light
lateral chapels, while the upper ones are partly screened by a
vaulted gallery which runs above the level of the chapels. This is
a happy effect, and protects the church from an overplus of sunlight in this hot country.

The nave does not follow a consistent plan; for the arches move
from the round to the pointed style, leading up to the original
chancel with its seven radiating lights. But there are attractive
details in this slightly confused effect. It was Cardinal Mazarin,
for instance, titular abbot, who presented the magnificently carved
architectural organ. Beside it, in a wild contrast of styles, is a very
early crucifixion in carved and painted wood, about the twelfth
century. Calm, emaciated, still, the figure of Christ is all forgiveness. I cannot think of anything quite like it as emotion. And then
there is another aspect, this time of legend; for the trunk and the
arms of the cross are living, growing small convoluted branches.
It has some kinship to the legend of the Holy Hay, which
'blossomed again as it were not dead'.

A little before Mazarin's day work had been going on to
enhance the dignity of the collegiate church. New seats of the
miserere type were erected in the chancel, attractively sedate work
of its kind, and a screen of white stone in the classical manner was
set round it, concealing the ambulatory. All the wealth of pilasters
with Corinthian capitals, of frieze with broken ornament contain
and crown traceried lights like a half-wheel; almost they anticipate
the fan-light of a London house designed by Robert Adam.

I have two final recollections of the abbey church; the first of
them I almost missed. In the south-eastern chapel is a remarkable
Pieta, rich with the donor's heraldry and with lion's masks, but
essentially decorous in its paint, elegant in form and emotion. But
I think I was more moved by the western gallery which I saw as
I turned to go out. I suppose it is a matter of the perspective, of
the building up of tier upon tier and one curve of arch against

E

another in contrast. This seventeenth-century gallery is carried far out over the nave from the western wall; staircases lead you to it from either side; round arches enshrine it from the back, making a rich and lovely recession. So often these late adjuncts work out fat and heavy. Not so at Moissac, where vital tradition has from the first spiced function with harmony.

III

Toulouse

TOULOUSE has the third largest population of the cities in France, and you see it afar, as you come from Cahors and Montauban, sprawling in a light-industry way over the vast plain in which it lies. The approach is unattractive, though the avenues are wide and tree-shaded. If, however, you come in from Auch and the western country, you have the pleasure of crossing the active Garonne. Once over it, you are soon in the heart of the old city, its age-old clamour of quick-tempered voices reinforced by specially noisy and antique trams. You gain the great central square, the Place du Capitole, which is a terrifying place. Obviously it is the city's 'Trams' Club'.

The trams circle round the square, then stop for a chat in a solid line. You turn to outflank them, and just as you get to the end of the line, off they move in convoy leaving space for other clattering monsters to bear down upon you. But your troubles are not done when you have dodged the trams. There are the cars seeking safety in the gigantic car park. It has only two entrances and as a result cars are always swooping round waiting their chance to go in. Equally there are only two exits, attended by the same risks for the pedestrian, who may have been fool enough to think that the quickest way from one side of the square to the other would be the shortest. It is a far, far wiser thing to walk round; and if your nerves give out as trios and quartettes of talkative Toulousains bump into you, there are plenty of cafés where ou could sit down and recover.

This vivid square is dominated by a grand mid-eighteenth-century Hôtel de Ville. Its beautifully proportioned, pedimented central mass curves back to wide flanks which in their turn curve forward to an emphatic finish at the wings. The windows are divided by Ionic pilasters and set in panels of yellowish stone and the local very red brick, all of which makes a fine flash in the

strong sunlight. There is an older courtyard within and a rich
display of heraldic carving which enshrines a statue of Henri IV.
A good staircase of pinky gold marble leads to the great reception
rooms of the first floor, which suffer from a good deal of nineteenth-century ornament, designed to set off vast canvases by
local artists, depicting scenes from the history of the city and the
life of the countryside. They were all in the *Gazette des Beaux
Arts* years ago, and are tolerable of their kind. The Hôtel de Ville
stands on the site from which the old Consuls and *Capitouls* of the
thirteenth century defied their Count, their bishop and even one
King of France when they undertook the defence of the local
heretics, the Catharists. By their defence of the Catharists they
produced a revolution of power in this part of mediaeval France,
and destroyed their own civilisation which had culminated in the
age of the Troubadours. This Catharist heresy provoked a
crusade in the thirteenth century, which battered its blood-stained
way all over the countryside with which this book is concerned,
and if we are to understand the genius of this part of France and
of its capital, we must know something about the ecclesiastical
rumpus which brought so many changes.

*   *   *

'There are,' claimed the Catharists of Toulouse, of Albi, of
Carcassonne, wearing their distinctive clothes, 'twin powers of
good and evil: God and the Devil. We have to fight the Devil who
created this sinful world.'

In the days when he was known more politely up in heaven as
Lucifer or Lucibel, the Devil (so went the theory) made some
human bodies into which he slipped souls he had stolen from
heaven, and left them to breed. So all forms of procreation were
devil's work, because the first men were created by fallen angels.
Therefore, one must eat no flesh, no eggs, no milk nor cheese.
Owing to defective biological knowledge—they didn't know that
fish had any sex life—fish was left on the Catharist's menu, as
were fruit and vegetables. The doctrine of the Virgin Birth, of the
Passion and the Resurrection were ruled out, since they involved
direct or indirect recognition of the devil-made, procreative world.

Christ and the Holy Spirit were only treated as emanations of God. The doctrine of the Trinity was not accepted and the Cross was denied.

All this is no more than a variant of Manicheeism, ruled as an heresy nearly a thousand years before, but still finding its supporters in the eleventh and twelfth centuries in far-away Bulgaria —the Catharists in France were often called Les Bougres, 'The Bulgars'—still sliding its way along the commercial routes to Venice, across northern Italy, and finally into France. If Catharists went up to northern France or to the Loire, they were pounced on and burnt pretty fast. But in the south men were so accustomed by trade to the vagaries of Eastern ideas, that they developed tolerance. For instance, they did not feel strongly about the Jews, of whom they harboured large numbers, while in England and Normandy King John was pulling out their teeth.

The Catharist sect was divided into two groups: 'Les Parfaits' (the Perfect Ones, who took on a higher degree of moral responsibility than their fellows and virtually acted as priests) and 'Les Croyants' (the Believers, who were allowed to indulge in such natural passions as eating meat, fasting only three days a month, having a wife, and fighting within reason). If a Perfect One even touched a woman by mistake, he was due for an additional three days' fast. He embraced the vows of chastity, not in the way of the clergy as a symbol of the marriage of the Church with Christ but to help in the ending of the human race which, since procreation was devil's work, was evil. No Perfect One could enter into judgment nor take oath, since oaths were a conception of the Old Testament, and in their view Jehovah was the equivalent of Satan, the power of evil. They had their own ritual, and their own form of sacrament, the *Consolamentum*, which only the Perfect Ones could receive. Inevitably this roused scandal against them and they were suspected of all sorts of immorality. But the many records of their trials do not suggest any foundation for such a common type of slander; and one may be sure that St. Dominic's Inquisition would have followed up a cotton-thread of evidence on such a point. Instead one concludes that the Catharists were entirely heretical, admitted it, and would not recant even under torture. They showed themselves much readier to die than to live in a world they despised; they flung themselves willingly upon the bonfires. There is the pathetic case of a Catharist who did recant under torture. He was brought up to sign his confession the next day, but refused to do so, and begged to be killed. 'I know that under torture I shall recant again. Kill me now, so that I may die in my faith.'

* * *

One royal and three noble families in this region became deeply involved in this heresy, which in time drew a crusade upon this lovely part of France. They were the Counts of Toulouse, whose immense dominions included Provence: the Viscounts de Tren-cavel who under the Counts of Toulouse held the land from Albi and Carcassonne to Béziers; and to the west, along the valley of the Ariège, the hardy Counts of Foix. Creeping up from the south, across the Pyrenees through Perpignan to Narbonne and Montpellier, ran the dominion of the King of Aragon, Pierre II, a handsome warrior, a wild lover, shifty for political advantage, but at this moment the darling of Pope Innocent III, since he had won a great victory over the infidel Moors of Spain. To him the crusade presented mostly a chance of extending his property at the expense of the others. The Counts and Viscounts were surprised by the vehemence of the crusade, since, as has been said, they were by nature tolerant, which is more than can be said even for the historians of the period as I found when, wanting to bring my knowledge up-to-date, I went in search of books.

The bookshops were at my hotel door, just off the Place du Capitole, where a relatively quiet, narrow street, the Rue du Taur, ran towards the university quarter and St. Sernin. I think I can still remember the individuality of five of the bookshops, much in the way that you remember your temptations or your sins. In the mood that it is more fun to find for oneself the perfect book with the unknown title, I wandered around these pleasant pastures, wondering at intervals how the owners ever put such good stocks together, seeing that their new books are mostly uncut and you can't flap through them. At least the assistants knew their stuff extremely well when I asked for help at last; and it was in a small but seemingly erudite shop, a miniature Black-well's, that I accepted defeat.

'What can you show me,' I asked, 'about the heresy of the Catharists and about what we call in England the Albigensian Wars?'

I was shown two books; but, said my assistant, there was a third, written from a different point of view, which really I must read to balance the others. Technically it was out of print, but he knew where to find the last copy in Toulouse. Could I come back at six-thirty and he would show it me?

So back I came at six-thirty and, miraculously, at six-forty the book was there, the last of its line. As I looked it over, perhaps a little injudiciously predisposed to it by the enthusiastic effort of the book-seller, I became aware of a man in his thirties reading what looked like a nineteenth-century transcript of a mediaeval chronicle, and he was reading it in a world of his own. The proprietor forked him out of it in this pleasant way.

'Monsieur,' he said, 'I have something here to show you which perhaps you will never have seen before—an Englishman who is interested in our wars of Albi. Have you ever met such a type?'

'No,' said the professor (for if he wasn't that already, clearly he soon would be). He surfaced through six centuries of history. 'Show it me,' he said, and I was presented first to his beard and then to his hand.

Now he was back in the 1950's. 'Where did you catch this local disease of ours?' he asked like a doctor.

'In my grandfather's library, assisted by a postcard of Albi sent me in 1923. I never knew my grandfather, since he died almost a hundred years ago; but I handled his books often, and he had a good mediaeval library of its date.'

We then became slightly technical, and I do not think I can have been a credit to my country, since the last thing of the sort I had read—a Franco-Spanish chronicle—had looked to me far more like Esperanto than good reading. I was rescued by the efficient bookseller, who came back to ask Monsieur le Professeur which of the three books I should take to make a balance. I was kindly and, I feel sure, well advised; and the don then fell back into his private, preferable world, dating around 1350, when some pretty nasty things were still going on, and Nuncio Pelegry, the builder of the Cahors tower, was negotiating some undurable truce between England and France.

With more than two books under my arm, I sought an aperitif in the Place du Capitole, to see if the tempo of the population ever dropped. You will have your drinks more peaceably in the Place Wilson (hated name). And then I began to think of what I should see the next day, and to think how clearly defined still was the old town, which had fought its battle for its favourite heresy out of sheer cussedness and killed the arch-crusader, Simon de Montfort, in 1218.

* * *

The last four Counts of Toulouse had died crusading; one had almost been elected King of Jerusalem. So, it seems strange to find their descendant firmly protecting heretics. But to find it so is to misunderstand the mutual obligation of feudalism, which to them made this as simple as a penny. The Catharists were their vassals. True, as they professed poverty, they were not fully valuable vassals; but, valuable or not, it was the overlord's duty to protect them and so their heresy, which seemed to him less dangerous to Christendom than the Saracens. Roger-Raymond de Foix looked at it just the same way; his wife and sister were open Catharists as was the Vicomte de Trencavel, in whose capital, Carcassonne, lived one of the Catharist bishops. All were agreed on one other point. Far too much land was given away to the church. All very well, of course, to buy your soul's salvation; but what about the overlord's revenue? This jealousy against the growing landed power of the church (which culminated with us nearly a hundred years later in the Statute of Mortmain) prompted reprisals to level the account. None of these great feudatories thought anything of keeping bishoprics vacant so that they could enjoy their revenues, nor of raiding church property.

To illustrate their manner of life, here are some of the points on which Raymond VI of Toulouse agreed he was guilty, and for which he accepted the humiliation of a public ecclesiastical flogging, dressed only in his shirt and his pants—the accepted costume of a penitent.

First he swore to accept the orders of the Pope or any of his legates touching the sins for which by all or any of them he had been excommunicated. Then he went on to admit:

(1) He had double-crossed some friends over a peace treaty.
(2) He had not kept his promise to clear his lands of heretics and of those who favoured them.
(3) He had not observed the 'Peace of God'—the days, including Sundays, on which the Church had decreed that no hostile action might be taken by man against man.
(4) He had not regarded the requests of his enemies to have peace.
(5) He had given public offices to Jews and kept the revenues of the Monastery of St. Gilles and of many other churches.
(6) He was suspected of complicity in the murder of the Papal Legate, Pierre de Castelnau (of blessed memory) as having harboured his murderers. . . .

And so the list goes on for fifteen points, the last of which concerns the beating up of religious persons and other forms of brigandage—a minor item, one presumes.

To Innocent III these affairs had a sinister complexion. He found that the enthusiasm which had brought victory to the first crusades had dwindled; the latest, the third, had degenerated into a monstrous commercial enterprise. Threats, sermons, theological disputations led by the future St. Dominic had left the Catharists unmoved; few conversions had been made (despite Fra Angelico's fresco); the great lords still preferred the physical to the spiritual safety of their vassals. Against this background the Pope decided to leave the Saracens alone and to launch a crusade against the Catharists. Those who did not repent of their heresy were to be destroyed. He went further. He named Raymond VI as their protector and put his lands to the possession of anyone who should take them. Pilgrims and crusaders were further bribed by indulgences. This was indeed to whistle the vultures down from the north.

So in the name of Christianity began a most hideous contest. The 'Lightning Crusade' as it is called was directed against the dominions of de Trencavel. Owing to the folly of the citizens Béziers was captured in a few days, and a massacre of such unprecedented fury took place that the whole countryside was aghast. The chroniclers say that twenty thousand were killed in one day in hot blood, and that those sheltering in the cathedral were killed there regardless of age or sex to the number of seven thousand. This at once tells us to take these figures with a grain of salt. The dimensions of the place are known, and it could not have contained seven thousand people.

Whatever the true figure, this horror set the standard for both sides. If prisoners were taken at all, they were maimed irreparably in hands or feet, eyes, or less imaginatively—and left to die in a dungeon or by the wayside. I know only of one maiming, not obvious but so horrible that after the Catharists had used it once and the northern French had sent back a party of prisoners similarly damaged, the practice was stopped. At last these combatants for faith had found a limit of inhumanity which shocked them both. The forces of the Crusaders were drawn mainly from northern France, with contingents of English, Flemish and Germans.

The 'frightfulness' of Béziers led to the early surrender of Carcassonne after only a fifteen-day siege. To save the inhabitants their Viscount, Roger-Raymond de Trencavel, to his eternal honour gave himself up as a hostage, in exchange for their safety provided they took the road to Toulouse, to Spain, to anywhere out of the area. He died in prison, as he must very well have expected, within a few years and Carcassonne became the Crusaders' capital.

Here is a feature peculiar to mediaeval warfare, which gave a twist to this crusade. The period of feudal military service was a matter of forty days, 'la quarantaine'. After this length of operation not only the captains and the kings but the sergeants and the majors departed as well. No result could be gained after the forty days, unless one of the two commanders could pay for a lot of mercenaries. This moment was reached by the 'French', as the crusaders were always called, just after the capture of Carcassonne. The Duke of Burgundy and the Comte de Nevers were definitely going home with their men: what was to be done? The affair was left in the long run to this brutal, heroic, profoundly devout Simon de Montfort, with whom stayed an exceedingly small backing of relations from Normandy and their following, some skilled English under the intrepid Hugh de Lacy, and a few from the Ile de France. All these men had taken the Cross for their faith rather than for indulgences. What their trained soldiering accomplished is astonishing.

The military history of this crusade is one of the dullest things one could read. It was no more than a series of siege operations, reminding one very much of the first war—the reduction of strong points. Siege methods had advanced very little beyond Roman times, and it is odd to find that Pierre, Archdeacon of Paris, called in as the chief expert in siege warfare. There was only one decent open battle at Muret, southwest of Toulouse; and there de Montfort showed real tactical ability, backed up by Hugh de Lacy. For the Catharists Pierre II of Aragon took command and, against the sounder opinion of Raymond VI who at last had pinned down all de Montfort's forces in a bad position and wanted to starve them out, challenged battle and insulted Raymond's opinion. Pierre II was killed fighting an unnecessary battle and lost the cause of the Catharists, to which he had never been much attached. But he lost as well an enormous number of bourgeois and petty nobility from Toulouse, drowned, for the most part, in an unauthorised attack on the town. The Toulousains unjustly attributed this loss to their hated count. Stiffnecked, they would have nothing to do either with him or with de Montfort, whom the Pope nominated as Comte de Toulouse in Raymond VI's stead. They set themselves to a passionate and for a time successful resistance.

Now the future of Toulouse and all the count's wide lands became a focus of international intrigue. Though the Pope had created de Montfort the new count, he ceased to support him, preferring to give aid to the King of Aragon in his wars against the infidel Moors of Spain. Indeed, there is strong reason to think that the grasping, political pontiff intended to leave de Montfort in difficulties, so that the whole county of Toulouse should ultimately fall into the papal lap. But Simon de Montfort was too good a Frenchman to allow this to happen. When he found himself left in the lurch, he appealed to the French King, his suzerain for his Normandy estates, and paid fealty to him for the county of Toulouse. When he was killed in 1218, his colourless son, Amaury, by processes too complicated to relate here, transferred to the French crown the Duchy of Narbonne, the Marquisate of Provence, the County of Toulouse, the Viscounties of Albi, Béziers, Carcassonne, the rights of election to the bishoprics of Cahors, Toulouse and many other sees: a kingdom about the size of England, mostly the theme of this book.

The English had already been thrown out of Northern France after the battle of Bouvines (1214), and were left with only a small enclave in Aquitaine; by now the Kings of France were on the way to uniting their country for the first time since the days of Charlemagne. This was the practical outcome of the crusade against the Catharists, quite counter to the expectations of the popes concerned in it.

All this took place in a great age of faith. The immense length of the church of St. Sernin at Toulouse is a tribute to the crowds of pilgrims who visited that shrine of relics on their way to St. James of Compostella. Had the church closed the gap between the prelates and the lower clergy (almost as wide as that between noble and villein) they could have prevented the spread of heresy by good teaching. By contrast the Catharists, with all their faults, were teachers par excellence and successfully fed something at least to the hungry sheep who looked up in desperate need of spiritual consolation. The action of Innocent III brought the papacy to a purely mundane level. His conception of the church was fundamentally temporal—*Imperium Mundi*, the Empire of the World. He matched faith with faith only by scholiastic not by spiritual measures. Soldier of the church that he was, he preferred St. Dominic the Inquisitor to his contemporary, St. Francis of Assisi.

Had the dynasty of the Counts of Toulouse preferred administration to display, to infructuous generosity, to psychopathic idealism, to the romanticism of frequently underbred and spiteful troubadours, they might have kept the affection and respect of the vigorous Toulousains. Despite the efforts of Raymond VII, the dynasty failed to re-establish itself. How the city of Toulouse tackled the future we shall see.

* * *

You can beat the bounds of the old fortifications by walking at a steady, heating pace along the boulevards which replace the old walls: Armand Duportal Lascrosses, d'Arcole, Strasbourg, inevitably Carnot (the 'organiser of victory' has needed somewhere to walk in every sizable French town), Lazare. Then come three later but romantic 'Allées'—Feuga, Jules Guesde and Forain F. Verdier (whoever they may be)—which enclose some of the oldest historical monuments of the city and include the site of the Château Narbonnais, now the nineteenth-century Palais de Justice, where Simon de Montfort's men died or surrendered in 1218.

Within this corner of the city in a sad, pebbled square which no one has weeded for some time stands the cathedral, set off by fine, faded, classical houses and a pretty fountain with an obelisk. In its basin four small children are prettily struggling to coerce geese to spit the water the right way; nicely studied naturalism, slightly Rabelaisian. For me, the cathedral personifies whatever you are bad at doing—crosswords, pools, or mathematical puzzles. Nothing is in centre. The great tower is not on speaking terms with the north transept. On the west front, the main door, the rose window and the controlling arch all have different political opinions. When you enter, a similar experience awaits you. The chancel lies off line, a little to the left, and a gigantic single pillar confronts you in an exclamation of protest. The place is as inconsequent as if a succession of pretty society women had come in to do the flowers and had left half-way through. How right Lutyens was when he said it was easier for doctors than for architects to bury their mistakes.

But the detail pays for all. First there are the choir stalls; their miserere seats, carved with all the fancy of which their age was capable, include a rude one of Calvin preaching disguised as a pig. This Toulousain country is at home to good woodwork, and so you get a later, lay expression of what is a suitable seat for worship—the walnut pews in the nave for the *Capitouls*. These are early classical, lightly handled and well proportioned. Perhaps I have a northerner's liking for plain stone as such, and so am not accustomed to tapestry in a church. But the tapestries in Toulouse cathedral must have been designed expressly for each position above the choir stalls. They tell you the story of St. Stephen in handsome early sixteenth-century language. There are some good tombs, some relics of fine mediaeval glass and of glass from the early sixteenth century—the painted and etched kind, if that is your taste. It has a local interest in that it probably was made by the same family as worked for the cathedral at Auch, which we shall visit later. But pleasing and even splendid as some of these details are, I left the cathedral with the sense that it was the epitome of committee work—and seven hundred years is a long while to tolerate a committee. Why, even the boss bearing the arms of Count Raymond VI was not hoisted into position till the very year in which the Pope dispossessed him.

*   *   *

In the nineteenth century Toulouse went modern, and built two axial thoroughfares, cutting through the old part of the town. The Rue de Metz runs from the Pont Neuf (over which you drive in from Auch) almost to the cathedral; at right angles the Rue de Languedoc runs from the Palais de Justice and continues as the Rue d'Alsace Lorraine up to the Place Jeanne d'Arc. If we are to look for something more positive and consistent than the cathedral, we should look first for the old houses of the merchants and small nobility south of the Rue de Metz. Despite the inevitable destruction of modernisation, a surprising quantity of these houses has survived, so many in fact that we can take only a few examples. But those who risk life and limb on foot in the by-ways of Toulouse, will be liberally rewarded—in the extremity, by their insurance company no doubt.

* * *

It had never crossed my mind that Toulouse should have made part of its fortune from woad—the herb with which, as we all know, the ancient Briton dyed his skin. It still grows wild in England but very few people have attained the bravado of Monty Rendall, the old headmaster of Winchester, who cultivated it in his garden. But here is the truth. Around Toulouse, in all that nice sunshine and occasional rainstorms, the endearing little plant will crop six times a year. Then you harvest it, you boil it, you pound it into a paste, do it up into the shape of an egg, call it 'paste' and ship it abroad. Until indigo was imported in quantity from the east, woad was among the best exports of Toulouse as the finest blue vegetable dye in the world of its day. Out of this blue weed, you might say, many of the best houses were built in the sixteenth and seventeenth centuries.

Let us think ourselves back again at the Palais de Justice, and start out a different way, along the line of the Garonne through the old parish of Notre Dame de la Dalbade ('of the whiteness'), and we will keep in mind the peculiarity of Toulouse—that it is a brick-built town, since the fields round it are clay and you had to fetch the stone for decoration from the Corbières mountains some way off. The combination of the two materials produces a fine sparkle.

Close to the church, on opposite sides of the road, are two great palaces, the Hôtel de Pierre and the Hôtel St. Jean, an exciting contrast of styles. The Hôtel de Pierre has all the effulgent, restless energy of the south, ennobled with trophies of arms and fruit. Deeply channelled pilasters flower into Corinthian capitals, above which rises another storey of little broken pediments, cornices, friezes and windows. Nothing stands still for a minute. Yet the disposition of all this brilliantly cut stone ornament is so well set off by plain areas that it invigorates rather than overpowers you. The courtyard behind all this *brio* is beautifully quiet and calm. Here brick predominates and stone only intervenes in the doors and fenestration. Figures of philosophers and prophets carry the lintels; and there seems a conspiracy of silence to leave them quiet at their already three-hundred-year-old task of supporting the doors.

Across the street is the departmental office of the Ministry of Agriculture, a very different proposition. With its peaceful brick arches and the long façade three storeys high, this place has the air of a monastic suburb of the Church of the Dalbade. It is for the most part mid-seventeenth-century work; the staircase to the first floor is quite fine. This corner of the city is rich. Shouting at the quiet of this building is the Hôtel St. Clamy, tremendously ornate with heraldry, trophies, pilasters, all bustling about the front in their carved stone. And then, as the key to the quarter, is the church itself, Notre Dame de la Dalbade.

One sees only a tenth of what it was, since there have been such a sequence of fires, of rebuilding, and similar disasters. The whiteness of the stone is quite astonishing in the bright sunlight so that the tall interior seems to swim in a vacancy contained by the simple ribs of the vaulting. After fire, one other disaster awaited this aspiring thing. Destruction. Some time in the nineteenth century the old spire had been repaired and, apparently, unsettled in the process. Without warning, it collapsed in a night, spreading devastation not only on the nave but on surrounding houses. There is a story told of a young girl in a nearby house who was awakened by the crash of the falling masonry. Thinking it was the end of the world she rushed to her more heavily sleeping parents, who at once disbelieved her story. They told her she was mad, but got her to sleep in the long run. Another shock was in store for her. All she had ever seen from her bedroom window had been this remarkable spire. Next morning it was not there and the frightened child thought she must have gone blind. At length, so we hope, she was comforted.

An endless richness dignifies these merchant prince houses, some of the best of which are on the river side of the Place du Capitole round the Rue Gambetta. There is the Hôtel Bernuy, for instance, built by a Spaniard from Burgos who became fabulously wealthy in the early sixteenth century. The place has now become a *Lycée*, and I trust the pupils develop some sense of the beautiful surroundings in which they work. The courtyard has all the architect's wiles; four-centred arches with amply coffered ceilings contrast with round arches; inventive balustrading is there, pilasters and medallions. The stairway to the first floor recalls one at Toledo in the hospital of Santa Cruz.

The Hôtels Dahus, Beringuier-Maynier, Palaminy, Tournier, Gaspard Molinier all attest the invention and the art of the Toulouse architects of this period. But before we look at the greatest of them we should consider two churches, one the church of La Daurade ('the golden church'—*dorata*), in whose parish most of them belong, and the Eglise des Jacobins, close to the Hôtel Bernuy, all that is left of the great Dominican monastery, the seat of the Inquisition, hated by the Toulousains.

The Daurade is the most extraordinary place. Things architectural have been going on there since classical times. It began as the temple of Minerva, and the Visigoths when they had settled into Christianity covered it with gold mosaics as sumptuously as any church in Ravenna. It became a focus of legend—that Christ himself had descended from heaven for its consecration; that the Emperor Theodosius wished to be buried there; that Clémence Isaure (of whom more later) actually was, and so on. Add a miraculous Black Virgin, protectress of pregnant women, and you have a prosperous mediaeval pilgrimage centre. But none of it, except the miraculous statue, do we see today. They had neo-Greek ideas in about 1770, which condemned all this desirable antiquity, replacing it with a structure, notable in its fashion, which would serve admirably as, say, law courts.

A more sinister fate overtook the splendid church of the Jacobins, as the church of the Dominican Monastery was known. Desecrated in the French Revolution it lost all its statues. The renowned stained glass was torn out and put into an outhouse, of which the roof subsequently fell in, crushing the treasure to splinters. Its ruin was not even yet completed. Napoleon took it over as barracks, divided it into three floors, using the ground floor for stabling, which completely destroyed the paving.

F

Though restoration work is now in progress, the place is a desolation. But none of these accidents nor the calculated endemic enmity of the town can destroy its majesty. Down the centre of the nave runs a single line of seven slim circular columns, rising from plain hexagonal bases to simple capitals, from which spring the ribs of the quadripartite vaulting. The seventh column, the most easterly, is called The Palm Tree, since from its capital spring like leaves the thirty-two ribs which bind together the seven tall, narrow, pointed windows of the chancel. Apart from the engaged columns on the north and south walls, which in themselves are necessities, there is no decoration; the loveliness, the aspiring height of the place, is the achievement of pure architecture. Outside one sees a stimulating tower of the type much favoured in this district, changing after four storeys from the square plan to the octagon with pairs of pointed windows to each facet, a brilliant effect in sunshine. There is one other feature, again very typical here. I know it only from a photograph, which looks to have been taken from a high room some distance away; at least I could never find the position myself. The buttresses are linked to one another by tall pointed arches, like an immense arcade high above the windows. They cast dramatic shadows.

*   *   *

Before the revolution the extent of the monasteries in Toulouse was quite prodigious. All of them, of course, were sacked by the insurgents. The Augustins survives in part, including, thank heavens, its two exquisite cloisters and chapter house, now a museum. A very admirable museum, too, specialising in Romanesque and Gothic sculpture, quite indispensable for anyone interested in those periods and in the individuality of the local style. The cloisters and the delicately vaulted hall make a perfect setting. The picture gallery is above average, and the attributions less optimistic than is often the case in a provincial collection.

But of the Carmelite monastery not a stone remains from its vast buildings. Even the Place des Carmes, the largest square after the Place du Capitole, does not cover its whole area; yet it is spacious enough to contain easily a very large market indeed, housing within its hideous exterior those pleasing heaps of exotic fruits and vegetables of unfamiliar hues, those banks of flowers, those ordered rows of the desirable *charcuterie* festooned with sausages, the inevitable stalls of cheap ready-made garments in execrable taste and heavy 'sensible' shoes and boots and Wellingtons.

It houses something else, down a little alley-way, the Rôtisserie des Carmes. This is a small restaurant of irregular shape in a little courtyard. We had the impression that most of the other people were regulars, since, unless by divination, their habits seemed to be quickly known. Of course, as English clients, our habits would be unpredictable even by the Delphic Oracle; but our every whim was gratified by quite admirable and unfussing service, which I have seldom found bettered. While the food we ate there did not sound particularly adventurous, it was perfectly cooked and a lesson to those who say that French cooking is always so complicated. Something new to me was a local cheese, *Prairie*, a be-herbed cream cheese of delicious flavour lighter in taste and consistence than a Camembert.

I was entertained, too, by finding framed on the wall a French doggerel poem on good manners equivalent to our 'Please remember, don't forget' type of thing some people used to put up in their bathrooms. As it is French, the advice on married happiness centres round the kitchen. It contains a good many French weights and measures, which cost me some dictionary work; so I asked my wife and Cyril Butterwick to do a verse translation for me. Here it is.

RECIPE FOR MARRIED HAPPINESS
Rôtisserie des Carmes, Toulouse

First in a pipkin put no less
Than several pounds of hopefulness.
An hundredweight then add to these
Of constant readiness to please
And small attentions, all a part
Of kindness springing from the heart.

Add to a quart of confidence
Five cupfuls of obedience.
Scatter in gaiety to taste
And do not think it woeful waste
Of sweetness to use countless grains.
But to disperse the growing pains
Of boredom, mind you bring to it
A milligram of madcap wit.
Mark that in cautiousness you halt
At more than just one ounce of salt,
Which to dispense without restraint
Would try the patience of a saint.
Simmer this on a steady heat
Until your mixture is replete
With love and friendship. In this wise
A cake celestial will rise,
A daily slice of which will leaven
A marriage that is made in Heaven.

RECETTE DE BONHEUR CONJUGALE

Mettez d'abord dans un bocal
Deux ou troix livres d'espérance.
Puis vous y joignez un quital
De petits soins, de complaisance,
Une mesure de bonté,
Un quarteron de confiance
A la discretion de la gaieté,
Quatre ou cinq pots d'obéissance,
Cinq ou six livres de douceur.
Et, crainte de monotonie,
Ajoutez à la bonne humeur
Un milligramme de la folie.
Quant au sel, n'en mettez qu'un grain.
Car, si vous passez l'ordonnance,
Au lieu d'une once il faudra bien
En mettre deux de patience.
Cuire tout au petit feu
D'une chaleur bien soutenue,
Qu'amour et qu'amitié tout deux
Ne le perdent jamais de vue.

Vous obtiendrez par ce moyen
Une galette bien pétrie,
Dont un morceau cheque matin
Suffit pour embellir la vie.

*   *   *

From one corner of the Place des Carmes you might just
discern in the distance the noblest church of them all, and you
have not too long a walk down streets of ancient names and
ancient houses—Filatiers (the spinners), des Changes, St. Rome.
Then you cross the Capitole to my booksellers' street, Rue du
Taur, where the legend of St. Sernin (the local form of St.
Saturnin) begins.

St. Saturnin was martyred in Toulouse in 257 during an
uprising against the Christians. He was tied to the tail of an
infuriated bull, which raced away with him from the Place du
Capitole, then as now the centre of the city. The saint did not
long survive; his followers marked down the place of his death
and erected a humble chapel where they buried him, quite close
to what is now the Eglise du Taur, the Church of the Bull. Inside,
the church has no remarkable feature; but the bell tower outside
set a fashion which suited the neighbourhood for a long while.
It is economical and makes a brisk skyline. Between twin turrets
is set a pedimented wall, pierced for the hanging of the bells; it
is a brick builder's technique, not a stonemason's. In a village
church, it can be quite a humble but decorative piece of work to
hold a single bell. The archetype at the Taur accommodates three
bells and has another embattled storey above pierced with
lozenges. At any time of day the silhouette is spectacular.

And to digress for one moment more before we reach St.
Sernin—the lozenge is quite a favourite form in this individual
land, so different from northern France. It is true that the tower
of the Jacobins seems to be ornamented by pointed arches with
a roundel above; and it is easy to mistake their forms in bright
sun. Actually what looks to be the 'roundel' is a diamond fitted
into the 'pointed arches', which in fact are half-diamonds. The
Toulousains and the men of Languedoc like their shadows

violent, just as they like to stripe their brickwork with courses or dressings of stone: they must have felt that for decoration at a height this rectilinear treatment gave a stronger flash to the shadows, which the subtler curves and mouldings of the northern architects would not have achieved.

Now we must move on past the alluring windows of the book-shops, the sole attractions of the Rue du Taur, down to the great abbey church of St. Sernin, infinitely larger and more splendid in every way than the cathedral, St. Etienne. As it was originally an abbey, Napoleon took his usual short cut with the subsidiary buildings, pulled down what he didn't need, and used the rest for barracks, for horses and for stores; for Toulouse was a main base during the Peninsular War. Indeed at the back of the Hôtel de Ville, on a wall lightly wounded by bullets, you will find a plaque commemorating the savage bombardment of the town by General Hill—the last battle of the Peninsular War. Now, except for the little College of St. Raymond, which houses a good museum, nothing is left of all these glories.

People's ideas differ on the best entrance to the abbey itself. Entering by the fine south door, you do get, it is true, an imme-diate impression of size, mystery and shadows from this forest of columns. I went in this way for the first time for the low reason that it was the nearer and that I then knew no better. But the singular purity of the west front—its twin doors, the little group of arches over them, the great, uncompromising roundel above —gives you a quiet enough mind to survive what is almost physical shock, the impact of the nave.

Tall, long, grey, the round stone roof and the round support-ing arches of the nave and triforium move your eye towards the distant altar, as if you were part of a procession. The abbey's architecture itself seems like a procession of worship, with its disciplined ripple of arches, the steadiness of the piers, the Damascus light which falls at the transept crossing. Then—a subtle piece of artifice—beyond the crossing come the wonder-fully carved choir stalls and the abbot's stall, their dark sparkle showing jewel-bright as detail upon detail catches the glint of sun, enhancing with their low tone the radiance of the crossing, and giving you the breath, as it were, to take the last strides to the altar steps, to the high, baroque altar, which contains the saint's tomb supported by bronze bulls, condemned to this task in perpetuity for his martyrdom.

The choice between offering you a long series of guide book details and writing the full description, which a professional might expect but will not get from me, is simply made. I shall do neither thoroughly. There is one technical device which I shall mention because of its beauty. The architect of 1075, the St. Raymond whose little College lies across the square, set himself the structural problem of supporting this heavy stone arched roof, and he solved it by his beautiful triforium. Above the main arches of the nave and directly over the inner aisles, he set a corridor the width of the aisles. This, too, he arched over, thereby distributing part of the weight outwards on to the walls or columns of the aisles. The only flaw that one can pick in the whole is the thickening of the piers of the crossing, even though it adds to the perspective. But it had to be done to carry the extra weight of the storeys added to the tower after the Albigensian wars.

But there is detail enough and to spare, worth any man's time if it suits his taste. There is the original altar table, a Roman slab decorated in the eleventh century, which Urban II consecrated in 1096. There is a wonderful copper Crucifixion of the twelfth century, the sculpture of the Ascension over the south door, the door of the Counts of Toulouse, and beside many other delights there are the two crypts. Beautiful in themselves they have been lightly painted in the spandrels and vaulting with floral designs, so that you descend into a coloured half-light. Then you are in a reliquary world; for originally the abbey was founded as a repository of relics of the saints beginning with St. Sernin in a coffer of silver-gilt on which are *repoussé* the offending bull and escorting angels. Against the faded colour of the decoration glimmer or shine these reliquaries in enamel, in gilt, in blue and turquoise, in silver-gilt and gold. Sometimes there are great coffers plated in silver, wondrously decorated and inscribed, containing the relics of several saints. Together they form a miniature history of reliquary design, and their multi-coloured tone in the very quiet light was oddly exciting.

A last look outside at the spectacular tower, model for so many others, a last wander round the exterior, and the huddle of supporting apses at the east end, which Viollet-le-Duc coated over with stone roofs as a tortoise's shell instead of leaving them covered with decent drain-pipe tiles; and we must be away.

*   *   *

We have a last assignation. It is with a lady but, I hasten to add, a mythical lady: Clemence Isaure. It takes place at the Hôtel Assézat, the noblest architecturally of the merchants' houses. So we go back to the parish of Notre Dame de la Dalbade to look over the place that this fortunate and unfortunate man, Pierre Assézat, built probably before 1550, for that was the climacteric of his life.

He came from the Rouergue, that romantic, hilly country around Rodez, north-east of Toulouse, and he slid into wealth. He was a Midas of a man, who could not help accumulating money. His two sons-in-law made wills in his favour and predeceased him. This was the kind of fortune which attended him. In a single year he sold to the Bordeaux market alone woad to the value of 150,000 gold francs. He was a *Capitoul*; he was the profiting receiver of the rents in Rouergue for the Queen Mother and the President of the Chamber of Commerce (as we should put it). Soon he would be consul.

And what did it profit him? This is a moral story. Conscience, not slim practice, was his undoing. He was entirely devoted to the cause of humanism and the Reformed religion; an Erasmus among merchants. The men of Toulouse had had enough of heresy; so they exiled their Midas, their Croesus, their patron of exquisite taste. But before misfortune quite vanquished him, he had summoned a French architect, a pupil of Michelangelo, Nicolas Bachelier, to build him the town house which is his uncompleted memorial.

Italian, of course, the house is in respect of the orders of its Ionic, Doric and Corinthian columns, Italian in the twisted columns of the entrance door. But still, how French! One thinks of Monsieur Nicolas going to sit at the feet of Michelangelo, but still swaggering in his French heart—'I shall learn all that these Italians can teach me and then build the French way'. The entrance to the courtyard is undeniably Italian, but the balcony on your right, carried on rather heavy consoles, is certainly French, and so is the delicious loggia and its double stair on the left. In front of you, at the angle of the two completed wings is a projecting square tower, housing the principal staircase, which you will find nowhere in Italy but everywhere in sixteenth-century France. Behind this rises a tower and turret which are pure Toulousain. The whole is a perfect example of a foreign idiom genuinely absorbed into the local dialect.

The Hôtel Assézat is so much more than a fascinating architectural curiosity. It is staggering, it is brilliant in every way. Bachelier may have bought his costume jewellery in Italy, so to speak, but he knew where to pin it on his building. Not for nothing has the Syndicat d'Initiative chosen this place for the local display of *Son et Lumière*—that pleasant technique, so acceptable on a warm summer night—which puts over the history of a floodlit town or building by playlets recorded by distinguished players. Every facet of the Hôtel gains value by this method.

It is now the Burlington House of Toulouse. It houses the learned societies of the district, which are varied—from the Académie des Sciences, Inscriptions et Belles Lettres, down to, say, Société de Médecine et de Pharmacie or the Société de Géographie. In this *galère* an Académie des Jeux Floraux (of floral games) seems as much a contradiction in terms as a battle of flowers. Yet it is the lineal descendant of the oldest literary society in Europe, perhaps in the world.

As far as history is ever true, it is perfectly true that in 1323 seven gentlemen of Toulouse wrote to the surrounding nobility and troubadours inviting them to a party in their very desirable meadows from May the first to the third and offering a prize for the best poem; the seven were to be the judges and called themselves the Consistoire de la gaie Science.

The party was a great success. All literary Southern France
turned up; and the thing became an annual event. After a generation had passed, it was felt right to codify the practice of the
society which by now granted degrees in 'Gaie Science', and a
document was drawn up, of which the preamble reads like a
miniature of its own date (1356).

> To kings, princes, dukes, marquesses and earls, dauphins,
> admirals, and viscounts, doctors, masters, licentiates, and bachelors
> of arts, knights, barons, justices, citizens, merchants and artisans.
> This is written and given at Toulouse in an orchard decked with
> flowers of divers colours, furnished with numbrous plants of mar-
> vellous perfume, with fruit trees large and small, with evergreens
> where we hear the song of countless birds.

The constitution of what now became the Consistoire du gai
Scavoir (why, I don't know) need not detain us. It is a pity, it
might be said, that at this peak moment of the new amatory poem,
the Consistoire should have pinned the competitors down to
religious themes, preferably drawn from the life of the Virgin.
After almost two hundred years of this fine drawn thread, perhaps
because of the increasing competition of poets from the north of
France who wrote in the Langue d'Oil, not the Langue d'Oc of
the south, the Consistoire began to look for new subjects. And it
is here, I suspect as others do, that forgery creeps in.

In 1558 Jean Blondin, a *Capitoul*, got up and addressed the
citizens. He told them of remarkable new evidence, just discovered, concerning the will of a lady long dead, a renowned
poetess, Dame Clémence Isaure, whose tomb was in the Daurade
church. This paragon woman of entire chastity had, as was known
(said Blondin), made bequests, not to the poor only, but to the
town as well, comprising all the rents from the various markets
she had built for the sale of fish, of vegetables and what have you.
But here was the news. A condition had been attached to the
bequest and all citizens should know of it. It meant that every
year a prize must be given for the best poem, and it should take
the form in which kings had given it to Dame Clémence—golden
flowers of the violet, the eglantine, the marigold, the rose, the

carnation. Should these conditions, including the May Day feast and the poets' contest, not be observed, then the rents passed to the city treasury, a thing no sensible man could wish.

Now there was subtlety about this idea of Jean Blondin. It suited the Consistoire (who gradually shifted their name to the Académie des Jeux Floraux), since it gave them a run of new subjects, including the encomium of Dame Clémence; and it sewed up the town's interest in the continuance of the Jeux Floraux, which was developing into valuable tourism with all these literary characters coming down from the north. If the thing proved a wash out, then 'the rents of Dame Clémence' reverted to the city treasury, from which actually they had come in the first instance. That's accountancy.

No evidence has ever been offered of the existence of this touching document; so from forgery we pass to malice. About 1623 some nasty-minded antiquary (local history was a nice new game in those days) pointed out that her funerary statue showed Dame Clémence clasping to her bosom not the royal flowers but a mere rosary. And (he added) what pray was she doing with a lion at her feet? In those mundane days they knew well how bogus relics had hit the pilgrimage trade at some of the monasteries. So the *Capitouls* commissioned two good sculptors (recording their names) to give her effigy new marble arms with hands holding her favourite flowers and to remove the equivocal lion. That is what you see today.

The scholars got at poor Clémence Isaure later in the seventeenth century; but their critical efforts were smothered by a young man who in 1809 sent to the Archbishop of Paris two documents, found (so he said) at the fine monastery of St. Savin in Poitou, which proved that she was known and respected as early as 1496.

Many reputable people, however, still keep their faith in the old romance. Still the old society flourishes. Still it meets at the Hôtel Assézat in a charming first-floor room with beautiful parquetry, Louis XV décor and Louis XVI furniture. Still the annual banquets are held at the expense of the city; still are presented the vases of flowers in silversmith's work of vile nineteenth-century design. In the Library are the records from the earliest times—anything but forgeries—and copies of the winning poems. And the medals, too, are there, which are given to the runner-up in the competition, displaying the mythical Isaure in profile, clasping to her right breast her bogus flowers.

IV

Armagnac Land

IT was a romantic mood which enticed me to go from Cahors to the confines of the kingdom of the Bearn and Navarre. On the slim shoulders of Stanley Weyman I clambered to the attics of my memory to *A Gentleman of France* (or so I think) in which the name Nérac occurred—or was it one of those endless manors to which the foundling of the *Man in Black* laid claim? In fact, I went to Nérac because its name and history attracted me, although I was dangerously near crossing the self-imposed frontiers of this book. And yet there was something to be said for seeing the northern capital of a minor kingdom of France, Navarre, the shield and buckler of the Huguenots, from which broke out what was unpuritanically called 'The Lovers' War'. There was also more to be said for seeing the best Armagnac country.

If, as I did, you attack Nérac from Cahors, you turn back to the Paris road, and then branch off as if to Bordeaux (N.111), and follow the valley of the Lot. You will meet some delightful landscape. At this stage in his journey to meet the Garonne below Agen, the Lot is rather like an old countryman telling a story with a wealth of detail, which always seems to be curving away from the point. Fifty or a hundred feet below you, he ambles along at the foot of the cliff. Then with a dyspeptic's grunt, he lurches off to the left from a rock he cannot digest, and comes back again to provide *Virages sur 2 Km.* while tree-clad hills, sharp as miniature mountains, rise from the further bank.

You pass a tiny village, Castelfranc, with a gem of a twelfth-century church, and suddenly enter upon a wide valley, an ancient conquest of the river. Then again the hills give battle and their last stronghold is ecclesiastical—Puy L'Evêque, 'Bishop's Peak'. Rounding a bend, you see the heavily restored east end of a church, mutter to yourself 'that's no good' and accelerate.

Then you see a sort of Ruskin-dream village translated from Italy to the French mode. The church is no nineteenth-century fake. Instead it has rather a fine square tower over a vaulted porch between buttresses; it boasts a complicated rose window, above which are two courses of amateurish pointed windows. There is a circular tower set in the angle of the south aisle and some good sculpture.

Surprise does not end here. In a few hundred yards you find yourself on a large triangular *place*, with a mediaeval fortress off to the left and to the right, far below, a plain dotted with farms and villages and small talk, a wider world than the narrow valleys we have traversed. And below you to the left is the ancient townlet, a place still vivid. If you look up at it from across the river, it rises up the steep hill, a diversification of geometrical shapes by squares and oblongs of grey stone; uprights with tiled roofs, old round turrets, the square tower of the château; then cypress and cedar and ivy right up to the amateurish arches of the church. The place lost touch with history centuries ago, but the narrow rough-paved streets are lively with flowers, which are potted out on racks outside the houses in any old disused earthenware, bottomless saucepans, untrustworthy cans and so on. They may have to live on the cheap at Puy L'Evêque, but they live gaily.

In fact I had made a mistake when I chose this road. A confusion possessed my mind that somewhere I had read of the colourful charms of Villeneuve-sur-Lot. They were non-existent; for I do not think that as maximum quality one stack of red-wood by the river with a saw-mill background and a minor street and gateway of sixteenth- and seventeenth-century brick would suffice to pass even tourists' 'eleven-plus', that debatable frontier. Neither did Agen give me much comfort. The cathedral will do, particularly if you like sixteenth-century stained glass windows; but the town was so busy keeping alive that it had no charms for me. It did, at least, give me a laugh against myself. We had had an excellent lunch at the Restaurant Basque with a dry white wine, Placiot, from the Corbières Mountains and a *pâté* which both of us had admired. Could we buy some, we asked.

Oh, yes. No difficulty about that. And out it came, no home-made joy—in a tin.

But Nérac at least we found and its little royal château, which was rather a Castle of Dalliance than a Castle of Indolence. Glamour it must once have had, when one thinks of the ladies, the poets, the warriors, the statesmen who gathered there. The peevish might say that today the percentage of surviving glamour stands in direct ratio to the surviving portion of the château: twenty-five per cent. I will not argue with them. I do not regret my visit.

It is so small. Half of one of the Louvre's courtyards would comfortably contain the whole original castle, which would still be about two storeys the lower. There was no room for the ministers. Sully and the rest lodged in the small houses of Old Nérac across the river, which offered no more grandeur than a successful wool-merchant's house at, say, Chipping Campden. As you contemplate these grey relics on the opposite slopes, you start wondering at and admiring the stamina of Henri IV and his entourage, who with so little money behind them, with nothing really except faith and intelligence and courage, survived the pressure of the Catholic League, of all-powerful Henri Duc de Guise, of the twisting policies of Henri III, and finished triumphantly with Henri IV placed on the throne of France, one of the great French kings.

Henri had married Henri III's sister, Marguerite de Valois, a saucy girl, and when first they set up together at Nérac all went well, since they amused one another and they amused themselves. Mistresses came and went. There was La Corisande, an intelligent creature, dark-haired with a tall forehead, a notable collector. There was a character who comes straight from musical comedy —Fleurette, the baker's daughter, who drowned herself in the river for love of her faithless king and to whom there is a rather low-grade academic, marble monument in the lovely *Promenade de la Garenne*, by the river's bank—the setting for *Love's Labour's Lost* some say. But Fleurette herself was no character of fiction. She was enough of flesh and blood to sell her body for a document of concessions to the bakers' confraternity, which still exists in writing. And then there was Françoise de Montmorency Fosseux (familiarly called 'La Fosseuse', which I take to conceal a faintly rude, lost joke). When Henri asked Marguerite to supervise the lying-in of his illegitimate child, she did it; but then their loose devotion snapped. No one could say after that that the Navarres were a happily married pair. Marguerite was sterile, and France needed an heir; divorce followed.

*   *   *

The merry arched balcony of the Château retains a great deal of character from the days of the Vert-Galant. It is quite charming, and the scale-model of the complete building conveys the air of a pocket palace for a pocket kingdom. The balcony or loggia is sixteenth-century and the earlier ground-floor rooms are prettily vaulted. But my most treasured recollection is of something necessarily ephemeral—a conversation.

An old woman with severely bobbed grey hair—she was a pioneer of the fashion in 1916, she told us—takes you round enthusiastically. She starts you on the first floor, and I should tend to doubt whether all the names she gives the rooms—*Salle Cathérine de Medici* and so on—are absolutely justifiable historically; but by this method at least she reminds you of the distinguished or dashing people who have stayed at the place. Then there are the pictures, which Madame enhances with optimistic attributions. '*Voici, Monsieur, deux véritables Tournères (Turners).* . . . *Voilà—deux Poussins.*' She does not dwell on the question of attributing them to the older or the younger Poussin, and scorns the conservative official label on these rather dull classical landscapes: 'French School; 17th century'. It would be cruel to disturb her. The privileged wand of age has turned her flock of geese into a white pride of swans swimming gracefully down the river of her memory.

What a memory she has: Her volcanic fires of protest are not yet extinct. The ground-floor room containing nineteenth-century lithographs and watercolours of Nérac as she first remembered it (by deduction, it would be not later than 1884) touches her off finely.

St. Sernin at Toulouse:
'The Abbey's architecture itself seems like a procession of worship'

Condom: the Cathedral crowning the hill above the river Baïse

'What idiots we all are, idiots!' she exclaims with rising passion, pointing to an indifferent oil. 'Never to think of the consequence of what we do! I remember this house, a noble house with servants, horses, carriages, a fine house fine. Now the roof is down and they live in a corner. No! No! No! I say.'

'What are these?' we asked about a frame of topographical drawings.

'Those were Old Nérac, Monsieur-Dame, where the principal courtiers had their houses across the river. That one belonged to a mistress of Henri IV, who used to meet her in the Pavillon d'Amour, which you will see down there by the river. But now what is her house? Idiots that we are, a barber has bought it—*a barber*. No! No! No! Impossible!'

'And this one—(pointing to another drawing)—this one is a worse case. It was the Duc de Sully's house and now a modiste has it for a shop. What could be worse than a *modiste* for such a great house? No! No! No! I say.'

She was fascinating as a character, so firmly entrenched in the past but armed with flame-throwers of vituperation ('Ils sont des sauvages, les Néraçais'). The least we could do was to cross the river to spit upon the modiste's shop on her behalf and to scorn the barber's scissors. There it was, as she said, this charming group of ancient houses scrambling up a hill from the river. The river is crossed by a very old and beautifully arched bridge, a river which can spare time to turn the old mill. These fighting Huguenots were never rich and you see in this group of small houses, so disproportionate to their owners' political influence, a token of their devotion and their faith.

* * *

From this sentimental detour I made my way back towards the Armagnac country, which I had longed to know, ever since my first acquaintance with the liqueur at a greedy but not exhausting lunch in 1930 which included to the tune of Château Yquem sweet Virginia ham and pickled peaches; and then followed Stilton and Croft's 1908 with the ancient armagnac to seal our content. I got a contract for a year, out of it. Coming from Nérac you drive through smiling, well-watered country, filled with orchards of plum-trees which supply the confectioners of Agen with the material for their speciality—a sweet, half-dried plum. And if a thing as subtle as that in texture and flavour can be made, I can only be sorry for the husband of the woman who invented prunes; she must have had a nasty mind.

The approach to Condom from this side gives you the more impressive view of the cathedral. If you come in from the south, from Auch, you may not recognise how firmly it stands on its hill above the river Baïse. There is its great square tower with its set of double pinnacles and round-arched windows; the stolid, solid buttresses make a resounding play of light and shadow on the long flank; at the north-east corner is the slim octagon of a turret, the watchtower over the valley. What we see today was built mainly between 1507 and 1531; and you could scarcely find a more splendid example of the regional style of this date. Like those of Cahors the buttresses refuse the northern technique of 'flying'. The native taste is omnipresent: the preference for breadth rather than height in the proportions, the pleasure in rosette windows sometimes used in combination with other decorative forms of flamboyant tracery, the zest for bosses and capitals, deep carved and shining. Within this invigorating space its celebrated bishop, Jacques Bénigne Bossuet, afterwards Bishop of Meaux and tutor to Louis XIV's Dauphin, trained the production both of his voice and of his wonderful cadences in ecclesiastical oratory till no one of consequence could be said to have been decently buried unless Bossuet had pronounced over the corpse one of his resonant *Oraisons Funèbres*.

Within, each of the six bays contains a lateral chapel, which by contrast with the nave is relatively dark. Their solid darkness almost simulates support to the great, broad windows above the arches which fill the nave with light—a most stimulating piece of design. Some over-carved nineteenth-century stalls, of which the ornament recalled unpleasantly the radiators of the old-fashioned gas fire, supply the only defect. But you soon recover from this set-back by going out into the cloisters, which you enter through a double arcade. The vaulting here is rich, and the ribs meet in heraldic bosses, which alone are worth the visit. Formerly the place was an abbey, and the cloisters carry the monks' old quarters above them: a single storey divided by pilasters above the height of the buttresses, with rectangular, mullioned windows between them. An intricate balustrade finishes the otherwise severe elevation with an unobtrusive flourish.

Condom is not a place of any great size. It has a pleasant arched market against the side of the cathedral, which dates from about 1800 or before I should say; and there are some attractive eighteenth-century houses scattered about the unpretentious town centre. If you were French, you would go to it for the sake of the Armagnac, for it is a principal centre of the trade. We went to see the *caves* of one of the most famous marks, Laressingle, and their wisely generous proprietor insisted that we should taste an old bottle. How unlike my nurse, who was always saying to me: 'You don't have to touch it to see it, Master Andrew'—a manifest untruth.

Though the basic process of making Armagnac is very much the same as that of Cognac, there are necessarily some local differences. The first is historical. It was the Moors who first introduced the alembic, the still, into France; and since they were longer at large in Gascony than in Poitou, the Gascons learnt to use it first. This leads on to a fact that has not only astonished but profoundly shocked me. For three hundred years these Gascons were making Armagnac before brandy was invented—and did they drink it? No! They used it to wash out wounds. What a set of sober-sides they must have had for doctors! No doubt in those days Armagnac tasted no better than *eau-de-vie*, the water of life, serviceable enough as a primitive steriliser but, *surely*, still drinkable. It maddens me to think of three centuries of men who never drank Armagnac and had the chance to learn. Could it have been the influence of the English occupation down to 1453? Melancholy thought.

The second difference is one of local materials, and this falls into two parts, the justice of which I cannot judge. It is well known that the fine brandies are kept in casks of Limousin oak, while for Armagnac the black Quercy oak from the district

around Cahors is used. I have been told that the oak of the casks
has nothing to do in distinguishing the flavour of the two liqueurs;
I have also been told that it is half the answer. Where French
expert speaks against French expert, there is no scope for un-
educated English intervention.

Then again the districts matter. The accepted best is the
Tenarèze, really the valley of the Baïse from Nérac through
Condom to a little south of Vic-Fézensac. To the left is the valid
country of Bas Armagnac with Aire-sur-Adour as a western
point, embodying also strange-sounding names like Mogaro,
Fusterouau, Parlebosq, Courresan. Beside the valley of the Gers,
along the main road from Agen to Auch through Lectoure, you
get the district of Haut Armagnac, which despite its high-sound-
ing name is reputed the inferior country for the grape. And when
I say 'the grape' I am not really accurate, since in the best makes
three different types of white grape are grown to blend by distilla-
tion into Armagnac.

So, after this quick trip round the country we can find ourselves returned to Condom and its *caves* and can drive the humble
three kilometres which takes you out to Laressingle, from which
this mark of Armagnac to which we had been generously introduced takes its name. Unbelievably, the locals pronounce the
village name as if it were an English, not a French word—well,
you can hear the sound, like 'Larry Single'; but if you want to buy
a bottle from a merchant forget your native accent and try to say
the name the French way; then you will get it.

The little village stands lost in biblical fields of corn and vine, a
thirteenth-century fortified village—town in those days—with its
strong tower and gateway, its circuit of stone walls, the church,
the donjon and a few intact houses with a few inhabitants. Much
of its ruins lie within the walls, and I don't know when it came to
its death. But there is enough to explain in stone the meaning of
the word 'bastide', which is as common in these parts as on the
Dordogne. It was a feature of the Hundred Years War that both
sides built themselves these fortified towns or villages as garrison
points or strongholds for raiding or resistance. These places still
have the air of a single professional interest and the closed mind

that often goes with it, of which one can be conscious today in a place like, say, a mining or fishing village, where everyone follows the same occupation, and there is no conversation since everyone is dominated by a single idea.

It would be presumptuous of me, who have done no more than drink as I find, to pontificate in this matter of Armagnac; so I will say only that I found Laressingle always reliable, sustaining its flavour right to the end of the sip and making the most beautiful offering to your nose. I enjoyed very much another, Fert, which came from Vic-Fézensac; I met it at the Lion d'Or at Albi (an admirable hotel, we found, about which there must have been some mysterious quarrel, since it is listed neither by *Michelin* nor by the *Club des Sans Club*). It was presented, very aged and beautiful, dateless, '*hors d'âge*', with an astonishing bouquet but a slightly grapey finish. In its five-star form Fert has not so fine a bouquet, but a more consistent flavour. Then again we were introduced to a charmer, La Fontaine, at a little restaurant run by a young couple on the market square of Auch, 'Chez Bébé'. But the general truth is that if you watch the district from which the bottle comes you should be happy in your 'digestif', provided you do not expect Armagnac to taste like brandy, which would prove you a fool.

*   *   *

Some place-names are pictorial or evocative even when seen on a map. 'Auch' was in this class for me and until I had been there I could not tell whether the name would prove to express a most intemperate word such as one would use to correct a dog or a sigh of relief. In fact it is the latter, since you climb quite a sharp hill to reach the city from the north (N.21) and there on the summit the city lies in repose.

Instead of making my fanciful detour round by Nérac and Condom, you could drive much more easily direct to Auch from Agen. It is not a very interesting road until you approach Lectoure, an ex-cathedral town, and see on your right a ruined château, St. Mère, a gigantic cut-out silhouette of a place. It gives you the first touch of the drama, which you find better from a side road like D.36 whence you can see the city as set on a hill and unhidden. For in this part of Gascony the rivers—the Gers, the Baïse, the Ariège—run from the Comte de Foix in the south northwards or north-east to meet the Garonne in its westward course; and their valleys are separated by chains of upland on which stand such eminent places as the archbishopric of Auch and the bishoprics of Condom and Lectoure. So heavy and fertile is the black land of the valleys that after the thunder rains in which the climate specialises it becomes impassable. It is a comment on soil conditions that no real road was built between Bordeaux and Auch till 1753. The market towns are in the plains; it was only worth dragging a market cart up a steep muddy track to a bishop's see.

Seen from the valley of the Gers, which it commands, Lectoure is an impressive site, and one can understand why in late Roman times, with marauders pressing up from Spain it was so frequently besieged. In memory of its ancient state it retains in a side street the fountain of Diana vaulted over in mediaeval times. It has also a splendid and talkative tower to its ex-cathedral; buttresses set at the angles and flashing pinnacles carved above its ogee arches. A round watch-tower is set into the angle of the main tower and the north wall to keep an eye for forces on the move from Agen. Inside you find a strange contrast between the short romanesque nave, which might originally have been covered with flat domes like those at Cahors, and the flamboyant choir with its radiating chapels rebuilt after a sack by Louis XI. This is fine stuff of its kind; and it offers, too, a salute to the dignity of bishops in general which I do not remember seeing anywhere else. Above the central arch of the choir, filling the space between its point and the clerestory windows is an immensely tall crucifix, which is flanked by bishops' croziers crossed in saltire with a tassled mitre to mark the crossing. The proportion is splendidly exciting.

And now I must confess to a dereliction from duty. Somewhere in an intelligent book I found a reference to the remains of an early chapel attached to a château just off the road to the right as you go from Lectoure to Auch. I found it; I saw it; but can I find the book with its name? No. But if my memory is right you turn

off just before you enter Fleurange, and there is some kind of sign
to draw you to it. You go down a rather rough road between trees
and halt naturally at the bottom of the slope, which rises again to
a walled garden, and on your right beyond a good wrought-iron
clairvoyé is a calm, smallish, pedimented château with the date
1745 (or perhaps 1751) carved on it. But the right-hand flank of
the courtyard is far, far older, the relic of a monastery; its chapel.
There it is in stone, with its transepts and the most beautifully
trussed wooden roof. It was a strange experience; and that is why
I record it even in this imperfect way. For I could find only one
thin giant of a man about the place, whose dialect was a good deal
too much for me; but he was a genial type and agreed to let me in,
although I gathered that it was as much as his life was worth.
From his attitude when we were inside, he seemed to believe that
I was afflicted by heaven as I contemplated with unconcealed
admiration the windows, the roof under and within which they
kept their tractors and other farm implements. It was a singular
sight under the side-long mediaeval light (it was latish in the
afternoon) and took my memory back to those sepia drawings by
Cotman of those mediaeval Norfolk barns and tumbling-down
churches, which he made for Dawson Turner. I saw some casks
of wine out of the tail of my eye. My giant advised the white and
we had a happy glass together in this peculiar setting of petrol
and the Middle Ages.

* * *

Auch lies above the Gers, and you have the most dramatic
view of it from the east across the river. From that quarter the
cathedral is seen to its high advantage, with its watchtower and
the monumental staircase which ascends to it. Here, too, I have
been lucky enough to see the place in tears and smiles. The stone
of the cathedral, which sulks in grey half-mourning under the
rain, takes on an ivory gleam when the sun shines; indeed I do not
yet know another countryside, where sun and rain create such
glorious contrasts.

The reputations left by most French 'Intendants des Finances'
(the officials who collected the local revenues) are for the most

part tales of corruption and the well-feathered nest. But at Auch
there was one exception, Mégret d'Etigny, who set himself to
beautify his town. He planned a miniature version of the Place
Stanislas at Nancy, built by the exiled King of Poland, Louis XV's
father-in-law, with a splendid apparatus of planned façades and
wrought-iron gateways leading off to formal parks. The Place de
la Libération at Auch is d'Etigny's memorial, a better one than his
statue there, and even though his design has suffered some interference one can still appreciate its conception.

It never achieved the formality of the Place Stanislas, since the
Hôtel de Ville here is not placed on the axis of the cathedral to
which it looks down; but it has amplitude. The Hôtel de Ville has
pretty proportions and near it is a broad flight of marble steps
which lead to the long tree-shaded Cours d'Etigny, where all can
walk and talk at ease upon the height of the town. As you look
down to the cathedral, which lies beyond another, but irregular
square, the Place de la République, you see the abutments of the
great iron gates which once honoured the approach. It took me a
little time to divine this, since one of them is embedded in a
violently modern shop-front. The glare of modernity blinded my
eyes to the comfortable stonework of the upper storeys, the old
shuttered windows and tiled roofs of the ordered town architecture, which formed the angle of the square. Once observed, this
sets you a pleasant problem of reconstruction, a lesson, too, on the
importance of the roof-lines in French towns. You miss so much
if you keep your eyes pinned to street level, where ground floor
reconstructions can distract you from an older beauty.

Not far from the Hôtel de Ville is an attractive little museum,
housed in a secularised church with graceful vaulting of the
fifteenth century, full of light. There was a considerable collection
of Peruvian pottery, a subject of which I have no professional
knowledge whatever. Ignorance itself can be a liberator and I
found myself care-free in a world of new shapes and symbols,
which conveyed to my imagination ideas of unfamiliar mysteries
and obscenity. Yet the forms at times were singularly beautiful.
More intelligible to my western mind was the 'Oliphant of St.
Orens', the horn of elephant ivory such as Roland blew in vain at

Roncevalles, sculptured with birds and deer and fabulous beasts.
There is talk of starting a Folklore Museum, and the authorities
have already bought for the purpose the most ancient house in the
city, the Maison Feizel, its heavily carved mediaeval timbers set in
stone foundations of at least the fifteenth century.

But it is the cathedral which forms the glory of Auch, and it is
nobly displayed by the two wide spaces of the Place de la
République on the west and the Place Salinis on the south side. At
the east end the ground falls abruptly to the river Gers, and the
ascent is managed by a monumental staircase of white stone.
Nineteenth-century work it may be, but scenically it is immensely
effective. The steep climb is broken at intervals by balustraded
platforms, backed with a grotto and a fountain and planted with
dark trees or bushes. At these points the steps break into two
flights, like a river lapping round an island.

If you cross the Gers to survey the scene, you see across the
peaceful waters, which reflect the weeping willows and the trees
of the Avenue Sadi Carnot and the long mass of the brick and
stone Préfecture, once the Archbishop's eighteenth-century
Palace, while to the left the slim watchtower of the 1300's seems
to pin the Monumental Staircase into position. Higher still
dominating the two surges of the ascent, the windows, the buttresses, the flying buttresses and carved parapet of the great
cathedral sing in the heavens.

Both south and north doors of the cathedral have their Renaissance charms, though the carving of the detail round the north
door was never completed: the blocks of stone still await the
mason's chisel and look modern in their lack of finish. But the
true approach is to the western porch across the Place de la
République. The towers carried by the porch project beyond the
old west front, slightly shrouding a fine rose window. They rise
in three recessed storeys, symbols of the Trinity, and the firm
balustrade which encompasses each storey makes a strong contrast with the rather solid and imposing uprights, reinforced with
engaged columns and pilastars framing low-relief arches, pediments, roundels, festoons—the *parure* of the French classical style
of the 1700's. The three high arches of the entrance porch are

closed by lively *grilles* of ironwork, painted and gilt. Altogether this front is full of light and movement.

The interior impresses you by a sense of height, which is gained by the absence of capitals from the nave. The ribs of the vaulting spring as it were from the ground, and the force of their spring is so convincing that it defeats the balancing horizontals of the triforium with its flatter arches and scrolled balustrades, and the string-course which separates it from the windows of the clerestory. It is a triumphant blend of Gothic and Renaissance before the Renaissance style with its classical preference for the horizontal finally takes charge of French and European architecture.

There is the nave and two side aisles with lateral chapels; and you will remark that mouldings of the arches of the nave are cut with the same directness of angle as we have noticed at Toulouse. This way of handling bright light belongs both to Gascony and Languedoc, while it does not seem appropriate to the gentler northern light. In the chapels is a good deal of attractive detail, including one of those elaborate Entombments which were so popular in the sixteenth century. I am bound to say that I often find them over-naturalistic; the grief of the mourners has what may seem the slight hysteria of the Counter-Reformation emotion. But here is an intense degree of control which only a great artist could evoke from stone. All the figures are looking down on the body of the dead Christ as it is lowered into the tomb. Only the Virgin is turned in profile with just one line to show the compression of her lips as she looks for the last time on the face of her Son. The contrast in demeanour of the centurion and St. Joseph of Arimathea is equally striking. I found this version of a scene which can so easily be overplayed really memorable for its spiritual quality.

The effect of the nave's height is enhanced, so it appears to me, by the rood screen and choir stalls in carved wood. At Albi, with the authority behind us of Prosper Mérimée, the novelist and the saviour of so much mediaeval work in France, we lean to the idea that a rood screen could break the flow of a nave. The proportions at Auch make the acceptance of the screen very much easier, a little because you come in by the west rather than the north and so see the screen in a better perspective. Once you have passed within it, you are in another world.

The general conception follows a pattern familiar enough. There are the twin rows of tip-up miserere seats; the richly carved panels which confront the gangways; the emphatic emplacement of the archbishop's stall; the uprights which divide one canon or precentor from another—all this is to the old idiom; a décor of fretted canopy and cusps framing ranks of coupled saints, of ogee arch and of pinnacle. Held within this secure background is a new world of art and faith. The martyrs and the holy ones, sculpted in low relief, stand on plinths supported by arabesques which in a book would form a splendid *cul-de-lampe* at the close of a finely printed chapter. The figures show a sharp realistic modelling. The flurry of sacred scrolls, the flutter of drapery, firm contrasting lines of sword and spear and sceptre, emblematic caskets, towers or wheels are all so placed as to provide a movement which is quite new. Adam, Eve and the Serpent are types familiar enough, heaven knows; but here one sees the old story with a new twist. For all his horny spine the serpent is man-headed and holds in his hand the second fruit from the Tree of Knowledge ready for Adam to take. Eve has her fruit at her lips as yet untasted, and both look towards the serpent wrapt in fear of the future, the fear of the risk. It is a perfect interpretation of its age, which for all its drive and power and discovery lived in the shadow of the fear of death, the problem to which they could envisage no solution.

This grand series of stalls was carved—you can see the generation's difference by the type of mask above the ogee in the canopies—during the endless deliberations of the Council of Trent, a sort of religious UNO of its day, which tried to make sense of the damage done to the Roman Catholic Church by the doctrine reformed. I can attest the weight of the doctrine, for if my father had a new idea about the arrangement of the library at home, it almost certainly involved the position of *The History of the Council of Trent*. There were not less than thirty—perhaps a few more—sixteenth-century folio volumes bound in exquisite calf, richly tooled and gilt—and quite unsalable. I frequently toted them around. So I, being externally familiar with the idea, do not resent the kind of high altar, which followed as an architectural interpretation of these long arguments and decisions, set out in such fine printing. Auch provides a beautiful example of this style, the climax of certainty after the doubts and the fears of the choir stalls.

Within the mediaeval chancel is interpolated this poem of classical emotion. It is wonderful as colour, since Auch is not far from the marble country of the Pyrenees. Grey, grey-blue, red and variegated marbles have been combined most happily, particularly when a boss or diamond of colour is inlaid as a jewel in a veined setting. But the composition impresses even more than the colour. A complicated use of columns—some higher, some lower, some connected by arches or knitted together by pediments, a variety in rectilinear and curvilinear projection, combine to make a climax of the high altar, which is one of the architectural expressions of the Counter-Reformation. This is a thing which is not second nature to the average Englishman with his Protestant up-bringing or background; but it is an expression of worship not to be despised.

There are the windows of the apse, done by Arnaud de Moles in 1513. They, too, are in the new style, vast figures of prophets, apostles and even sybils established in a painted architectural framework. Splendid in their way, they probably belong to the same family as designed the windows in the cathedral of Toulouse which we have seen. They have parted from the mediaeval tradition, and are, in effect, more modern than the choir stalls even though they were started almost a generation earlier. Whether or not you like them—as opposed to admiring their quality—is a personal matter.

A tail-piece to Auch: for it is not really worth running around the town, searching for the antique house in alleys. Unless you are a great deal luckier than I, you find vistas and façades which are agreeable rather than exciting or distinguished. But there is a statue of a second local character besides that of Mégret d'Etigny.

Statues with the romantic, academic swagger of the nineteenth century are not, I must confess, meat and drink to me; but in this instance the subject excuses the swagger, indeed demands it. For it is d'Artagnan of *The Three Musketeers* who decorates the street which bears his name and bears it without undue bluster. A man of this name, born at the neighbouring village of Lupiac, existed outside Dumas's imagination: Charles de Batz, Comte d'Artagnan (1611–73) who was killed at the siege of Maastricht. As a quick-paced historical novelist, Dumas telescopes his hero's career. If you remember the story, d'Artagnan becomes a member of the Royal Guards in des Essarts's company and serves in that capacity at the siege of La Rochelle (1628), still a young hero of twenty-one, prudent and virginal despite the attractions of Constance Bonacieux and the temptations of Milady. Soon after the siege Richelieu gives him a lieutenancy in the Musketeers. These mathematics beat me. He had a much easier career in fiction than his historical namesake in fact, who had to wait till 1654 to become captain of the Royal Guards, and was promoted only to a sub-lieutenancy in the Musketeers in 1657. At length his ship of promotion came home, and he died a brigadier (*Maréchal de Camp*).

All of course was considered fair in a period novel of those days. And yet it is strange to think of the friendship between such opposites in style and intellectual conscience as Dumas and Flaubert, who could quote chapter and verse for every episode and detail in *Salammbo*, his novel of the Carthaginian era, the result of immense research. Though the cool side of Flaubert's nature could admire the warmth of Dumas, he could—a surgeon by heredity—dissect the other's character, and his gift for dissections was not always kind. As a novelist he often attended funerals to observe the reactions of the bereaved and of the expectant profiteers from death. Dumas did not disappoint him when they met at Georges Sand's funeral. They assisted at the obsequies; they heard the will read; they walked away together. Dumas plucked Flaubert by the elbow: 'Tiens, elle ne nous a rien légué,' said the bourgeois.—She hasn't left us a penny.

*   *   *

Alas, after this divagation, we must now take a fresh view of our direction, if Bourg-Madame is to remain our western outpost.

Already the lure of the Pavillon d'Amour of Nérac and the nectar of Armagnac have carried us too far to the right of our objective. I should have liked to see what a village looked like called Ile de Noé; but it is out of the question; one would only arrive at some horse-fair at Tarbes. To gain the eastern passes from Auch the road lies once more through Toulouse.

V

Foix to Bourg-Madame

IF you are using the Bourg-Madame pass into Spain, you will most probably approach it either direct from Toulouse through Pamiers and Foix or from Perpignan up the lovely valley of the Conflent by Prades, still resonant of Casals and his festivals, up and up to the mountains of the Cerdagne and the Capcirs. The first route is the shorter of the two, and, when you are a few kilometres beyond Pamiers begins to form a quietly moving prelude to the grand scenery which follows.

I have been several times at Pamiers, but despite the lure of an ex-cathedral church—that curious ecclesiastical status—the town has never much tempted me. Its face is that of a woman from whom at a cocktail party you would instinctively move away, however well dressed she was, expecting no interest from her conversation. On the other hand, I remember with delight a June-day picnic on the hills outside by a field so bejewelled with wild flowers of every colour, that as we sat we counted twenty-three varieties. The ground fell away sharply to a wide valley, beyond which floated like clouds above the forest the greys and purples of the distant mountains. Obstinately, I was anxious to see Foix. Photographs of its staggering castle had whetted my appetite; Miss Nina Epton gave it a pleasant enough commendation in her reliable book, *The Valley of Pyrene*; and there was a third circumstance, which should be a lesson to me for the future.

The late Reverend S. Baring-Gould, a very intelligent man, made this ugly comment on the place.

> The town occupies a triangle where two rivers unite. It is a very dull place, its sole feature being the castle, like a plain man with a prominent nose. That it should be the capital of the department is due to association, not to size, for Pamiers, where a cathedral was, exceeds its population. It has a theatre, in which a performance is but rarely given; a public library, open for a few hours a week, into

which an occasional reader saunters; baths, better known from without than within; an abattoir, where oxen past work are slaughtered
for consumption by those of the inhabitants who have digestions
that could dissolve leather; a promenade which lacks promenaders;
a vast prefecture, in which the prefect is daily dying of ennui. The
Hôtel des Gouverneurs has now become the Palais de Justice—'un
édifice banal, malgré ce nom grandiloquent'.

As contempt, this paragraph ripples off very nicely; but it was
the last sentence which tripped me to fall in a puddle of self-
conceit. Obviously, I argued, this Hôtel des Gouverneurs is an
eighteenth-century building, a period well out of fashion in the
days when Baring-Gould formed his remarkable mind. After all
he published his *Book of the Pyrenees* in 1907 and could write
without affectation 'It was fifty years since I first rode over this
part of the country'—before the opening of the railway, in fact!
I concluded smugly that if his generation-blinded eye had missed
this building, it would have missed other beauties, too. But a
further confirmation of the old man's view awaited me in an
unexpected quarter.

On my first visit to Foix we did not come straight from
Toulouse but from Castelnaudary, where at the Grand Hôtel
Fourcade they prepare the famous regional dish, the cassoulet, in
the most resplendent manner. Authorities differ as to its origin,
some claiming that it is of Moorish descent, others that it merely
dates back to the Hundred Years War. However that may be, it
is the noblest and subtlest of ragouts, cooked very slowly for four
hours in an earthenware dish (the cassole) over a fire of furze-
bush. Antole France maintained that the Fourcade Cassoulet
was like a brandy—kept cooking and topped up for twenty years.
The dry white bean is the foundation and the other essential
ingredients are pork (or pig in some form) and lamb—and,
according to the district you are in, other delicious native sundries.
For instance we had tried with delight the Toulouse version
where they throw in some of their wonderful local sausage and
confit d'oie. At Castelnaudary they use as well pork rind and
bacon. The whole dish is highly spiced, and no one in his senses
would call it a light dish. A wise course for beginners to pursue

The Cathedral at Auch: detail of an Entombment in one of the chapels

(*below*) choir stalls and rood screen

Château des Comtes de Foix

is to order one portion between two (which the French never seem to mind when you are ordering *à la carte*); you can always call for another if you are still at full strength.

Moving, thus pleasurably burdened, towards Foix along N.119, we traversed a country of villages clustering round the tops of little hills with their tall church tower in the ascendant, mediterranean in their grouping, mediterranean in their prevalent cypresses. We felt leisured. Turning left to cross an innocent-seeming river, the Hers, we saw on the right a temptation I can never withstand—a well-defended mediaeval gateway hedged about with old walls. From the map I remembered that this should be Mirepoix, a name I vaguely connected with a military eighteenth-century duke without marked military talent. In by the gate we turned and sat down at the Café Moderne to consider the situation. This day was too full of a number of things. First, my bill had been added up grossly at the Castelnaudary restaurant—and it was the fourth bill I had seen returned for correction; my redoubtable cassoulet was still admiring itself within me; and then outside the Moderne I saw, or thought I saw, two irresistible objects at the same time—the glimpse through an arch of an arcaded square and, crossing towards us, an old peasant in blue overalls walking a boxer puppy, boneless and bendable with extreme youth.

Simultaneously, with the busy eagerness of a spaniel, Lucette emerged from the café to take our order. Back she came with it and, figuratively, put up her paws, licked us, sat down and wagged her tail. We asked about the place, the least we could do as manners. No; we had never been to Mirepoix before, and had only turned into the town by chance.

'But, how wise of you,' Lucette exclaimed. 'So many savages drive past outside the walls; the direct road, of course. What? You have not been to the squares? Nor to the Cathedral? But they are famous, Monsieur-Dame; and of course now that you are here, you will wish to see them. I will fetch you a postcard.' In a sudden access of commercial caution, she added, 'But not till you have rested sufficiently. *Encore un Dubonnet?*'

'Well,' I said in my dismal, scheduled way, 'we really have

H

planned to dine and spend the night at Foix. We must, of course, see the squares and glance at the cathedral now that we are here; but we are dedicated tonight to the glories of Foix, which I have wanted to see for so long.'

Lucette burst out laughing.

'But you're joking! "The glories of Foix"—that's rich! Who on earth would stay at Foix where there is no shop with a fashion later than three years old? Incredible! No one shops at Foix. Nor for that matter do they at Mirepoix. But here at the Commerce you will be better fed and better served at half the price of Foix.' And she went on, like a conspirator giving a password, '*Et c'est très propre—tout à fait propre.*' Then, briskly, 'Madame there is a friend of mine. I will run and see her.'

And off she started at her eager spaniel's lollop; and I swear I saw the long black ears streaming out behind her.

While Lucette was on her errand of mercy—or, more exactly, of publicity for Mirepoix—we wandered round the small town. Its cathedral is not great, though it has a very fine crocketed spire, which one sees from a distance; the broad proportion of the nave is characteristic of this region, which never lost its sense of the romanesque any more than it lost its taste for garlic. I rather liked the bishop's palace, clinging to his cathedral's south wall, discreetly hidden from public gaze by a screen of later buildings. The whole place was strangely endearing, a quality which I think contains the little things of friendship.

When I think of the word in connection with Mirepoix, I start with a negative—that there is nothing there of earth-shaking importance. You could balance this with a positive—that nothing pretends to be important. Personal pleasures of my own (which others might not find on a wet day, for instance) were the endlessly moving coloured shadows on the ceilings of these fourteenth-century timbered galleries. The trees in the centre of the squares give sensible shelter from over-bright suns and project, as they flicker in the breeze, the illusions of coloured shapes moving within the shadows of the arcades, '*the Couverts*', changing their intensity with the angle of the sun. To elaborate my conception of 'endearing' are the snatches of broad-handed, country carving which mark out such an important house as that, for instance, where lived the *Capitouls*. To all this one is further 'endeared' by the ephemeral, faded sound-track of murmured conversations behind doors, in shops, between upper stories, pertinacious bargainings, age-old gossip. I find it easy to make a successful excuse to see Mirepoix again; and friends of mine have liked it too.

There is a further absurdity. We all of us say at intervals 'Before the Flood'. But can we date it? Well, the men of Mirepoix can. They know that their flood took place in 1342. It washed away the whole of the old town on the right bank of that innocent seeming river, the Hers, conserving only as if by a mediaeval miracle the porch which sheltered the Holy Well of the Cordeliers Abbey. You reach it by a path which even on a fine day can be still muddy as if it was not so long since the flood had receded. I fancy that the time cycle for Holy Wells may be slightly slower than ours.

Long before we had got back to the Moderne, Lucette had returned. She was quivering with good news.

'Madame at the Commerce has a splendid room free; and I assure you that everything is *"très propre"*. I have seen for myself.'

The standard of Lucette's life could be summed up in those two words—'*très propre*' (very clean). Next day, for instance, she directed us to the *charcuterie* woman, the size of an hippopotamus, who also was guaranteed to be '*très propre*'. I dare say Lucette would have married an orang-outang, had he been certified as '*très propre*', a quality in which her first absconding husband had been notably deficient if all is to be credited.

Having learnt all (or so it may be hoped) of Lucette's first marriage, we wandered along to the Commerce, where we were received very easily. Nothing in that place goes on in a hurry but everything is up to time. Madame has grey estimating eyes, which look at you with a dignified curiosity. An unobtrusive drive goes with her natural dignity, which is well set off by light curly chestnut hair and lips which twitch easily to amusement. Her father-in-law, a talented chef, is running his son into the kitchen, from which flow a sequence of delights—not always complicated delights but those as well which can equal elaboration by simplicity and perfect cooking. Until I had been to this place I should have made a rude noise to anyone who told me I should live to think roast pigeon worth eating. And oh, that *escalope pannée*! My experience there cannot be unique. Over too short an acquaintance I have watched the plaquettes of recommendations grow on the front of the hotel like self-seeded flowers. With much the same pleasure I have watched Madame's handsome and well-mannered children growing up, and hope for another generation of good hoteliers to embellish the endearing charms of Mirepoix.

*   *   *

Despite Baring-Gould, despite Lucette we paid our call on Foix and its trinity of towers, memorials of its obstinate counts. The county of Foix originally formed part of Languedoc rather than Gascony, and so the counts were vassals of the Counts of Toulouse. But the slack administration of Toulouse left them virtually an independent principality. The territorial ambitions of Foix moved towards the Pyrenees rather than northwards; on their native mountains the men of Foix ('Fuxéens' is their patronymic) moved as fast as cavalry on a plain. They were as hardy as the bears whose steaks formed their principal delicacy, and as hard as the iron they mined. Even in the seventeenth century after Richelieu had blown up their Huguenot castles, a French Governor could write 'these people are as difficult to tame as their own bears and just as ignorant'.

Warfare was the local sport of the counts and in consequence you see ruined castles crowning high peaks throughout the territory. In times of trouble, the local landowner retired with the best of his men to the heights and let the current of war lap round his mountain's foot. This constant evasion of danger was reinforced by another circumstance to leave the city of Foix a place of little aesthetic value. Towards the end of the thirteenth century Rogier Bernat, Count of Foix, had married the heiress of Gaston de Béarn and on the death of his father-in-law inherited the kingdom, which subsequently passed to Navarre. Foix now ceased to

be a capital town and degenerated into a provincial governorship.
Indeed to this day it is the smallest departmental capital in the
whole of France. There has been no encouragement to the arts in
this place, and as you traffic your way round narrow twisting
streets you find antiquity without refinement. The old church of
St. Volusien, the local saint who was carried off to martyrdom in
Spain by the Moors, is built of a good ochreish stone, but otherwise has no particular distinction; you would not trouble with it
elsewhere. Next door to it is the prefecture which filled old
Baring-Gould with sympathy for the préfet; his quotation about
the Palais de Justice I found justified—banal it is. In fact the two
hotels are the best feature of the place and we should have done
well but expensively at the Barbacane, which stands high and
commands a fine view. People have spoken well of the XIXᵉ
Siècle, of which the terrace looks down on the swift Ariège just
by the bridge; but it had a paint-starved air to me. The best view
to take of Foix is that it is so much dramatic scenery, a necessary
prelude to the long pass into Spain at Bourg-Madame.

*　　*　　*

But before we start the long ascent, there are two essential
things to see if you have the time. One of them, the underground
river at Labouiche I will consider later; but the last stronghold of
the Catharists at Montségur stands so romantically and commemorates such a story that one cannot omit it.

You can only reach it by car from a gay little town on the road
between Foix and Quillan, Lavelanet, unless your legs are strong
enough and your sense of direction good enough to walk over
high mountain tracks by the Pic de St. Barthélémy some 7,000
feet up, where from a distance you discern blank, white-faced
mountains which are quarried for that essential to good soap,
talc. At the village of Montségur, seated lifeless at the foot of the
peak on which the castle stands, the road also expires. In a valley
at right angles runs a little stream, the Lasset, with a track beside
it from the ruined chapel on the Pic de St. Barthélémy to the
headwaters of the Hers, a way for sheep and pack mules. A foot-
path climbs the 3,000-foot mountain, which the castle ruins crown,

a calcareous mountain looking mangy with patches of scrub. It is a kind of Catharist heaven on earth remote in the void. As we picnicked on a shoulder of rock perhaps 500 feet below the castle itself and below the point of the road from which one could see the inanimate village, no sign of life met our eyes. It was a June day of brilliant sunshine and sparkling air. Long deep valleys flowed away from us, their sides compounded from this prevalent torso form, which I have already tried to describe. Thin upland pasture to which the sheep are moved for the summer months clothed the ribby valley sides with a middle-grade velvet, through which sporadically burst rocks.

Such is the setting—sky, rocks, thin grass and scrub—in which the last devotees of the Catharist heresy came to their end. Their natural leader, Raymond VII of Toulouse, had been so oppressed by the Pope and by the King of France that to keep a crust in his family's mouth he must toe the line to royal and papal orders, even though he still used every art at his command to keep the English and the Lusignans in Gascony in action against the central power. His final dishonour came when he was forced to lead an army to besiege the castle of Montségur, the last refuge of his former vassals, who had been provoked by the misgovernment of the French King's representatives and the continuous persecution of the Dominican Inquisition to a final revolt.

For some time the Catharists had been provisioning the castle of Montségur to withstand a long siege. After a declaration by Pope Innocent IV at the Council of Narbonne Raymond VII and his vassal the Count of Foix were ordered to reduce the castle and perforce had to besiege it. This was in 1242. The garrison withstood the attacks for another eighteen months.

As a mediaeval background to this ecclesiastical tumult we detect the groundbase of rapine. Not only were the Catharists heretics but they had a treasure: booty for the devout. This treasure had been transferred over the years to Montségur. No one doubted it. It became a matter of acute concern as the besieging lines crept up the steep hillside, till there was no longer space for the garrison to grow the lowest grade grain crop. The story goes that the heretics, as they saw the bonfires building for their extermination, determined that they must hold out until their treasure had been safely evacuated. Once they saw a beacon blazing on the Pic de St. Barthélémy, they would happily throw themselves on the flames. And so it was. No one, so far as is known escaped from the desolate peak of Montségur except the party with the treasure.

But where is the treasure? Of what did it consist? From that day to this men have been searching for it; but it has left not a wrack behind. There was an episode some years ago, now claimed as a sort of Piltdown Skull hoax by an archaeologist, which resulted in infructuous diggings in the shallow soil of the Pic de St. Barthélémy. It was said, too, that the escapers and their treasure had been walled up in a cavern at Lombrive nearby. Human bones indeed were found there; but of treasure no trace. Realist as opposed to romantic historians point out that the Catharists were professionally poor and that their treasure was more likely to be celestial (books of liturgy and dogma) rather than hard terrestrial cash, and that such things are perishable. Pierre Belperron, that admirable historian, tells in his *La Croisade contre les Albigeois* (Plon, 1942) of a manuscript recently discovered in the Vatican, but then not fully published, which purported to be the only known liturgical document of the Catharists. Or did the refugees of Montségur send off their escape party as a blind with nothing in their pockets, while they themselves leaped in willing matyrdom upon the flames, sure that their secrets would burn with them? They were quite capable of it out there at Montségur, removed as they preferred by nature from the human life which they despised.

*   *   *

At Foix you stand, if not in the midst, at least on the approaches to the underground world of which the devotees are called spelaeologists. Strange people, subverted geologists, people who certainly in this district of France—as in Derbyshire and Somerset—find adventure just below their doorstep. There are three places nearby in the region, which I have seen myself, and quantities of others which pander to this strange passion. And it is, of course, a kind of fairy land, because it is the hard core of folk tales. In '*The Princess and the Goblin*' Sir Walter told the children to 'stamp on their feet'; much living in wet, sandy earth had given the peoples of the caves, the primitive hairless goblins, soft feet. It is to such circumstances that you may descend in safety to tourist caves at Mas d'Azil, Labouiche with its wonderful underground river, or Niaux. And in the upper regions of the Ariège there are scores of caves and grottoes for the skilled explorer. Sometimes when I read in the summer that people have been killed climbing relatively innocent mountains or have been rescued by the exertions at great risk to themselves of far more skilled persons, I am slightly shocked by the exhibitionism of the victims. They were only doing badly something which had been done well before, but it had pleased them to test their strength. But these men who plough the bosom of the earth, also at infinite risk which with care they steadily minimise, are true explorers in the old vein. They are opening up a new country to us, a fruitful country, fruitful of effortless power.

Pioneers of underground exploration, such as Norbert Casteret, are slowly tracing these underground rivers and water-forces with a view to harnessing them to hydro-electric power, just as the French government have steadily worked above ground on the great lakes and tarns that lie in the high mountains. But it is not just a matter of the explorer's skill. I learn that before you can make an underground exploration, let alone put any water-power you may discover to commercial purpose, you must find out the government department empowered to empower you to do so; and that this can range from the equivalents of our ministries of Fuel and Power, Agriculture and Fisheries, to the Coal Board and so on. When you get into the higher reaches of the Pyrenees, the problems soar to the diplomatic sphere. Is it French or Spanish water, to take the simplest example, that Casteret found flowing in the Caves d'Attout? If the water is Spanish, should the French pay the Spanish a royalty on every power unit they create from it? I suppose that in principle this is no more difficult than an eighteenth-century decision on the Newfoundland fishing rights, because the latter could be determined in a much simpler way—you sank the opposing fishermen.

This countryside is calcareous and pitted with holes, caves and grottoes, all of which drip water which slowly takes on the forms of stalactites or stalagmites according, one might say, to its masculine or feminine nature. From the days of prehistory, where it has not been too wet, men have sheltered in these caves; and as at Mas d'Azil you will find traces not only of prehistoric culture, but of Catharist and Huguenot remains as well. Whole cycles of religions have left a seed behind them. Slowly scientific evaluation dissects the epochs and habits of the occupants. Was this cemetery of bears' heads the symbol of a tribe's worship, or the proof of its vitality. This is the problem for the archaeologists, not for the spelaeologists.

For these modern conquerors of the antediluvian world a new prize lies ahead. Take, for instance, the caves of Niaux, a few miles south of Foix (and you must get a permit twenty hours ahead from the Mayor of Tarascon in order to see them). These caves are a fairly recent discovery, in the sense that though they were scented in 1867 their cathedral, the grand cave, was not traced till 1936. Then was found one of the most astonishing series of mural paintings, akin to those in the Spanish caves of Altamira. Except for the horse—a cob, rather—and a trout, the animals depicted are extinct; but owing to their long isolation from the upper air, they are in much finer condition than those at, say, Les Eyzies, gawped at for too long. Let us hope that the curators of Niaux will show a developed sense of preservation.

There is water in the Niaux caves; and so there is in the caves which lie below them at Sarbath and to the side of them at Ussat. There is learned speculation that if some blocked passages were cleared, then a conjoined underground river of some fifteen kilometres would be opened—far the longest known underground river in the world. For after all, Labouiche, so beautiful in its progress between gardens of transparent limestone flowers and trees, is no mean river for Pluto's kingdom. For an hour and a half you descend in hooded darkness but for the thin light of bulbs, devoted usually to some stalactitic growth down a dark,

Lethe stream, your iron barque pulled or ferried by a modern Charon along a steel rope, until he hears the sound of danger, the changed note such as we heard above ground in the Gorge du Vis, heralding a waterfall. And so your Charon's boat turns about and you leave the churning sound behind you, wondering perhaps whether at some obscure point in the darkness it is joining the waters you have already seen lower down the mountain side.

As you ascend the picturesque valley of the Ariège towards Tarascon and ultimately Ax-les-Thermes you will be, if your fancy takes you that way, in and out of grottoes all the time. The old Romans knew of all the hot-spring business that could be made use of in these parts; in the mid-nineteenth century the knowledge was picked up again and littering around the main road you will find old-fashioned spas falling and flaking away, whatever the curative value of their waters; little spas first praised then contemned by Louis Philippe, that fickle Orleans, until the businesses which thrived through his influence, were reduced to accepting parties of ageing nuns. And such are the water condi-tions at Ussat, so wholesome, so hygienic throughout, that it is quite impossible to have a private bathroom in case you use the curative water without payment to the authorities of the Bains Thermales.

If you wish to see the caves at Niaux, you will inevitably stop at Tarascon—not Daudet's literary place by the Rhône, but a place addicted to Turneresque storms. One greeted me my first evening there, a thunder and rain storm which circled the neigh-bourhood. Just south of the town is a tremendous rock, like that on which the Foix towers are poised, the Roche Bedheilac, almost a pyramid of rock with its base so hollow that the Germans in the last war began to excavate it as an emplacement for a safe under-ground aircraft factory. This daunted the local archaeologists, since the caves were all prehistoric burial grounds. This strange rock, on the evening I witnessed this storm, was its focus. It stands upright in a valley among eminences. And round its head swirled a cloud dance of the seven veils, the shifting shafts of light illuminating now one face and now another. The variation of colour was extraordinary, changing from the dark purple-greys to the pinks and golds, as the rainclouds were drifted and convoluted against the true sunlight, still operative about six o'clock of the evening. Seldom have I seen a spectacle more exciting, accompanied as it was by an orchestra of torrential rain.

Tarascon endorses the judgment we have already passed on Foix—that the further you go up the mountains the less there is to see of an aesthetic kind. Tarascon has only folk-talk for you. If you look carefully at the houses high above the east bank of the river, you will realise that they are not like those you have been seeing lately. If someone has put you on to it, you will recognise a faintly Spanish look, and a carelessness for the proprieties which makes it acceptable to dry your maize and your tobacco on your first-floor balcony. This gives the whole place an unshaven look. And now, as you advance upon your steep climb, you must decide which, if any, of the side valleys you will explore. If, for instance, you have gone to Niaux, you may care to carry on up the valley of Vicdessos, from which, if you like such things, mountain tracks will take you on foot across the frontier of Andorra. You will be passing through the old iron-mining valley, which once was governed by mediaeval charters, frequently renewed. For the miners were a close corporation, and the right to mine passed from father to son; an heiress was, if possible, married to someone from the valley to prevent the rights passing to some foreigner from across the mountains. The miners were part time workers, spending the rest of their time on their farms. It was an offence to work more than a set number of hours a day, and when you had extracted the permitted quota of ore you had to stop work. The object of these prohibitions was not, however, restrictive in the trade union sense; they were made in the common interest of preserving the life of the mines for as long as possible. But nothing would induce the owners to accept any form of industrialisation, and in the nineteenth century the workings no longer paid. Now a gigantic plant at Tarascon forms a belching memorial to the old charters.

Though the scenery is fine, there is little of real architectural value to tempt one along this route. So after Niaux you would have to return to Tarascon and the practical road, N.20, which has carried us all the way from Limoges. This is the main road to Bourg-Madame and the frontier. If you were staying in the neighbourhood, and were feeling adventurous, there is a byroad to a pocket of small mountain villages picturesque in themselves, buried in remote antiquity, and among them the ruins of a tremendous castle, Lordat, with a triple enceinte too large a problem even for Henri IV's engineers to destroy, who had made a thorough enough job in the rest of the neighbourhood.

The road by the cheerful Ariège, dotted with little villages, indeed a pleasure of fine trees and high wooded hills—mountains indeed one might call them since some of the peaks are over 4,000 feet. The engineering is extremely good and the gradients present no difficulty to a light car. A small railway, which ultimately finds its way to far-off Catalan Barcelona, keeps you company, disappearing below ground at difficult moments, but for the most part climbing doggedly along on the right bank of the river. You reach a town with the recollections of a Roman name, Ax-les-Thermes, the Waters for the Hot Baths. Apart from the situation which is delightful, it has no message for me. I can take no joy from the inbred conversations of these 'thermal stations' or watering places, where everyone's mind is introverted to his curious condition—'such an interesting variant'—where the creak of bones is drowned by the local Palm Court Orchestra, where the inmates wait for the kindly opening of the jaws of death—or the end of the season. But there is one thing worse at Ax than the smell of mortality: the smell of sulphur. I could not think what had happened to my beer, left it unfinished and ordered another brand from another café. This too tasted bad; and I then realised that the whole place smelt of rotten eggs (or sulphur) and there was no hope of enjoying food or drink in it, unless you had a really good reason, one of those 'interesting variants', to indoctrinate your nose to disregard this insidious smell. The inhabitants show as little awareness of it as, I am told, do Macedonian peasants in the malarial valleys of the Struma and Varder, where they work happily in the fields showing every symptom of the illness without feeling its effects. But in Ax-les-Thermes even so reliable an English paper as the *Sunday*

Times turns yellow (physically, of course) within twenty-four hours.

Let us then proceed, proudly conscious that Ax-les-Thermes can do nothing for us but turn us yellow—oh yes! it has a romantic line in all the wrong kinds of architecture—and continue our ascent to the grand pass, the Col de Puymorens, something over 6,000 feet up. Steadily you are climbing above river and rail level by this superbly graded road, which defeats by compromise seemingly impossible situations. So well are the curves calculated that on the return journey, you can safely run your car in neutral for fourteen miles with modest applications of the brake. Now and again you are forced to change your direction as suddenly as a minor statesman, owing to the pressure of events; but on the whole rather than twisting the road swoops down its kindly but fantastic path. Inevitably you leave behind you as you climb the deciduous trees, so dear to English eyes; ilex and arbutus console you for a time, but inevitably as you come within sight of the snow-line the countryside is starker. You are after all a little man in your little car, looked down on by say Pic Pedroux (9,201) or the Pics de Font Vive and Font Frède, a few pitiable hundred feet lower. Conifers and poorer soil are now your company. But if you are approaching what is to me a less interesting tree-scape these generous, wide-handed, civilised mountain valleys still have variety to offer you. A legend as a start.

Pyrene was the beautiful and, until the start of the story round about 1500 B.C., virgin daughter of a Celtiberian king named Bebryx, whose headquarters were Lombrives, probably in one of the caves, since so little is known above ground of Celtiberian architecture. On his return from setting up his pillars in the Mediterranean Hercules looked in, luckily for him, just as feasting was in season. He liked the look of still maiden Pyrene; but I fear that the inevitable desertion replaced matrimony. Worse still one of the local bears got hold of her and though the absconding Hercules put on his best turn of speed, he was too late to effect a rescue. Every hero has a hairy heel. The sequel justifies the opinion of a certain type of intellectual woman, who might argue that Hercules' penance of clubbing all examples he could find of *ursus speleus* hardly affected the case and was just typical of male muddled thinking. But at least the old tough gave this range of mountains something they have never had before—a name, the Pyrenees.

Then there is another prodigality in the uplands, butterflies and flowers, things of which I have no knowledge in the sense that though I can see and enjoy them without knowing what I have seen, I remain incommunicado as it were. But fortunately two friends, Betty and Richard Fairbairn, were in the district this summer and along this very road, climbing at suitable intervals the hills on either side in search of the appropriate treasure. On the whole the weather quelled the butterflies, who are not like the late Neville Chamberlain professional umbrella carriers. So Richard did not see his prize, the Parnassian Apollo, who is only to be found fittingly in the high places of the world. But he was consoled by a wealth of butterflies, some of which like the wood white are uncommon. British species of fritillaries were found in variety—the pearl-bordered, the Glanville, and the Marsh Fritillary, together with several continental species, such as the exquisitely marked, Melitaea Didyma. A species now extinct in England, the green-veined white, flourishes in these parts as in the whole of southern France.

You are high enough on the plateau around Bourg-Madame for the rain to turn to sleet even on a June day, and so surprisingly Betty found sheets of narcissus displaying their fat whites against the flake ice around them. On a better day on these same heights she found a great variety of orchis ranging from the dark red nigritella nigra to the pale pink field orchis, well enough known here. If you climb the side valleys you find natural rock gardens with yellow orchis, pink saponaria, green hellebore and grape hyacinth growing in the crevices. As you descend from the Col de Puymorens to Bourg-Madame, gentians of many sorts decorate the slopes and clumps of bright pink rhododendrons (ferrugineum) and the blue aquilegia alpina which grows as big as the garden flower. In every way a paradise for the eye in the hue of flower or wing.

*   *   *

And so by more lethargic, less exciting curves you drop slowly
down from the vigours of the Col de Puymorens to the upland
plateau on which stands plump Bourg-Madame. The countryside
seems to live in a trance, as if expecting something to happen.
Green in season, snowbound at times, it is simple upland pasture
country; not comparable to the sharp determined shapes of the
Cerdagne plateau (off to the right) nor of the harsh Capcirs on the
left as you descend to Prades. But Bourg-Madame is a breathing
space after your long climb from Foix. If its too many, too small
bits of public gardens strike you as fussy and in bad taste,
remember the countless knots and frills of the Duchesse
d'Angoulême's clothes, and forgive the nice little place which has
tried to dress above its station.

VI
The Rouergue

SALESMAN that he is, Demas is not a man to be dismissed; and if you were a genuine traveller from Burgundy to Perpignan and the Eastern Pyrenees or were on an early pilgrimage to St. James of Compostella in Spain, you would rightly have taken his advice to go by Clermont-Ferrand, through the Rouergue, where you would see the fine towns of Villefranche and Rodez, the amazing—no, the world famous—treasure of relics at the remote abbey of Conques. And when Demas said: 'Ho, turn aside for I will show you a silver mine,' he would have told you no less than the truth. The mediaeval silversmiths of the district in which the silver was found were men of quality; we know a little about them and can identify some of their work— more than can be said of their English contemporaries.

The old province of France which bore the rough-sounding name of Rouergue corresponds more or less with the modern department of the Aveyron. It is a favourite holiday country for those of the French who like to arrive at a place and then use their legs. The geology of the district is confused by the break-up to the west of the central mass of the Auvergne and the Cantale mountains (where they make that delicious cheese). This is not motoring country for the fellow who likes to keep at or to a steady sixty; the roads, though well engineered, are narrow and slip hither and thither in their courses as they discount by circumnavigation and hairpin bends the steepness of the wooded hills. And this goes for the smaller as for the greater hills; they have a sharp determination.

It was frontier country for a great part of its history, notably in the struggle of the French kings against the Counts of Toulouse and their vassals, the Viscounts de Trencavel, or against the English in the Hundred Years War. It still wears from habit the slightly secret, poker-face of frontier lands, where tree-silenced, folded hills conceal smugglers' tracks as easily as fast brown streams. In the wider valleys which the course of stronger rivers have eroded you meet with the strangest landscape effects. Some outsize Cyclops has at intervals cast down upon the valley floor a pyramidal rock or two high enough to be lost in the clouds. Rodez, the modern capital of the district, stands eight hundred feet above the plain, which itself is already a thousand feet up. Villefranche-de-Rouergue is elevated, though not to such a degree. Tucked away in remote valleys, preening themselves on high peaks or in recessed secrecy, are ancient abbeys ruined or conserved, fortified towns and citadels, from which you can learn much about the practices of mediaeval France. Scattered in small local sacristies or concentrated in the treasury of the Abbey of Conques is such a wealth of French mediaeval silver as one could not find in any comparable area of France, perhaps of the world.

* * *

They complain of the cold and of the perpetual wind at Rodez, this cathedral town on the high hill which the road circumambulates quite three times before it attains the summit. Far below in the plain lies the railway station; and if you are well advised you will lunch or dine there as often as is convenient. This sort of idea is basically repugnant to the Englishman, who knows what happens even to reasonable food once a railway official has even thought about it. But in France, though they consider their railways charge too much for the quality of their meals on the train, they demand serious food at the station if sometimes the timetable compels them to descend from the train either some way out from the town, as at Rodez, or because, as at Dijon, you may be left with time for a meal while waiting for your connection. Both these *Buffets de la Gare* get commendation from Michelin and the Club des Sans Club; so when I report favourably on the Rodez *terrine de grives*, a thrush pâté, which tastes so light and flavoured that you know instinctively who had the soft fruit from your garden, you will recognise that my testimony is not unsupported. They have also a butter which they serve with steaks or

I

with veal, compounded with parsley of course, but also with tarragon, chives and garlic. It is a homogeneous butter to which the garlic gives no more than the faintest whiff. I asked how this was achieved and was given this simple answer.

'The boy sits down with the necessary quantity of garlic and a clock. When he has chopped it for an hour by the clock, it is ready.' And of such are the dishes of heaven. You never bit anything in that butter which you could challenge as garlic: the achievement of an hour's monotonous work.

Rodez is now a busy town, a pushful town, one might say. The hotels are not winning. One of them must have been the very latest thing in 1890; and this summer another latest thing will have been opened, the Moderne (how true) where all the youth of the town meet for their beers and their juke boxes, well behaved and accompanied by pretty girls, some with the red hair which by derivation gives Rodez its name. Their patronymic is 'Ruthenois' —redheads. It is an administrative centre, a position which it has taken Rodez centuries of political enmity to win from Ville-franche. You have the feeling that though they maintain their old monuments suitably, the men of Rodez do so for tourism, not from affection. Their heart is in the present and the future.

I should not class it as a town of faith in anything but the material. Rodez stood out from the Albigensian and Huguenot wars so far as it could. Even its Renaissance buildings lack courage in decoration, as one sees in the flat façades above the shopfronts in the Place du Bourg, the Place d'Olmet, the Place du Cour-comtal. Consequently in this old and unloved part of the town— for that was the feeling it gave me—it is easy to miss a Roman-esque church concealed under an eighteenth-century overcoat: St. Amand. It looked worth no more than a minute's purchase, until buttresses of an antiquity far greater than two hundred years caught my lucky eye. I went inside. Four round-arched bays confronted me, and a perfectly good Romanesque cupola covered the central crossing. I have seldom had such a shock. Engaged columns with richly carved capitals supported the arches at the crossing and in the nave the columns fled up to the spring of the roof and its simple quadripartite vaulting. I found nothing of interest in the lateral chapels, but the over-all colour effect of the stone, ranging from grey to rose, was something quite strokeable; so soft, so delicate. I am still surprised, writing necessarily some months after my visit, at the warmth of my recollection. It was not '*grande dame*'; it was not 'peasant' either; yet it had some of the dignity which inherently belongs to the best of both classes.

I can't say that Rodez ever gave away its central secret to me; I'm prepared to look again, to listen again, because the permanent wind blows so much away. It always has a trick in hand to keep you in suspense. At the corner of the Rue Bosc and the Rue du Touat, for instance (now we are out of Le Bourg into the Bishop's town) is a square fourteenth-century tower on a house decorated with trefoil windows and somewhat effaced heraldry, which still retained the odour of heraldic tinctures. Its old name, the *Tour des Anglais*, recalls our brief occupation of the town in the 1360's. Round the corner from it is the Place d'Estaing and the delightful courtyard of the Maison de Benoit. But the restorer boys have got after it without too much tact. Their new gargoyles are mental defectives.

Take a wrong turning, or ask to be directed (as I did) to the Chapelle des Pénitents and you may easily find yourself inside the Chapelle du Lycée. Originally it was the chapel of the Collège Royal, a Jesuit affair, when education was in the news in seventeenth-century France. But whatever may have been its history, it still retains one essential in an educational building; a quality of affection, an atmosphere of which there is no plausible proof. It has, of course, the traditional long nave, white walls, dove grey stone, a barrel vault crossbanded; simple and correct. Placed between the arches are the painted galleries, their panels decorated with episodes from the lives of saints or with portraits of saints, all in peaceable tones of colour. I think it is the galleries which give the quality to this church, an overflow of religious emotion which somehow escapes the English Church, where galleries seem to express only a Malthusian excess of population. Here they told a story of success and an increasing flow of pupils, ranged in these galleries according to their juniority.

Meandering to the right, you find yourself back in the main square, where the ground slopes uphill past a dangerous crossroad to a regrettable First War memorial before the west front of the cathedral. Off to the left lies the pleasant old bishop's palace and park (now something to do with Roman Catholic nursing) and beyond, the great dominating clock-tower. It is early sixteenth-century work, replacing an earlier tower that had collapsed. Storey by storey the ornament grows richer and richer. Hexagonal pinnacles at each corner shelter in their niches heraldry and sculptured saints right up to the profusion of the traceried balconies, which crown the final stage. Finely done, even if possibly overdone—a very near thing. The noble tower still looks out episcopally over its wide diocese, as it did before the Huguenot problem surged round at its feet.

The north and south elevations, with the great rosettes in the transepts, again display decorative windows; but it is the west front that produces the most interest. In the towns we have seen so far, the churches have eschewed that northern device, the flying buttress. From Burgundy to Clermont-Ferrand and thence across the mountains of Le Puy and Cantale the idea must have travelled to Rodez as a frontier outpost of the style. Indeed, the whole of this front is a précis of history. At first, like Moissac, it turned no more than a blind fortified eye on the enemy—just a couple of slits in the lower part of the central block. The decoration of the rest is relatively late, as if the process of relenting from the tumult of war was grudgingly slow. Yet it culminates in a high and complicated rose window, surmounted by a classical pediment flanked by crocketed pinnacles.

Up rather a huddled street lies the south door with its finely sculptured gable forming the entrance to the cathedral. The moment before going into any great church has always a breath-holding quality. Will you find excitement, disappointment, or the true solemnising hush of worship? Judged on this purely emotional approach, Rodez gives you large scale and a continuity of effort, which carries a variety of style. Despite the sharply pointed arches of its choir, which recall Albi, despite the lofty nave, it is not a great building. On the other hand, in it are some very beautiful things indeed, some of which speak once more of Burgundian connections.

There are the choir stalls, a wonder of carved wood fashioned into architectural and human form. They belong to the latter part of the fifteenth century. There is a wealth of detail in the lateral chapels. The early Renaissance screen in stone to the chapel of St. Raphael, a ripple of arabesques; two early sarcophagi, the tombs of St. Naamas and St. Dalmas, who died towards the end of the sixth century; the statue in the chapel of the Holy Sepulchre of the Tiburtine Sybil with her enigmatic smile and her long plaited hair; the strange Agony in the Garden, in which tufa stone is employed in naturalistic simulation of rocky Gethsemane— almost baroque it looks. Then the inevitable sixteenth-century Pieta (but an exceptionally controlled one), the painted faces modelled in broad sharp planes; and a predecessor treating the same theme, this time from Burgundy in the mid-fifteenth century. Though I am no Ruskinian in principle, this moving bas-relief made me reflect how almost English was the harrowed silence of the mourners; how this was the sort of thing Ruskin could best interpret to us by articulating in his rich prose the cadences which already lay mute in our hearts. These things were made in the days when Europe was all one church, and deep down we recognise them as part of our inheritance, even if we don't admit it often. Does our antipathy to the Counter-Reformation sometimes cover a sigh?

* * *

Suppose that we have reached Rodez by this slightly complicated but still realistic route, via Villefranche-de-Rouergue, a sizable place, and two mediaeval townlets whose names spit defiance through gritted teeth—Najac and Cordes, both built on stupendous sites.

If we had gone that way, we should perhaps have spoken of mountains and mediaevalities, since the wine of these parts does not make a leading topic. All three towns have a similar origin in the combination of politics with its active expression in military science.

Dotted about France, and particularly in this area of it, you will find a good many towns called 'Villefranche de something or another'. You translate this name quite literally as 'the Free Town of Rouergue' for instance, and you tell from that that a king founded it for military defence as a fortified town. In this case, it was founded on the instructions of St. Louis in 1252. Henry III of England was weakening, and this would make a strong point against his holdings in Aquitaine beyond the Garonne. It stood in moderate elevation at the junction of the rivers Aveyron and Alzou; it commanded a fertile valley and chestnut forests to supply the necessities of the garrison. Better still it guarded the approach to the silver, lead and copper mines of the district. A rich and well-chosen position.

They built a bridge in 1321 which still survives, but without the original fortress towers such as we still see at Cahors. They built in due course their Hôtel de Ville and an Augustin monastery with an extremely pretty cloister; they built in fear walls against the murderous English in 1351, when the Black Prince's campaigns laid this part of France open. In the process of time they became a very royalist town. When they were handed over to the English in 1360, they soon won back their freedom. They minted their own coins from the silver mines in the neighbourhood. They had their own assay office. They felt royalist and grand. But the wars of religion provided a character as well as a theological test for the three towns of Montauban, Rodez, Villefranche-de-Rouergue; and their futures depended on it, as we can see now, and as they probably knew themselves at the time. Montauban, as we know, was a Huguenot stronghold, and finally died of wounds in 1629. Villefranche, the town of the Most Christian King, was sacked by the Huguenots in 1568. It lived to rebuild its splendid belfry, which rises above a buttressed porch at the corner of the old arcaded square. Shut-faced, worldly Rodez kept away from it all, just as it had done in the Albigensian wars, and in the long run scooped the prizes of administration and the fruits of office under the Revolution. By the seventeenth century, Villefranche was a spent force. In the eighteenth century its mayors slipped a rung or two further down the ladder of morality and regularly bought from the king the monopoly for the sale of wine. This may have enhanced the royalism of the town; but as the century advanced, royalism infected its supporters more and more with the political blindness which proved fatal. When the revolutionaries came to re-organise local government and to break up the old provinces into departments, Rodez not Villefranche secured the position of the capital of Aveyron.

I came across one trace of the manners and character of the women of Villefranche. They were pretty, records a French tourist, Jouy, of the 1820's, and easy-going; and their husbands liked them that way. '*Qu'importe à quoi tienne la vertu des femmes, l'essentiel est qu'elle tienne à quelquechose.*' Should one tie to this the illuminating fact that the itinerant wine merchants addressed their call to the women, not the men?

'*Accourez, petites bonnes femmes, car les cerceaux éclatent.*' ('Come quick, little housewives, as the hoops of the wine barrels are bursting.')

Of the quality of the modern Villefrancheoise and her zest for the joys of wine and life, I have, alas, no personal experience; but I can contribute one observation. During the various showers and obliterating storms which fell on my head and—worse—on my spectacles during each of my three pertinacious visits to the place, I used to shelter in a better-class café near the church, over-looking a sixteenth-century house, whose doorway proudly announced that its designer had been to Rome to see Michel-angelo shortly before his death. On my first visit a dark-haired girl looked up from her ironing at the back of the storm-darkened room, asked what I wanted, brought it me and, without word or smile, returned to her ironing.

The rain still fell; by now I could have made a detailed drawing of every moulding in the house opposite, once so attractive; I felt as I gazed through this lake of falling water rather like a fish whose aquarium has been tilted unexpectedly. I ordered another drink and asked out of boredom: 'What are you ironing, Mademoiselle?'

'Napkins, Monsieur,' she answered without enthusiasm, and returned to her ironing board.

It was the same at my next visit, and the same at my third, all storm-bound. With a bogus claim to being, for a foreigner, a regular, I would ask with false heartiness when she brought my drink: 'Still napkins, Mademoiselle?' And I looked at the rather repulsive high pile of shapeless, coarse off-white linen, creasy indeed but without a crease in the right place, utterly depleted of the power to give pleasure of the most modest kind, tasteless, stuffy, smelly.

'Yes, Monsieur, still napkins,' and she went back and picked up her iron, turning its face to her cheek to test its temperature, before her lightly muscled forearms went to work again. The single naked light bulb above her threw her cheekbones into a high relief and cast shadows below her eyes—both false effects. The unreality of the whole thing nagged me. It was poor school of Caravaggio. Where did this Babel-high tower of napkins come from? Who had used them and where? Obviously not in the modest restaurant of the café, where they would not run to white linen. Had the girl got the town contract for washing linen napkins, and had she arranged with the patron that she might iron on the premises when trade was slack? Could there have been a first-floor banqueting room where the little housewives of Ville-franche met every so often to discuss the eternal problem of husband-management?

There was a saying that the English won the first war on the playing fields of Eton, but the French on the beds of the Paris tarts. Did this concentrated girl look for success in the battle of life to training on the ironing-board alone? Did she, aware that she was plain though strong, look forward in bedroom imagina-tion to the time when she would overhear her husband say to a friend: 'She's a beautiful ironer, you know'?

*　　*　　*

If you were going direct from Villefranche-de-Rouergue to Najac, you would drive roughly east along N.111 and then turn north when you make the junction with N.88. This is Mr. Easy's route. If you want a more amusing time through some out-standing country, you will leave Villefranche by D.47 for the south along the valley of the Aveyron, whose course here twists and loops like the marks made by a salesman proving to you that the ball-point pen works. You have a riverside journey to start with, and the hills descend on you pretty smartly. As you drag up higher from the valley you gain a stone-wall landscape, small fields, small hedgerow trees, small farms, faintly reminiscent of the Gloucestershire Cotswolds except for their height. You drop down again after all this effort to make height, and then by Mazérolles turn left to D.39 and in no time you are clambering in the lower gears one of these high rocks which Cyclops cast to force the Aveyron into yet another loop. This time he cast a rock selected with especial care, no more pyramid but a cone with a chine attached, an astonishing sight, a natural place for defence.

This, of course, it soon became, as the great round tower attests to all the world around, higher by far than the subsidiary walls and turrets, higher than the church which it protects. It stands, in fact, some twelve hundred feet above the river. The castle always seemed to attract an able governor, and it has become almost a dictionary of mediaeval defence methods—machicolations, curtain walls and flanking towers with their slits first for bowmen and later for artillery; staircases contrived within the thickness of the walls so that any danger spot could be reinforced without loss by exposing your troops to enemy fire.

Najac had a brief but adventurous career. In the days when the clergy were fully interested in the exercise of temporal power Raymond IV of Toulouse built it as a security point against the Bishop of Albi. In the Albigensian struggles it played the same contra-episcopal part; but though it came out of this first stage victorious, with the final defeat of Raymond VII of Toulouse Najac passed to the French crown, as a frontier fort against the English. We put Najac through its paces; captured it, held it, lost it, recaptured it again, though by 1400 it was back in French hands, so to remain. But this was not the end of its troubles. A place so finely sited was an embarrassment even to artillery in the sixteenth century. Guns were heavy things to drag into range up a very steep hill; even when they were in position, the uphill trajectory was against them. Najac held firm and inviolate for the Catholic League until its last years. Then that determined man,

Henri IV, who had the greatness to choose when to be violent and when to be patient, starved Najac to surrender despite its famous well.

From that time on its only importance was that of a stone quarry, and through the centuries a good deal of dilapidation has occurred. Even so its unconquerable quality prevailed. The revolutionaries swore to destroy it. The place passed to a local publican, named Bach, who licensed for his profit the removal of more stone. What followed has the flavour of mediaeval legend. As the workmen set upon the old bones of the castle a vast block of sandstone fell on them killing or maiming the lot. After that there were no takers, and the piece was virtually taboo to the vandals. Now it is in safe hands as a *Monument Historique*, and we need fear no more.

It is well worth visiting, not only for itself but for the village as well. One word of warning first. As you twist round and round this twelve hundred foot hill, when you are just within the fringe of the 'built-up area', you see on your left a sign in amateur lettering with an arrow pointing up to an impossible turning to the left 'Château et Eglise'. Anyone in his senses would take it to indicate a short cut for pedestrians. But do take it literally; otherwise you will find yourself (as I have) in the old village on the top of the chine from which there is no access by car to the château's conical hill. Yet this was a mistake worth making, for it remains a pretty authentic picture of what a fifteenth- and sixteenth-century garrison town must have been. Soldiers are soldiers all the world over, and few of them find time for the refinements of life. Quite right, too; they might get out of training. There is a fine broad street with an avenue of trees down the centre, designed after the military function of Najac had disappeared. But the little half-timbered houses, their first storeys often propped up on roughly shaped wooden pillars, the meanly lighted cobbled lanes, the absence of a decorative instinct all are the equivalent (without the conscious planning) in their period to the meanness of Aldershot banality.

*   *   *

On the 4th of November 1222 Count Raymond VII of
Toulouse promulgated a charter for his newly founded fortress
town of Cordes, some twenty-four kilometres from Najac. His
situation politically and economically was appalling and he needed
a fortress in the north of his dominions to replace one he had lost
to the French king. All this part of the Albi territory had been
systematically ravaged by the 'Crusaders' under de Montfort,
by royal troops, and above all by the mercenaries employed by
the forces of both sides. In those days in that part of France what
most men wanted was a stout city wall about them; and this
accounted for the successful foundation of Cordes.

> Anyone who wants to set up at Cordes shall not be liable [so ran
> the charter], for annual tax on such houses as he puts up.
> Everyone shall be exempt from every form of service.
> The people of Cordes shall not have to pay any tolls through the
> length and breadth of the Albigeois. On the other hand they shall
> have rights to use the Count's woods and quarries in the district.

This was the way to start up a fortified town, a 'bastide'. Walls
went up, fortified gates, houses; and within seven years the
population had risen from nought to 5,500, proof enough of the
need for security and shelter caused by the Albigensian crusade.
With this solidification, with the building first of one set of walls,
then of another, then of a third, planned with all the ingenuity
known to the mediaeval military architect, local government
went hand in hand. But let us first take a general view of the
little town.

It also stands like Najac on a Cyclops rock, which strikes up
from a fertile plain, surrounded by bare or wooded hills, a very
striking panorama. Seen from the central point of Cordes, their
slopes do not seem too hostile, though they are formidable
enough when you are battling your way past their curving roads.
The old charter gave them some right to the land within a rough
radius of fifteen kilometres from Cordes; and in those early days
of primitive agriculture the land was to a great extent devoted to
the cultivation of three valuable vegetable dye-plants—woad,
madder and saffron—and also to the main product, flax and hemp.

So Cordes was an early textile town and, since the Catharists were for the most part weavers (they were familiarly called 'les tisserands'), industry and heresy went together. Some of the latest cases of heresy came out of Cordes long after it had passed to the crown of France.

There is a central street, the Grande Rue, with a powerful gate at each end. The little town clambers up to the summit of the steep hill, originally crowned with towers, like a French San Gimignano: a bold site. Curtain walls with their little turrets for the protection of two sentries connected the towers which covered the few gateways into the town. As you circle the ascent to its height it still wears the dress of a strong old site.

It had other advantages besides those man-made for the purpose of defence—underground rivulets which filled subterranean cisterns; a well two hundred and fifty feet deep, explored and tested so recently as 1951; natural caverns into which mediaeval man had the wit to pack the winter snow so that it lasted as cold storage past the worst of the summer. Every device was employed in guttering to conserve the rainwater, which when it falls falls very heavily. To this day Cordes is largely a rainwater town.

All this was organised, including a special ice house for the official slaughter-house in the thirteenth century, when they drew up their own articles of self-government first under the dominion of the last Comte de Toulouse and subsequently under the Baily (the provost) of the French Kings. One thinks of the middle ages as primarily dirty. At Cordes they were advanced in their day, since there is a good deal of sanitary legislation in their '*Livre Ferré*', the beautifully illuminated book, originally chained ('*ferré*') to the wall, which embodies the town's constitution and by-laws of the thirteenth century. This still exists and can be seen on application. There were provisions, for instance, for seeing that the streets were regularly swept; you could not keep fowls within the city's precincts. Keepers of hotels and taverns could not buy in the market before ten o'clock in the morning, to give the housewife a chance, nor might they sell drink while Mass was being said. All the areas of communal life were covered from the protection of the vines to the percentage which the miller might

charge for milling your flour. Annually the magistrates surrendered office, each nominating a choice of two successors from
whom the Baily could choose. The man elected then took the old
oath on his knees swearing on the 'Evangile du Libre Ferrat' (as
they called their charter), *suivant l'ancien usage d'estre fidelles
serviteurs du Roy, de procurer le bien du communauté et de rendre
compte loyal, de les adminstrer et de nommer des gens de bien et de
probité pour succéder à leur charge*. Good God! How old an hold
have the bureaucrats upon us!

An interesting idea, which we might do well to study in these
days of agitation over penal reform, is that the men of Cordes did
not believe in imprisonment as a sentence, though a prison was
a useful place in which to detain a man while his relatives were
paying up his fines. Otherwise, they declared, it costs the town
a great deal and does the individual no good. Prison conditions,
it was thought, were not good. The 'Basse-fosse', known locally
as 'little hell', was so damp and so dirty that often prisoners were
in danger of their lives owing to the infected air and the stink
from the water, which was so prevalent that you could not put
your foot on an inch of dry ground. General opinion favoured
summary punishments of the most drastic kinds or fines rather
than imprisonment. I'm not at all sure they weren't right.
Another window on their attitude to life is the fact that, whereas
they might use 'little hell' without approving it much, they also
ran three hospitals in the town and provided for the orphans.

For two hundred years the town prospered. It was safe: it had
its textile and its dyeing industry; many fairs brought wealth to
the place. In addition they had a glass factory, as is still attested
by the name of the Rue Boutellerie—Bottle-makers Street. And
the name of the town itself, borrowed from Spain as so many
names are in this part of France on the pilgrimage route to
St. James of Compostella, is a version of Cordova, a leather town.

They did beautiful things with their money, building superb
town houses in the fourteenth and fifteenth centuries. And in this
way the little place makes its personal contrast with the rest of
the countryside. Perhaps because of its Catharist origin, it paid
no more than minimal respect to Mother Church. It resented

interference from the Inquisitor Bishop of Albi, took a high-handed line with his emissaries and left the ecclesiastical element in the town at a discount. The tower of St. Michael's is good enough; but that is all you can say. It was for the priests to undertake watch-tower duties on it for the town's defence.

Now let us start at the end of the Grande Rue, to which we have climbed by narrow streets, paved with sets, winding our way between the ancient walls of sandstone houses. At the top you reach the first open space, the covered market, which dates back to the mid-fourteenth century (1353). It was not the ordinary market with which we are familiar in France and Italy today, where flowers, vegetables, meat and *charcuterie*, butter and eggs and cheese are offered. This was the cloth market, which needed protection from the sudden storms of the climate. Twenty-four massive pillars carry the roof, all but one of them octagonal. The well-head of the vasty well is there; and a lovely iron cross, a compromise-relic of some disapproval registered by the Bishop of Albi. Here were displayed the linens and the 'hempen-home-spun' of the neighbourhood, dyed yellow, blue or madder from the local products. Here were the stalls of the leather-makers too; and some scholars attribute a specialisation to the leather-makers of Cordes, which is otherwise unfamiliar to me. Their 'Cuir de Can' was in high favour on the Albi market; dog-skin they say it is, perhaps a light form of chamois leather.

Across to the left is the Place de la Bride, from which you look out over the edge of the old ramparts to see a segment of the area of country which fell under the blessings of the charter of 1222, villages, woods and vines. But opposite you, to the right, is a run of such fourteenth-century façades as you would not dream to find in so small a place. Such is the rich arcading and the grouping of the windows on the first and second floors that, in a half light, you could think yourself to be in Venice or perhaps Perpignan. This may sound ridiculous, when said of a place in the mid-southwest of France; and of course, when you look at the detail —the carved birds eating the grapes, the familiar hounds and so on—you would not hesitate to say it is French work. Yet these groups of tied Gothic arches, pierced with rosettes between the spandrels, the intervening courses of sculptured animals, masks or gargoyles, seem to be the work of an architect who had seen Venice.

Whatever the origin, this style, first developed in the Maison du Grand Fauconnier—the Grand Falconer's, as it is called romantically but without the shadow of historical justification—pleased the rich merchants of Cordes: and you find other capital examples of it in the Maison du Grand Veneur and the Maison Fontpeyrouse. In short the place is full of good architecture. If you want the sixteenth century, you find it beautifully represented by the Maison Gorsse. It is difficult to find anything later than the seventeenth century. You clamber up the Paternoster Staircase (one step for every word of the prayer) enshrined in the middle ages. All over the town you find noble ground-floor pointed arches which originally led into shops, stables or storage places. The place never ceased to be a garrison town for two hundred years and a great deal of what you see belongs to the original conception of what a mediaeval garrison town should be. Even at your pleasant hotel, with its challenging collection of statuary and local prints, you will climb to your comfortable bedroom by a spiral staircase and cross the old courtyard for your dinner. No. Cordes is a place to be respected and it can command affection. Even if it is now outwardly romantic only, it has been immensely practical in the past, and one can sense the ancient briskness.

An attempt was made some years ago to revive the commercial prosperity of Cordes. Albert and Marcelin Gorsse brought back from Switzerland, where they had been interned in the 1870 war, a mechanised process for embroidery. They put up a modest capital and set all the old people and the young people of the town to this practice; and the place prospered. The success was phenomenal. From a start of a foreman and two operatives, finally two hundred and thirty were employed. The crash came ironically just when in 1926 they were about to hold an Embroidery Festival in the town. Order books which had been full now turned white as an empty winding sheet. Prosperity ebbed, perished. Not even the light railway could think of climbing Cordes' rocky emplacement; it passes five kilometres away through a village without character. So Cordes is left again to its memories, to a fading population. I do not conceal my hope that so beautiful a place, which has had the courage to steer round so many difficult bends, will still plan a future of a lively kind for itself.

*   *   *

If you ever have the sense to go to this part of France, you will kick yourself for years if you do not make the journey to the village and abbey of Conques. It is most easily reached from Rodez; and you can imagine yourself if you wish as forming part of the great pilgrimage of 1878, which commemorated the re-opening of the abbey and of its precious treasury of relics at which the Archbishop of Avignon and eight other bishops officiate! They did the forty kilometres on foot in three days and as they passed through the little villages on the way were comforted by wine, dancing and reinforcements at Salle-la-Source, Marcillac and St. Cyprien among others. It is a charming and varied road. Soon after Rodez you pick up a brisk little stream, and before long the hills begin to crowd in upon its little valley, forcing their way in closer and closer from right and left like bids at an auction. Short of Salle-la-Source, you are right under the cliffs of rock, soft rock which breaks off to make all sorts of designs. Sometimes the breakage is vertical, and produces small cliff faces; in other places the fission is horizontal, forming something like the gigantic battlements of an imaginary castle.

Salle-la-Source is a pretty place, overhung by cliffs, from which bursts out a fine cascade of water ('la source'), turned inevitably in these prosaic days to hydro-electric purposes. I wonder what the old slate roofs, the monastery and church of the village think about it all, as they lie picturesquely listening to the chord of the waterfall, a chord principally of three notes, of which the employment is varied and modulated by the wind which plays conductor to this water music.

And then, the pilgrims gathering to the cortège would have moved slowly on, chanting as they went, to the little town of Marcillac-Vallon, where the hills open out and release another

Porte
des Ormeaux
at Cordes

Cordes: 'The Paternoster Staircase . . . enshrined in the Middle Ages'

valley. Snuggling up the hill-sides in terraces are copious vines, which produce a remarkably purple wine. Indeed, if I could find a jot of evidence that Keats ever went to Marsillac, I should argue that it was there he got his 'purple-stainèd mouth'. It is a smiling place, with its local river, the hard-paced Dourdou (a deceptively soft name) running off on a punitive expedition across the meadows to the left. And if you rout out the local curé, he will show you the processional cross of his parish. It was made by the Rodez silversmith Steve Frenchieu in the sixteenth century, the third recorded generation of this silversmith family at Rodez, whose work still survives at Conques, at St. Symphorien, at Mayrans and other small places in the neighbourhood. Again, when you reach Nauviale, perhaps another ten kilometres further on, you will find another of these fine crosses, this time made at Villefranche-de-Rouergue between 1498 and 1512. The results from the simple technique of this local school are frequently beautiful; the design is worked in repoussé and filled out with engraving on the thin plates of silver or silver gilt and pinned to a wooden core. The figure of Christ crucified is in solid metal and nailed to the cross in the traditional manner.

All this stretch of your pilgrimage is steep and rocky; but once more at St. Cyprien the mountains part for a while to allow a rich plain of surprisingly red earth dotted with trees and woods of great variety—oaks and chestnuts, beech and ash and plane all combining their differing greens in a changing pattern against the vivid earth and rock background. Again the hills close in upon you, leaving just room enough for road and river and, at one point, a mediaeval bridge to an ancient mill. Suddenly round a corner you see below the bare shoulders of a mountain the three steeple-crowned towers of the monastery rising above the slate roofs of the little village, clustered around and above it, protected still by its gates. Over a bridge of great beauty—and you climb the narrow road to enter by the arched fortified gate.

Abandon your car conveniently and for a moment slip your way among the old houses by staircases and mud-lanes which have been compressed by ten centuries of feet. They are remarkable for their endurance rather than for their architecture. The

K

fish-scale slate roofs are now as green as an old cassock; some-times you see an adventurous turret; sometimes some half-tim-bering with roughcast between the beams. The higher you climb the more gaps you find where within living memory houses have fallen in untenanted. It is a dying place. In the fifteenth century three thousand people lived, prayed and worked here; today a bare three hundred.

Yet in its heyday the abbey was one of the great centres of pilgrimage, both for its own relics and as a stopping place on the road to Compostella. Founded in the eighth century, it passed some time in obscurity, until Charlemagne visited it on his way to Spain; he is said to have made offerings, as did his descendants. It was not royal patronage, however, but the initiative of the monks that was to bring glory to the monastery, enabling them to build their incomparable church and to gather together a group of relics, reliquaries, monstrances, crosses, coffers of the earliest and strangest workmanship. But before we consider the treasure and the story of the saint by whose miracles it was acquired, or the changes and chances which overtook it, let us look at the church itself.

The placing of it strikes you at first as a little odd, since you go down to it by steps, whereas from the distance it had looked so dominant. The reason is simple enough: to accommodate the church and the monastic buildings on the steep hill-side, a level area had to be cut from the downslope of the rock. Before I had worked out this easy calculation I was arrested by the sculpture over the west door, the Last Judgment. It is one of the wonders of southern France; outstanding by the firm linear distinction between the different levels of the story-telling, and by the texts which help the pilgrim to gain the full significance of the sculp-tured story. Christ, a figure of superb majesty, sits surrounded by the four Evangelists, in glory and in judgment with Sainte Foy to his right. Even Charlemagne has to be introduced to him by the abbot; for Conques had by this time been made a papal collegiate church, and the pope and his abbot must in the twelfth century make plain the superiority of the papal case in its tem-poral struggle with the Holy Roman Emperor and the French

King. Choiring angels support the elect as they move to be admitted to the steps of the throne of grace; below on the left-hand side, sheltering beneath the dignity of arches are the elders of the church. No such shelter awaits those of this lowest tier in the centre and the right-hand side—only the devil's maw. For here are the damned.

The interior, despite the memories of desolation by sack, siege and neglect, can still transfix you. The great high nave of five round-arched bays to the crossing would be impressive enough even without the supporting aisles. But these are essential to carry the roof, a stone cross-banded barrel-vault and immensely heavy. Above is the triforium of coupled lights with their sills splayed so as to spread the light downwards to the nave. At the crossing a shaft of brilliant light flashes down from the octagonal tower above it, throwing the choir and retro-choir into a mysterious shadow populated with perspectives of arches and columns. And this is just as it should be; for in the choir behind the altar was the great object of veneration, the bones of Sainte Foy (St. Faith), virgin and martyr, protected from the fervent crowd of pilgrims by a splendid iron grill of the twelfth century. The material for it came from the fetters of the prisoners who had been released (so tradition says) at the intercession of Sainte Foy. The iron barbs, like arrow-heads, make a further deterrent to relic-snatchers. And the brothers of Conques had every reason to take a precaution of this kind. Which takes us back to the story of Sainte Foy herself and of the monastery's astounding success.

* * *

In the latter part of the third century A.D. the Christians had been having a fairly quiet time and were beginning to look forward to the peaceful conquest of the Roman Empire. Before the turn of the century Sainte Foy was born (c. 290) to noble Gallo-Roman parents with a vast estate near Agen. This was not a noticeably Christianised area, and it caused surprise that one of the principal Roman administrators in Spain, Dacianus, should bother to journey so far into Gaul to supervise the application of the Emperor Diocletian's anti-Christian edict of 303. However, in the forum of Agen, he announced his intention of putting to death all who despised the 'institutions of our ancestors'. The Christians fled to the solitudes round the town.

All but Sainte Foy. Brought up by her nurse as a secret Christian in a pagan household, she refused to make the required sacrifice to Diana, disregarding all threats and blandishments. She was condemned by Dacianus to be grilled; and according to the Roman law first to be scourged and then raped. And now the power of God intervened to convert the heathen. It was said that the stripes of her flagellation were miraculously cured; the temple in which the soldiers tried to rape her collapsed upon them; when she was to be laid upon the heated plate of iron, rain descended upon it and she arose unscathed. By now the pagan crowd were hurling insults and threats at Dacianus who, however, stopped up his ears and in a fury of frustration ordered her to be beheaded.

From his hiding place above the town, the Bishop of Agen, Çaprais, had watched this tumultuous sequence of events. Shamed by the girl's courage, he gave himself up and after submitting to the regulation tortures he, too, was beheaded. In the secrecy of night the bodies of the two martyrs were recovered and enshrined; later, when Christianity had within ten years become an officially recognised religion, a primitive cathedral was built at Agen, where miracles of the most varied nature were worked at the shrine of Sainte Foy, bringing many pilgrims and much profit to the cathedral.

In the turgid world of the ninth century, distracted by plundering Norsemen and raiding Saracens, devastated by plague and famine, ravaged by the senseless internecine wars of Charlemagne's descendants, men sought security, though by different methods from ours today. They, in their age of faith, literally looked to Heaven and to the saints and their relics as intercessors, a protection against adversity and a guarantor of prosperity in the fields. Now the monastery of Conques had made no great progress in the first century of its establishment; and the monks came to attribute this to the fact that they had no really notable relics in their shrine. In 853 they decided to remedy this by what one can only call the attempted theft of the bones of St. Vincent

from Saragossa; but unfortunately their representative was discovered before he could make good his escape. After a time in
gaol, he had to return to Conques to deliver his miserable report
of failure to his abbot. Not cast down by this reverse, nor by a
subsequent one, the monks of Conques seriously considered the
capture of the bones of Sainte Foy from Agen. All this is openly
recorded in an almost contemporary chronicle, which describes
the operation not as theft but as 'the furtive translation' of the
relics.

Aronisde, the curé of a neighbouring parish, was selected for
the task as a man of infinite resource. He was also a man of great
patience, since he waited ten years for the perfect opportunity.
He left with a companion in the guise of pilgrims for Agen, where
they lived exemplary lives. Aronisde indeed expressed his desire
to live out his life there, and such was the charm of his manner
and his obvious devotion that he came to be accepted by the
clergy of Sainte Foy. Time passed; Aronisde took his part in the
regular services and (his patience at last rewarded) was appointed
sacristan. Among his duties was the safe-keeping of the bones
of Sainte Foy.

With unhurrying self-control he still held his hand until
Epiphany, a festival after which it was customary for the monks
to stay longer than usual over their supper in the refectory. With
the entire goodness of heart which stamped his nature, Aronisde
declined the feast, saying that he must stay and guard the precious
relics. One does not require much imagination to guess the
sequel. The companion has the horses ready, and away the two
go with the skeleton of the little saint wrapped in a chamois
leather bag long since prepared. The pursuit goes astray; later it
catches up, but even in such a predicament Aronisde survives.
No, he says, he has seen no such two men as they describe; and
with the utmost unconcern stretches himself out with his face to
the ground and goes to sleep, while the chase continues. He was
much more alarmed, when at Figeac, a dependant monastery of
Conques, the saint's relics cured a blind old man. The news of
this would soon get about; even though the men of Agen had
travelled so swiftly to Conques as to get there before him and

find nothing suspicious, they might hear the news on the return journey. So from Figeac Aronisde travelled alone with his precious burden and at long last his patience, his resource, his charming manners and his spectacular devotion were rewarded by success in his somewhat questionable enterprise. One can only say that to the writer of the early account the whole thing appeared to be open and above board; nowhere is an excuse offered or a moral doubt raised.

Sainte Foy took happily to her new home, and in this remote corner of the Rouergue was soon working miracles. She does not seem to have been a specialist, though she had a preference for helping prisoners (to whom she would appear in a dream) and the blind. Remembering her extreme youth as a martyr, the locals called her miracles 'les jeux de Sainte Foy'—her games. If you are prepared to admit that we are not all of us equipped to know everything, you might side with a certain Bernard d'Angers, an early eleventh-century ecclesiastical schoolmaster at Chartres, who was disturbed and shocked by the stories he heard of Sainte Foy's 'games'. He went to investigate for himself. He might have been a journalist or a scholar rather than a schoolmaster.

He went to Conques three separate times, and wrote down what he himself had seen as well as some of the stories he had been told, for which he did not accept the evidence. He had a remarkable mind for his pre-Renaissance generation. When he came to send in his manuscript to his bishop for revision, he made the condition that the bishop was there to correct any stylistic tropes which might displease him, but he was in no way to interfere with the substance of the original material. Bernard d'Angers felt sure. And there is the same scholarly approach displayed by the man who wrote the continuation to Bernard's story of 1020. This man makes a point of telling us exactly where his additions begin 'for fear that any confusion might arise over the authenticity and authority of the (original) work'.

Bernard felt sure, for instance, that he had seen a man (before and after) whose eyes had been put out by his master, and whose eyes had been restored to him after he had been urged by Sainte Foy in a dream to make the pilgrimage to Conques for their restoration. There is the extraordinary case of the vassal unjustly imprisoned by his overlord in a fortress from which escape was really impossible. After some years of confinement he obtained permission to undertake on parole the pilgrimage to Conques. There he prayed at the shrine, received the intimation that, though owing to the situation of his prison the task was a difficult one, Sainte Foy promised his ultimate release. As a virtuous man, he surrendered to his parole, returned to his incarceration and passed some more years in his dungeon. Then the saint appeared to him one night, told him that the guards were relaxed and he could leave his cell. He did so—only to find that his one route of escape lay in throwing himself off the high battlements on to rocky ground. His heart failed him, and well it might. But the virgin martyr was at his elbow. He had only one condition to remember—she wanted his fetters. If he would bring them to her at Conques he would land safely. And so he did, says Bernard d'Angers, who met him.

One could continue for a long while such recitations. What fascinates me about them is the care which the author took in checking his authorities, his early instinct for the true against the false, for the importance of buttressing the true miracle, of confronting equally the credulous and the agnostic in an age over-emotional for faith.

Sainte Foy would, it appears, find things for you, cure you, exact restitution from thieves or dishonest merchants, even arrange the birth of an heir (but this I question). One cannot now be surprised at the consequent popularity of Conques, however much one may wonder at the casual attitude of the clerics of Agen —but then it is a town where they confection plums, and you cannot expect too much from such types.

* * *

Thanks to 'the games of Sainte Foy' the prosperity and reputation of Conques increased, increased one thousandfold, and as was financially common in those days they put their money into gilt-edged (i.e. precious convertible metal, gold or silver) or into land or revenues from glebe farms. For instance in the early sixteenth century the monastery owned forty-four benefices in Rouergue, seventy-three in the rest of France, three in Italy, two in Spain, and one in England. Thanks to the gifts of itinerant pilgrims, often of high degree, a treasury of relics was established, shrines or smaller reliquaries which contained the relics of one or more saints. What survives from the original treasure—by no means the whole—is now very beautifully displayed in a room formed from the remains of the old cloister; and it is worth many sabbath-day's journey to see.

It has not survived to these days without devoted attention. For instance, the Huguenots attacked the place in 1561 and the abbey withstood a four years' siege. So early as that they learnt to bury their relics in case of disaster. The touch point came in 1793. News came through that a body of revolutionaries were on the march to sack the place. Then a brilliant improvisation took place. It was pretended that a party of pilgrims who had passed through the day before had raided the abbey. By the time the republicans arrived, the story was ready and the *mise-en-scène* had been faked. Any fool could see how the building had been mishandled where the relics used to be kept; there was nothing to find. But all this was a blind for the rapid concealment in walls of houses of all that was important. They used as well a piece of walling which had been erected within the church itself as a result of the damage done by the Huguenots. It was here that the bones of Sainte Foy were immured, only to be discovered in the 1870's.

The contents of the treasury, as you see it set out today—I was told that they mean to use radar all over the town on the chance of finding more silverwork—includes fragments from the fourth century and descends to one 'very late piece' of the early seventeenth. It is overpowering, curious, and at moments exceedingly beautiful. As curious, one thinks at once of the 'Alpha', the piece of silver shaped as an A, said improbably to have been presented by Charlemagne, more likely by Louis le Debonnaire; of the 'lantern' of St. Vincent, more likely a monstrance with an unusual dome, resembling the domes of Sainte Foy at Perigueux, supported on arches which would have permitted a view of the relic enshrined; the strange hand and arm, draped as if naturally folded lawn were translated into silver. The hand is raised and the fingers bent in blessing. This contained relics of St. George. Then there are the earlier reliquaries, the coffers left by Pepin the Short, by Louis le Debonnaire; the silver figure of Sainte Foy, carrying her martyr's palm, her gridiron and the sword with which at length she was finally put to death. Portable altars, consecrated perhaps in Spain to be carried either on pilgrimage or on crusade, of onyx set in silver; bindings in silver to contain manuscripts of the Gospels. All this, a matter of thirty pieces of silver or silver-gilt, stands as a record of the sort of thing enshrined by piety in every church of standing throughout Europe and these islands before the Reformation, since the treasury contains such a degree of antiquity in workmanship, which elsewhere perished in religious and political turmoil.

To the antiquarian, to the curé of Conques, to the unreflecting believer, the most important and without doubt the most impressive thing of all is the reliquary containing the head of Sainte Foy herself, hidden within its chest. I believe that there are only one or two things like it in the world; and every inch of its surface testifies to the faith of the devotees of Sainte Foy.

The statue, seated on a throne with the slippered feet of a prelate, is of gold. The throne is of fine silver-gilt plating affixed to a wooden core. Of the saint's head, you must make your own judgment. It is of a dark stone, and the eyes are of black and white enamel. They stare at you, they hypnotise you from under the very elaborate, bejewelled crown—one could call it a diadem. This crown is perhaps a little later than the main work (but there are many dating problems) for at least you can see beneath it the very naturalistic treatment of the saint's hair. Many authorities say that the head itself is of Gallo-Roman origin and dates before the era of Sainte Foy. I am not qualified to judge; but the extreme naturalism of the hair is out of key.

It is hard to admit oneself completely out of sympathy with a statue of such religious importance as this. This is an issue I cannot dodge. As a sequence of details, the thing is incomparable. As a monument to the riches of an abbey deceased it is a light on the road to Damascus. But what are we to say of it as a whole, setting aside all thoughts of its value as a reliquary and judging it solely as a work of art?

It may embody for you all the panoply of such chronicles, or such historical novels as you have read but never entirely trusted; and having seen it you may be tempted to say to yourself:

'Well, after all that world did exist; here is something from it. All those ham-actor phrases of gold encrusted with rubies, with diamonds, with pearls, with antique cameos, ornaments with all the names from the jewellers' dictionaries are here, attached to gloves, to shoes, shoulders, crown, knees, skirts of the saint. The barbaric splendour of the world I read about did in fact exist, and it is here.'

And this is true; the mediaeval world was like that; not for nothing did Aronisde 'furtively translate' the bones of Sainte Foy.

So what you see here, now in the museum very well displayed but originally protected from thieving pilgrims by the lovely grill made from the iron fetters of the prisoners whom the saint had released, is, to put it brutally, the mediaeval balance sheet of Conques Abbey, Inc. There is its major capital asset, and the productivity record has long since been certified in the note of auditor Bernard d'Angers, latterly circulated through Europe by German and Swiss manuscript copies of the twelfth century. But artistically it is a hideous thing. And so are balance sheets.

VII

Albi to Carcassonne

TO reach Albi from Toulouse entails no more than the straightforward job of driving seventy-six kilometres (N.88) through country which is agreeable without making heavy demands on the emotions. There has been the occasional sharp geological snarl resulting in an unexpected hill, but nothing to require intervention by the police. At St. Sulpice the landscape grows livelier for there the Agout, flowing south-east from the Montagnes Noires, joins—you might say, hits—the sturdy Tarn. The Tarn, either reinforced or staggered by this conjunction, turns through a right angle from its south-westerly course to flow north-west to join the Garonne at Montauban. From here to Albi you have his dramatic company, but it is closer for the little scenes if you drive along the lesser road on his left bank.

If you are so minded, you can turn right up the valley of the Agout to Lavaur (N.530) where the cathedral will explain to you in small what happened over all this countryside in the thirteenth century. The Catharist town offered an heroic resist-ance to Simon de Montfort. Exhorting the defenders was a virago of a Perfect one, Dame Guiraude, who when it came to the surrender and the slaughter hurled the nearest thing to an im-precation she was allowed to use against the crusaders. They seized her and threw her down alive into a well. To make sure, the crusaders filled it with stones. The town was very heavily fined, on condition that the money was put to the rebuilding of the cathedral.

You see now the fear the heretics had caused the church, as it reflected on these terrible episodes. This is a fortified church. On either side of the west door project square, durable towers. The left one has no opening whatever on the outer faces, while in the right is one archer's slit for each of the five gaunt storeys.

The two towers are joined by a band of machicolations, another defensive point. You will find the same thing on a larger scale at Albi, where even till 1608 the guns of the cathedral were still kept trained on the town. After the heretical insurrections the bishops were frightened of the townsmen, from whom in consequence they extorted as much revenue as they could—too much to buy goodwill.

If we keep on the direct road to Albi, we shall run through a small, attractive town, Rabastens, another haunt of Catharists. It came as a surprise to me, since really I was on my way to find the Château de St. Géry where, I had been told (quite erroneously), Toulouse-Lautrec had spent his childhood. In fact he was no more than a remote relation of the reigning family. We found it at the wrong moment in the morning, when Madame la Comtesse in very smart tweeds was just off to lunch with friends in Toulouse. But would we not come back after lunch? We could easily be received then; meanwhile perhaps we could lunch in Rabastens; she had been told the Pré-Vert was reliable, though she had never eaten there herself.

It was not architecture that took my fancy at the Pré-Vert, for it was an ordinary 1860-ish country house, of which the hall and the wide staircase had been pleasantly modernised. There were big bedrooms on the first floor; it would not be a bad place for children to stay on holiday. The garden was large enough for them to run about. And I think it was just a part of the atmosphere that in fact they did cater for families with children with a sort of affectionate efficiency. Everyone about the place either was actively pretty or made herself look as pretty as she could. The food would be an inducement to go again, even if it was not outstandingly brilliant.

We had time after lunch to look over the little town, where we found an imposing brick built castle, some pleasant old houses, and another thirteenth-century church with a ferocious fortified tower and, inside it, exceptional thirteenth- and fourteenth-century frescoes. The church has rather a broad proportion, as so often in this part of France, with a dark-glowing apse like a cave. All the church is painted for the most part in the kind of scrolled designs which we saw in the crypt of St. Sernin, but as well with figures of Saints and Fathers of the Church and scenes from the life of the Virgin. In the chancel red, blue and black were the predominant colours, while in the chapels the backgrounds were a sort of dull turquoise. Altogether the little place turned out to be a quite rare wayside flower.

The Château of St. Géry lies a few kilometres towards Albi slightly off the road to the right. There is a long forecourt with welcoming arms stretched forward. It is made of brick covered with stucco, which is now flaking off—as unceremonious as a country gentleman in his old clothes. It is now 'classé' as a *Monument Historique;* consequently we saw workmen there darning the tiles.

The bell was answered by an elderly gentleman with a bright grey eye; white hair; corduroy suit. Discerning some sort of relationship to the pre-prandial lady, I shifted my approach from '*Est-ce qu'on peut visiter . . .*' to '*Madame nous a dit . . .*' I have met elderly French gentlemen before, but there was something to this one which I could not place at first. I will tell you why later.

So the ceremonies went through, and we realised quite peacefully that it was the owner who was taking us round. So much the better, since he would either be accurate—or wildly inaccurate, which could always be checked—but at least no parrot of a major domo would confuse us. We found ourselves in the French equivalent of a Tudor hall, complete with a mantelpiece old-fashioned even for these days, and off to the left a tiny domestic chapel—'oratory' may be the better word. It was not the original chapel of the house; but on the white plaster of its wall was a most moving Annunciation perhaps of the late fifteenth century, a recent discovery; that seemed to be the date of the modest vaulting. Like the arms of the forecourt, like the gentlemen in the corduroys, this small quiet spot had its own welcome. The noble altar, saved (I was told) from the wreck of the Jesuit monastery in Toulouse, had repose despite a wealth of gilt bronze; it too seemed to have learned a lesson.

To describe the house room by room would invite insoluble differences of taste. Though large, it is neither a great house nor a mean house, and consequently is something one does not often bother to see; yet it is a true historical document. I remember particularly the long gallery on the first floor, seven windows long with a pale yellow floor covering. It seemed to have the games-room atmosphere of the gallery at Chastleford or at the Deanery of Winchester, which Charles II, that inveterate walker, had built to keep himself fit while he planned his palace and avoided the Popish Plotters. Yet the grey white of the walls set off the pretty furniture to perfection; it may not be of Paris museum quality but how glad you would be to have some of it for yourself. Then there is Cardinal de Richelieu's room and the canopied bed from which he sent out the instructions demanding the surrender of Montauban in 1629. Again leading off the great gallery is an agreeable bedroom and a boudoir with grey panelling, light overdoors and Louis XVI furniture upholstered in optimistic yellow. There is a mass of good stuff all through the house, parquetry, Chinoiserie paintings, Sèvres porcelain, Cordova leather. And above all there is the view.

You could drop two hundred feet into the Tarn from the garden parapet; and the Tarn that day was angry with late rains, flushed red. How wise was the designer to leave this river front to the living rooms; you would never have kept your eye on the ball in the great gallery if it had been on the river side. The sound of the powerful Tarn in spate must be a wonderful soporific at night.

We saw all this with the good-natured comments and explanations of our host (rather than our guide) and we saw the last letter written by La Peyrouse, the discoverer of the New Hebrides, who is for the French a cross between our Lord Anson and Captain Cook. Then we were taken to something almost English, the dining room. The walls are, so to speak, upholstered in large Wedgwood plaques, blue and white; nymphs, vines, Bacchus, stirring about among Ionic pilasters under an oval blue ceiling. It seemed wildly improbable, until we remembered the eighteenth-century Wedgwood depot at Bordeaux and, until we learnt something of the family history, which also explained the quality of the light in our elderly host's eye.

In 1728 the property passed from its insolvent owners to the Comte de Rey. He was 'noblesse de Robe'—head of a good legal family, and his son, the equivalent of a Q.C. on the Toulouse circuit, protested hotly against the Revolution and was guillotined in 1794. This son started a tradition of marrying Irish girls. He married an O'Kelly. His son, also a deputy of Toulouse, married a Miss McCarthy, daughter of the good book-collector, whose name is commemorated in a Toulouse street for benefactions to the city. To keep the tradition alive the next son married a Miss O'Brien. But how should an Englishman know why the French and Irish were so mutually attracted, or why these Irish girls should have been about and around Toulouse during the eighteenth and nineteenth centuries in a perfectly respectable way? But it did explain our host's eyes. There was an Irish laugh to them.

We passed through a charming town, Lisle-sur-Tarn, with deeply arcaded squares, and went on towards Albi through Gaillac, where they make an excellent white wine, which is slightly sparkling. In fact I found the white wines of this district surprisingly good. There was an amusing advertisement in the square, a sort of booth where you could buy your glass of shining Gaillac, and on the top of it a large glass, endlessly refilled from a never-empty bottle some way above it. A light breeze sometimes blew the thin stream of wine aside in a playful way, gently perfuming the air. We did not go down into the old town, though it looks from photographs to be a pretty, old place, scrambling its way down the banks of the Tarn, where picturesque turrets and ancient houses rise from the water itself— or so the photographs tell me.

And so you come to Albi over the new bridge across the Tarn, from which you can see its predecessor, still in service. The great piers are of stone, and their upstream faces are trimmed to a triangle, of which the sharp point cuts the flood of water and sends it the more quietly under the brick arches. Further to the right on the far bank are eight circular bastions connected by curtain walls, the last remains of the lower defences of the mediaeval city. But you do not see all this the first time you cross the bridge, for your eye has already been irrevocably captured.

I remember once seeing the *Queen Mary* from the railway at Southampton West across what was then flat open land, and thinking that she had the look of a gigantic cut-out. Albi cathedral has the same uncompromising line against the sky; for from the top of her tower you drop 450 feet to the level of the river. The nave makes a long chine; and the walls of silk-smooth brick seem at a distance as homogeneous as the admirable hull of the *Queen Mary*, and will prove to be far the more durable. This great flank is broken by two tiers of slim, pointed windows, placed unusually high, and the upper tier is much the taller. Set between them are half-round turrets, running the whole height of the building, unbroken brickwork from the ground up, buttresses in fact though they look as frightening as bastions. Here too the craftmanship was so skilled that it invites you to pass your hand over the surface; and the design is so well planned for the creation of shadows that the façades will change their aspects from hour to hour through the day.

The colour can be staggering. I say 'can be' because I have seen Albi cathedral under such rainswept skies that you could have rated it for any brick thing in smoke-smeared England, and I cannot think how one could guess the height of colour latent under the rain. In the sun—well, people quarrel about the exact shade of red in the bricks. I have read an impassioned Frenchman's book, in which he would, if given the power, have excommunicated anyone who christened the brick a rose-red. The truth perhaps could be that it is a very red red indeed, and that in the sun it varies according to the background sky and the time of day. The excitement of the colour is proved by these hot contentions; no one has passed it by unnoticed. For myself, I will only repeat that I have seen the place, dead under rain and alive under the sun, as red as red against a pure but not a deep blue sky with few clouds sailing. Just down the hill-side to the left the old Bishop's Palace spreads out its bulk in a mutter of excommunications, heavily fortified against the citizens.

This approach from Cahors or Toulouse leads you by a broad,

The Cathedral at Albi

Château de St. Géry, near Rabastens

The Abbey at Conques

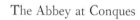

tree-shaded avenue, Les Lices, to the Place du Vigan, the irregular centre of the town, where all is bustle and colour. If you come in from the other end, say from Carcassonne, you must traverse the modern part. You pass a fairly reputable Park (Rochegude) in which various local antiquities have been unconvincingly dotted about among the trees, and reach the noisy Place Jean Jaurès, twice the size of the older Place du Vigan. All the new-money vulgarity is there from every class; it is as if every café had a juke-box imperfectly concealed under its awning, which might as well be a cowboy-shirt.

Unless you have determined to make a long stay at Albi (in which case the detail of the cathedral, of the Bishop's Palace and its contents will repay you an hundredfold) the programme is not a heavy one. The old town is a huddle of a place, only workable on foot. It is wise to peer into courtyards, into the courtyard of the Hôtel Reynes, for instance. It is a miniature and, I should judge, a slightly later version of the Hôtel Bernuy at Toulouse; the suitably placed medallions, the masks, the pilastered windows, the turret in the angle, make it a small but swagger thing of its period.

Then there is the Salle des Etats in the Hôtel de Ville, where the representatives of the Communes of the Albigeois province assembled to hold deep discourse on the affairs of the neighbourhood. It has a good roof and pleasant arabesque decoration in greens and browns; but there is some restoration. You have to ask at the office to see this, and for a guide you take your chance between an elderly secretary in glasses and an old lady in felt slippers. Neither of them professed to more exact knowledge than of the place where the key was kept. More exhilarating for me was the Pharmacie des Pénitents, on the corner of the street of the Pénitents and of the Rue Timbal. It, too, has been restored but inoffensively. The ground floor is handsome with Corinthian pilasters in carved wood, while the upper storeys are half-timbered in an unusual way; the subsidiary timbers are set among the brick fillings slant-wise between the uprights and give a very active look to the place.

As you go along the Rue Timbal into the Rue Mariès towards

L

the cathedral, a flight of steps on the left takes you up to the oldest church of the town, dedicated to their local-born saint, St. Salvy. Here alone there is calm in Albi. It was begun in the eleventh century, revised in the early thirteenth, when the beautiful arches of the nave and the shallow transepts with their apsidal chapels were introduced. The spirited tower was given its present form in 1385. The cloisters, incomplete though they are, epitomise the negligent grace of this church; and you stop worrying quite soon over the fact that no one has pruned the roses for two years.

A few yards more, and you are in the square designed to give the cathedral an air. It fails. Originally a genial huddle of old houses crept right up to St. Cecilia's skirts and lived there securely till the mid-nineteenth century, when it became apparent that the fabric of her cathedral needed a basic overhaul. It was decided then to make this clearance to show off the jewel. However wise the decision in principle, the proportion of the square went wrong, as did the colour of the paving. Nowadays the featureless houses displaying the jewel look cowed and bewildered, as if destruction by the bishop's guns could have been understood, but not destruction by architects.

I think this deaf-mute atmosphere of the square worried me more when I came into it from the side, than when I approached direct to the cathedral from the east down the Rue Mariès. This battleship-prow of a west end gives you all you need. To the left of it is an inviting gateway, elaborate fifteenth-century stuff with statuary for the most part modern. As you come up to it, you are forcibly made to recognise the fortress character of the church. The walls do not rise in the ordinary way, perpendicular from the ground to the pinnacle. These walls are in effect a military 'glacis'; for, perhaps, fifteen feet they rise straight up, and then they are sloped inwards so as to cause the maximum trouble to troops with scaling ladders. It is this purely military device which gives Albi such a dramatic character. Never was 'the church militant here upon earth' better illustrated.

The original entrance was on the north side guarded by the fortified episcopal palace. This was walled up later and instead a magnificent porch was made in the south wall, when life seemed safer (though this was to prove optimistic) in the sixteenth century. After you have passed the fifteenth-century gate, which leans one arm upon the cathedral and the other upon the last surviving tower from the old town wall—a true blend of the spiritual and temporal in brick and stone—you are faced with a flight of fifty steps, no less, to what is called the 'baldachin'. This word is commonly used of those copious canopies over Jesuit-style altars—there is also the baldachin in St. Paul's—and they are usually supported, as here, on columns. But it is also used of an elaborate porch, this aspect of the word implying richly ornamented Baghdad textiles, stretched as an awning to provide cover from the sun. Ornament is the basic idea.

And here is the *ne plus ultra*. Its white stone makes a vivid contrast with the red brick, though a friend of mine, seeing it again after twenty years, considers that the smoke from a modern factory below has slightly yellowed it. But how rich and flashing it still remains, some of the conception of the decorative way in which the arches are managed derives from the splendid rood-screen, which we shall see inside. This is natural since the origi-nator of this porch was Louis II d'Amboise, nephew of the bishop, Louis I, who commissioned the screen.

Louis I d'Amboise, a cousin of the cardinals who did so much fine architectural work at Rouen and in northern France, enjoyed enormous revenues and virtuous intentions. To keep himself in his place, he composed his own epitaph:

Homme! Alors que tu es terre et cendre, ou tend ton orgueil?
Pense donc sans cesse au moment suprême et tu échapperas le péché.

(*Man who art dust and ashes, whither leads thy pride?*
Think constantly of the last hour and thou shalt escape sin.)

In fact, he was a better aspirant than bishop—and, anyway, he cheated by borrowing these pious sentiments from the tomb of Cardinal Lagrange, who died a century earlier. More detailed study of his life suggests that south-western France was not illogical in its acceptance of the reformed religion, when such masters of ecclesiastical abuse as Louis I walked publicly before their eyes as they expiated their sins in beautiful stone. Yet in the arts he retained a very serious mind. For instance, when he commissioned a splendid altar-piece in silver-gilt for the high altar (now destroyed) from Jean and Adam Morant of Paris, he went in to the details of the design minutely in an instruction of 19 August 1485. The gryphon was to be similar to that at the Cordeliers at Paris; the cross should resemble the one at St. Germain l'Auxerrois and be of the same weight; but he would wait till Christmas before he decided whether the figure at the top should be God the Father or St. James. There, at least, his conscience was at work full time.

But we have left his nephew, Louis d'Amboise II, outside in the sun by his white baldachin. With what a flourish of vitality his men designed. Their rounded columns, which contrive to recall the turret-form buttresses of the main structure, support a thing so light and airy that it hardly seems to have been built of stone. All the artifice of decoration is employed. Cusped ornament masks the severity of the round arches. Above them a pair of ogees is controlled in its turn by more round arches, which then suffer defeat from the triumphant ascent of a final pinnacle. And within all these arches in their different forms is light tracery of sub-arches and sub-sub-arches till your world is all a flicker of light and shade with the rich columns and their canopies, their crockets and their pinnacles. The porch itself is open to the sky, in so far as the architect has been able to restrain himself; and indeed he gives way many times to fresh sallies of carved, curving stone, diamond bright against the blue southern sky. With the sculptured saints it might be an open air chapel, where you made more than a genuflexion before entering the shrine.

And when you do go in a warmth greets you, a warmth of colour, of frescoed colour. For all the lateral chapels, of which there is one to each window, are painted in some form of decoration, sometimes a pattern, sometimes an image. The roof, too, is painted with scenes and arabesques.

Your next impression is of breadth rather than height. For although the arches and the quadripartite vaulting is Gothic of the thirteenth and fourteenth centuries, the proportion of height to breadth is still Romanesque. The nave of Amiens cathedral, for instance, is 42 metres high by 14·6 wide, but the corresponding measurements at Albi are 30 metres and 19. Yet the date is much the same.

Here is one of the ways by which a mediaeval cathedral could be paid for. By 1247 the former St. Cecilia's Cathedral was found to be 'minée par les guerres et par les hérétiques', and the rebuilding fund was started by the bequest in 1275 of Sicard d'Alaman, a prominent crusader, of 20,000 " sous tournois" (not nearly so large a sum of money as it sounds, but enough to pay for the damp-course, so to speak). The Bishop of the day who was also Inquisitor for the district, Bernard de Castanet (a harsh man, so it was reported to the Pope, who would leave men in prison without light or air for five years at least awaiting sentence) dedicated five per cent of his revenues for twenty years to the building, and forced the canons to do the same. The contributions of the laity followed, accompanied by the sale of indulgences. They started the new building at the side of the old one, so that there should be no intermission of service, and by 1306 the choir was sufficiently advanced to permit the honourable burial of a canon. But the money cannot have come in as easily as that, since in 1310 Pope Clement V, the first of the Avignon Popes of the 'Babylonish Captivity', whose name is still commemorated in the Rhone vineyard of Pape Clément, sold indulgences for a hundred days in exchange for ten years contribution to the fund. And so it went on. A major benefactor like Bertrand de Fargis who built the retro-choir by 1334 was allowed to have his coat of arms splurged all over the place. Structurally, the building was going ahead well and the clock-tower was climbing up after almost a century, although in 1365 the raiding English interrupted the work. But the final consecration did not take place till 1480, in the time of Louis XI. It is the decoration of the following century that we must next consider.

* * *

A rood-screen can be a beautiful thing in itself, particularly if it is a light piece of woodwork. Transpose the same or a similar

design into stone and you import a major interruption into the
progress of the nave. This has happened at Albi, though there is
this excuse from an administrative point of view, that the choir
belonged to the canons, while the western half belonged to the
city, which has its altar under the tower at the west end. But
whatever one may think of rood-screens in general, this particular
instance is a stupendous piece of work.

It consists of five arches divided by columns each crowned
with a pinnacle; statues of the Virgin and St. John flank the
Crucifixion above the central compartment. The general form
of the ogee arches set the pattern for those of the baldachin. In
the balance of the sky-line lies one of the great beauties of this
masterpiece. The crest of the outer arches rises to the level of the
pinnacles; the crucifixion and the central statues make a grand
climax of height above the fretted balustrade which forms the
intervening link. Everything is carved with profusion, yet with a
touch so delicate that the richness never gives the eye indigestion
as it studies crockets and canopies and undercut mouldings.
This deep undercutting was achieved by a special technique.
The stone is soft and chalky, and the sculptors tackled it while
it was fresh from the quarry, while it was earth-damp and before
it had had time to harden. This wonderful skill never seems
obtrusive.

Of the statues which peopled the canopies only four survived
the fury of the revolutionaries, who destroyed seventy others,
when they made the place a Temple of Reason in 1794. Really
we are fortunate not to have lost the whole thing, and as we walk
down the Rue Mariès we should raise our hats to the man whose
name the street commemorates, since he was the preserver.
Mariès was a local engineer, who had the sympathy to appreciate
'the rood-screen and the choir with its inimitable sculptures'.
Hearing that they were all to be pulled down and sold to the
highest bidder, he wrote off at once to the appropriate minister
in Paris, Roland, and was in time to procure an order of protection for the rest.

For the choir with its sculptures and its stalls is another wonder.
It is enclosed by a noble traceried screen, openwork except where

it backs the stalls. The statues are placed under canopies on elaborate pedestals between each panel of the screen, and deserve detailed study not only for their intrinsic beauty but also for the conception they embody. For there is nothing miscellaneous about the selection of the subjects. Half way down the choir is an opening to the ambulatory, and above the screen is placed on one side a statue of Constantine and of Charlemagne on the other—the two Emperors who to mediaeval thinking did the most for the establishment of Christianity in the form they knew it. West of this point are the statues of the prophets, each bearing a scroll on which is carved his contribution to the message of the Old Testament. To the east are the saints and martyrs, similarly equipped. The lovely Virgin and Child forms by its composition a climax to the single figures. One finds the same conception elsewhere, of course, but seldom is the sequence of thought so carefully worked out in the choice of the individual phrases.

The sculptures have the most moving qualities: the slim beauty of Esther, the grief of Jeremiah, the grace of St. Cecilia. But their origin and authorship have provoked a good deal of argument, some pundits claiming that they are Burgundian work and quoting Cluny in support of their theory, while others bitterly show that the school of Dijon sculptors which worked at Cluny contained artists from Holland, Flanders, Avignon and even Aragon, and almost say 'So what?'. Let us leave them to it and enjoy the line and colour of the massive forms.

One last look before we leave the enclosed choir; the choir stalls. The seats of them are too well-mannered to have those rather rude carved jokes, on which the mediaeval joiner propped up the monkish backside. There is much good sharp turned work and broad carving well proportioned with crisp and simple panelling behind against the wall. And above this rises the glory of the place, the flight of angels under their light canopies which fret and arch their complicated decorative way up to the top level of the screen. The angels themselves hold musical instruments or scrolls, ready to break out as a heavenly choir; their rich swans' wings frame their heads perfectly. This course of sculpture, like the sequence of statues, is not without parallel; but has it ever been so well done?

If you are at all interested in past changes of taste or fashion, Albi cathedral will please you. After the various mediaeval styles we have considered, the frescoes present the contrast in another form. The Last Judgment, a huge mural at the west end, is a late Gothic piece fully characteristic of the French school, while on the roof we are switched to the Italian Renaissance. For these jewelled scenes from the Life of the Virgin are by painters of the Bolognese school, who conveniently for us signed and dated their work quite frequently. The arrangement of these panels in the Gothic vaulting is exceedingly ingenious.

Nor can one fail to see the resplendent organ over the west end, and as befits a place dedicated to the patron saint of music, it was one of the finest of its day in France. It has been enlarged considerably since it was first erected in 1734–6, when the principal organists of the neighbourhood used to turn up every St. Cecilia's Day to hear and to play its noble keyboard. Its maker, Christophe Moucherel, had a considerable practice in Lorraine, though he came originally from Toul. A French researcher, M. Charles Portal, has dug out curious details of his career and shows him as a man of wide interests. He began as a farmer, went on to carpentry, turned soldier, but tiring of that qualified as a master turner at Metz. It was after this that he took up organ building; but even that was not enough to satisfy his restless mind. He cast type at Paris, and invented his own moulds for type and his own printing press. Invention came as breath to him—various musical instruments, a carriage, a system of (so he hoped) perpetual motion. After this you will not be surprised to learn that his hobby was alchemy.

Compared with the soaring quality of the well-defended clock-tower of the cathedral, the defensive towers of the bishop's palace look like sordid northern dwarfs under their pointed witches' hats. It does not look quite as fierce today as when it was first built, since windows were introduced into the outer walls during the sixteenth century when, as we have seen before, people rashly began to think they were safe.

It is called Le Palais de la Berbie, as nice a corruption of language as one could find. Originally it was called 'Lo Bisbo,' that word being the Languedoc recollection of the Latin for a bishop '*episcopus*', so through the sieve of usage it was softened to its present form. Some of its ramparts have been softened, too, into an attractive garden, somewhat formal, of roses trained to arches, and fig trees interspersed with statuary. But the old parts are very severe and rely a great deal on the half-circle of project-ing brick tower, unslitted for archers, a blind defence, which seems to have been so much to the taste and the nature of the Albigensians. 'Modernisation' set in again in the seventeenth century during the reign as lay bishop of the Duc de Daillon du Lude. He was very much the great gentleman and bishop, for he kept a retinue of one hundred and fifty men. Clearly, no poky mediaeval staircase or chamber would do for them. So he built a splendid stair leading to noble rooms, in some of which now are housed the best reason for visiting the palace.

* * *

In the octave of St. Cecilia's Day, on the 14th of November 1864, in the family mansion of the Du Boscs, which had passed by marriage to the Tapié-de-Celeyran family, a son was born to the elder daughter, who had unwisely married her first cousin, Alphonse Charles Comte de Toulouse Lautrec Monfa. You can see the blind face that the big house turns on the street, which then was called the Rue de l'Ecole Mage. It is a run-to-seed street now; and when I first saw it I thought that Albi might have done something better for the memory of their great painter than to rename this sand-blown street after him. But I wronged the city; for after all it was in the big house that he was born, and if you slip your way down a turning to the left you will walk past the long garden wall, catch glimpses of an upper storey—perhaps nursery windows—and see the crests of fine trees with (I think) some cedars among them.

This is not the moment for a digression about Toulouse-Lautrec, his life, art, character and girl-friends. But it is the moment to say that in the Palais de la Berbie is a superb collection of his work in every phase. There are the early landscapes, the drawings and paintings of horses, the sea-pieces, the portraits in oil, in every medium, sketches, illustrations for books, drawings for *Le Rire*, the lithographs and the posters. Nowhere else, so far as I know, does one get anything like such a chance of pene-trating the quality of his mind and of his genius. I remember an exciting exhibition of his work at the Orangerie about 1951, which ranged over a wide field. But the strength of the Albi collection lies in its depth. You do not see one illustration of a particular mood or technique, but many; and that is enriching.

All these hundreds of beautiful things (with a few exceptions) were given to the city by the painter's mother in 1922, twenty-one years after his death. A fortune. But then, as another proud member of that family said to an American, chaffering for a relic of the painter: 'We are the buyers, not the sellers.'

Gifts of this order, particularly of an unorthodox painter, are sometimes slighted by provincial recipients. This is not true of Albi. The hanging is admirable, particularly of the posters, and the catalogue beyond praise. It contains, among other more specialist details, biographical notes which illuminate the sitters or the setting of the picture. For instance you find this about the portrait of the bull-dog, Bouboule (105), which belonged to Madame Palmyre, who adored him and (as happens oftener with women than with men) came to look exactly like him. She kept a bar, *Le Souris*, which was mainly frequented by women. But, says the exact cataloguer, Bouboule had not the same taste in women as his mistress; he barked at them fiercely and bit their legs. There are the small restrained joys of a cataloguer's life, and they are rare flowers. I once got into trouble with the late Cameron of Lochiel over a note in a loan exhibition catalogue, where I described Clementine Walkinshaw as 'Mistress of the Young Pretender'. I defended myself against his public attack by giving the *Dictionary of National Biography* as my authority, and followed it up by saying that I had considered this a more reputable title than the British Museum Engraved Portrait Catalogue gave her—'adventuress'.

*   *   *

At some time or another most people see a poster or a photograph of Carcassonne—'ses murs, ses tours, sa cathédrale'. It is not far from Albi—107 kilometres along N.118—and the drive takes you through some unexpected country, once you have passed Castres, on the Agout. To retain affection for a small town which you have seen once in rain and once after a heavy rainfall (but the streets and roofs were brilliant from it) is to argue that it has a quality. I think it is the sort of place which allows you to think that it commemorates the idea of government and opposition. For government you have the old seventeenth-century bishop's palace and its lovely topiary garden (Mansard and Le Nôtre in collaboration), where Molière's lines would comfortably flow; an outpost of government, the Chambre du Commerce at the foot of the main square blocks your view of the river. And then, for the opposition itself, the eager river and the irregular houses which rise and fall along its further bank, individual, unpretentious but upstanding, picking up the light from sky and water, arguing the reflections, tossing them around just for the pleasure of it.

Castres is the gateway to the sinister Montagnes Noires; but before you push it open, you should, if you care for these things, push open the door of the Museum in the bishop's palace. You delude yourself often as a traveller does by thinking that you have made a discovery. I was betwixt and between about the Museum at Castres. They have had the property for years, and so it is in the books. But it is only lately (after twenty-five years' effort, I was told) that they have reached their new display. The last room was completed in June 1956. And it is worth seeing. What is shown us today has been hived up in back-cellars and offices of the Mairie or Prefecture. The interest of the collection is in Spanish work, (and this impels us to think how close we are to the dominions of the Kings of Aragon). You find here remarkable Spanish armour, metal work, leather work, painting, culminating in splendid scenes and portraits by Goya and his imitators. This is really instructive, and, since I have never met personally the gifted curator, I can say that for me he has made, with so little money to spend, so logical, so allocutive a display that he brought my mind to life again after the rainstorms. Castres may well be out of your way, but it is more than a name on a map.

Driving out of this fundamentally pretty place—which had that day the air almost of a girl with her eye-black smudged with crying—you begin to climb into the Montagnes Noires, and that is a curious experience. They lie between Castres and Carcassonne; embedded in them is the now small village, Mazamet, almost a druidical place, near which is the Grotte de la Dévèze with stalactites of the most eccentric forms. And then you come, if you wander off the path, to rocking stones, and to things worse than that, rocks shaped as geese which sing in the wind and look like early Persian sculpture. It is high and ancient.

Because of that, perhaps as a disguise, it welcomes trees. A good deal of forestry goes on to preserve the normalities, and we recognised the oaks, acacias, sweet chestnuts and maples with rides cut through them; and above the deciduous trees, the conifers. With a deceptive suggestion of richness, grass, where it grows at all, grows lush. Wild thyme imperilled the edge of the road; bugloss, cotton-plant, thrift, campions, orchis, wild roses spread at their will behind and maintained their life until just below the summit.

The summit again is harsh. No one wants to live there. Only tracks lead off the road, and lead unwillingly. Then in a moment you can see a further range of mountains in the distance and, mid-way, a haze which conceals a town. This will be Carcassonne, looking irretrievably like a film-set.

*   *   *

Like most old places, Carcassonne owes its existence to geography, and in a secondary degree to politics, which are themselves for the most part controlled by geography. There it stands on a sharp hill on a bend of the Aude, a spot fortified since pre-Roman times. In the days of the Visigoths, of the Moors, of the Albigensian wars, it still remained in a sense a frontier fortress. The Visigothic walls still are incorporated in the defences, which have been overhauled several times since. It has not often been captured, since it was saved in the gunpowder ages by suddenly becoming politically unimportant. In the sixteenth-century wars of religion it was never a serious target, though some attempts against it were made; and a hundred years later, the Treaty of the Pyrenees (1659) deprived it of its last signifi-cance as a frontier town, by incorporating the Spanish-Catalan province of Rousillon with France.

However, military organisation has always been on the conservative side; so Carcassonne remained a garrison town into Napoleonic times, and indeed later. Suddenly, about 1850 the French War Office woke up to the fact that it had a quite useless garrison on its hands and ordered the outright demolition of the whole citadel. Overnight it became a sort of Crichel Down case. Fortunately that great preserver of mediaeval France, Prosper Mérimée, had already been down there and raised a healthy and successful opposition. It was handed over to the architect, Viollet-le-Duc, who was already at work on the restoration of the cathedral. Though he did preserve what was left, in fact he built into it a good many questionable ideas of his own.

These have to a considerable extent affected the skyline, since naturally the upper parts of a building perish first under the weather. And, as you do the tour of the ramparts, the modernity of the stonework intrudes itself unpleasantly. The surface has been faked to such an extent that I felt that if I were to touch it, I might catch some disease, leprosy perhaps. Still, the walk round is worth while if only for the landscape, the perspectives, and for the general conception of the place you gain. Though all of the towers are very much the same, you have to remember that for the defence of each one a different family was responsible, and that this was a characteristically French conception of civic obligation in feudal days.

The citadel is encircled with a double line of fortifications, the outer ones being within bowshot of the inner. This was the result of a lesson learnt when de Montfort captured the place by storm in 1209. Then there was an outer walled suburb, and this, though gallantly defended, was the first to fall because the central garri-son could not support it by archery from the walls; it was out of range. As a substitute and as a watchtower, the splendid keep, the Tour de la Vade, was built and connected with the outer enceinte.

It is really good value to walk round the space between the two lines, known as Les Lices, from which you can see the true quality of the old masonry. Originally the ground sloped gently up to the inner walls; and when the outer were constructed, the ground was levelled between the two lines and the old Visigothic foundations (never very deep) were carefully underpinned, as the size and bonding of the stonework very clearly shows. From the foot the frowning height and mass of strength is tremendously impressive. After the completion of this grand essay in the art of military defence, the place successfully withstood all attacks. The last tower you see on the official tour, a tower so fine that it is wisely kept to the last, is the gateway called the Narbonnaise. Over it are two magnificently vaulted rooms, with fine fireplaces and delicately pierced windows. These interiors have live beauty and, for me, were worth all the rest—they and the gateway itself, its twin, thick towers protected by an outer archway, heavily armed with portcullises. Between the outer and inner defence zones of the gate, apertures face inwards, from which the defenders could strike or shoot at any man hardy enough to have won the first door.

The story of Carcassonne is military and brief. It was once captured from the Moors by Charlemagne after an heroic defence led by a legendary woman, Carcas the wife of the chief, who employed all imaginable stratagems and wiles to deceive the attackers into thinking that the garrison was numerous and fully provisioned. She even flung a pig stuffed with millet into the moat. Astonished and impressed by such wanton waste in time of siege, Charlemagne was preparing to withdraw, when one of the city towers leaned towards him. Taking this to be an omen, an implication of obeisance, he made a last attack to find in truth that his host had been bluffed by the one solitary survivor from the garrison, Carcas, who had shot bows and flung spears from tower after tower. Believe it or not as you wish.

Then there was the siege and capture of the town by Simon

de Montfort, to which allusion has been made. It had been a
particularly hot August, flies fed and hovered above the corpses;
the wells were polluted. After fifteen days the heroic viscount,
Roger de Trencavel, surrendered himself rather than let his
vassals and the citizens be massacred as at Béziers. Carcassonne
then became the headquarters of the Crusaders until, by the
wish of the purposeless son of de Montfort, Amaury, it passed
after a number of legal and political complications to the
French crown. Then, of course, there was government by
underpaid Seneschals—as we should say Lord Lieutenants—
who were as corrupt as French officials always were until the
nineteenth century. One poor widow objected to a fine of ten
livres—so she was fined a further five hundred for having
objected. Louis IX, St. Louis, took notice of this, and the district
began to feel itself a part of France.

When the royal power was established changes took place in
the management of the suburbs, which were swept away, since
they were an impediment to the defence of the fortress. What is
really surprising in those thirteenth-century days is that the
citizens were actually compensated; and a new town, a prosperous market town, grew up at the foot of the hill. Soldiers need
victuals, and their wives need the sort of things that wives do
need, and it was essential to maintain the colony of merchants
to serve them.

This 'new' town is worth exploring. It has a pleasant late
fourteenth-century church, a very pretty eighteenth-century
market place for food and flowers, while in another square
another market is held for clothes and solid country implements
around a baroque fountain, where two tiers of dolphins with
amusing faces conduct an endless water-war against one another.
There are some good houses too, but just at the moment we will
turn off the main shopping street in search of food.

You can be very pleasantly served at the Rotisserie Périgourdine in the wide Place Gambetta, where if the skies are kind you
will eat out of doors, and you will eat well. Once we were there
on the feast of St. Jean, patron saint of the town. The dark sky
was pierced, slashed and pointed by fireworks. At ground level

the whole square was luminous with that yellowish light derived from lighted cafés and diffusing into the strange dark blues which Cosmo Clarke paints so well. The scene was actually a little garish, and slightly like a half-planned ballet. Strong lights from across the Place threw figures into silhouette so that you could imagine the cry 'Allo mon brave' from the tall gesture of a new arrival. All the figures were elongated like El Greco's. Coveys of people would flock across the Place, pools of dark shadow, then dissolve in pairs or little groups, as if leaving the stage free for the entrance of the principal dancers. Endless, unpredictable crowd-work, as fascinating as the drift of clouds.

On our way back to our rather dim hotel we were arrested by unfamiliar sounds, which came from a little open space by the hospital. A sound like castanets played very slowly does not make sense against a sound like ducks plaining; at intervals there would be a sharp sound followed by what I can only describe as a scuffle in sand. This was our introduction to the game of *Pétanque*. It is one of the many local French versions of bowls played on a rough piece of ground, where your knowledge of the pebbles counts for more than your capacity to use the bias. This form was exceptional because you played it with glazed pottery unbiased balls, decorated with fine lines or broad stripes, which gleamed nacreous in the artificial light under the trees. Slightly larger than a cricket ball, they would take finger spin to a marked degree. It was the noise of them striking one another that had reminded me of castanets. I never got the explanation of the duck noise, though I could see it was made by the player rubbing one ball against another. You could hardly bring up the seam on a pottery ball; so perhaps it was just a professional gesture.

The jack is laid, and a vast man puts his ball close to it by simple but infallible method; more balls gradually are laid round it, and then the team's dive-bomber is brought in. He it is who produces the report and the sand scuffle, as from a height his ball ascends on the group and scatters it. Then comes the turn of the white-haired old man with the long fingers, the master of back-spin. He throws the ball fairly high to land a little beyond the jack; a flurry as the spin bites, and the ball nestles the closest to the jack. Played, as we watched it that night of St. Jean, between the medical students and their preceptors it was robust fun.

At the Restaurant Auter you will eat even better than at the Périgourdine. It is one of those first-floor French restaurants which permit the fragrance of its cooking to percolate to street level. As you read the *Carte du Jour*, your nostrils twitch to smells from upstairs, and your fate is sealed. So my wife and I, drooling slightly with greed after a long day, climbed the easy-going eighteenth-century staircase to the dining-room and ordered.

It was the *Confit d'oie* that did it. This is a regional dish. The goose is half-cooked in a casserole and then stored in its own juice and sealed with its own fat, almost like marinading except that you keep the goose to a vintage term, never high since the corrupting air has no access to it. Then you complete the cooking of it in its own fat and serve it with peas specially cooked with little bits of chopped bacon. If you could not smile as you ate and if your smile did not embrace the next French table, it would indicate a morose, an introverted character. Through the fumes of food and through our smiles we became aware that an elderly Frenchman was dining a younger man, who was deplorably fluent in an accent which we did not know and who appeared to be teaching his grandfather to suck eggs. Obviously he thought he had done a good business deal with the old Parisian and had scored.

The older man's grey hair had once had a curl to it and did not disdain to say so; his rather full moustache hinted a swagger in days which he had put behind him. But his sleepy grey eyes missed nothing. There was a pleasant wrangle between the two over paying the bill, which the elder easily won—he was always three moves ahead of his guest—and then he took an unexpected advantage of us as he caught our eye. Inevitably we had slipped into conversation over a remarkable Armagnac—'*Hors d'âge*', which means that it must be over fifty years old. The restaurant was closing and we agreed readily to the suggestion of '*un petit verre*' somewhere outside. He was a nice, knowledgeable old man of the world and I looked forward to it.

M

It was the older rather than the younger man who took firm charge of my wife as we walked in pairs to the café, while I made the ordinary, uninteresting conversational passes at this very dark young man, who, admittedly, had a certain verve to him. He was, I learnt, a wholesale timber merchant, doing business in a little place, Quillan, in the Pyrenees on which all roads converge, and where all the restaurateurs batten on the fact that you cannot eat within thirty miles of the place. Imbecile that I am, I was urged to ask him what I considered the French equivalent to 'How's business?'.

I am not very much of a business man in English, and when it came down to the French terms for some banking and stock exchange processes which I barely know in English, I was in a desperate condition. Every now and again the sleepy-eyed old boy would throw in an explanatory word or two from across the table, so that the two of us should avoid an impasse, a situation which would mean that he would again have to listen to the atrocious voice of this insistent young timber-merchant from Quillan. For this young man was a tyrant in talk, and the old boy had spent the day with him.

Because of my shortage in technical terms, the young man gave me a long résumé of English methods of finance, which he declared were precisely the same as the French. If my eyelid quivered towards an objection, before I could voice it he shouted his battle-cry: '*C'est pareil; c'est pareil; c'est pareil*' ('It's exactly the same'). He told me, for instance, that in England as in France, all dealings in stocks and shares went through the banks. When, growing querulous, I told him I used a stockbroker myself and that I had seen the Bourse in Paris and asked him what purpose it could possibly serve, he again cleft my ear-drums as surely as Renaud of Montauban would have split a horse, with his verbal battle-axe '*C'est pareil*'. If you ever want to know what the accent sounds like in the Pyrenées Orientales without the expense of going there, find the nearest machine riveter at work or imagine a machine gun firing without the woosh of the bullets to soften the noise.

Yet there is one point of relationship between that dialect and our form of speech. As with us, in their blast and fire of talk all consonants are shot away, vowels are elided, and diphthongs rule the roost. It is not at all like French. Much as I had looked forward to this by-way episode, I was glad to finish it at no longer a term than the duration of '*un petit verre*'.

VIII

To Montpellier

MR. VIVIAN ROWE, who writes so delightfully about France, is a quietly persuasive man. He started to tell me that I must go to Montpellier, and before long he had mesmerised me into capitulation. I pointed out the extra mileage it involved, that it enlarged the frontiers of this book as planned to bursting point. He riposted that it was the home of one of the great universities of France. He forced me to remind myself that it had a very good museum. Then he trumped the rest of my hand by insinuating that its omission would be illogical, and went on to prove this grave statement. I was going to Perpignan and the Rousillon, wasn't I, all part of the dominions of the Kings of Aragon in France? Well, then, why omit one of that kingdom's principal towns?

I now can admit my delight at having taken his advice. Not only is Montpellier full of the breath of history and the pride of fine buildings, but on the way to it from Rodez we found many enticements: the home of Toulouse-Lautrec; the little village, sunless for six months each year, of Roquefort where since Roman times they have made their noble sheeps' cheese in caves air-conditioned by nature; the incomparable restaurant at Millau unimaginatively called the *Commerce*.

*　　*　　*

The Château du Bosc lies just off the road from Rodez to Albi (N.88), and one cannot pretend it is on the direct route to Montpellier; but its associations and the contents which evoke them are compelling. It is close to a little town, Naucelle, about which we need not bother our heads, and you can get an adequate lunch at the *Voyageurs* on the main road. You turn left when you leave and soon a signpost invites you to turn right down a tree-lined road to the château. Then comes a little plateau on which are grazing the local breed of rather feudal sheep wearing a distinguished livery of golden-brown. My own family, I am sorry to say, only specialised in pigs—Tamworths, and a now extinct strain, Stauntons; perhaps for this reason we did not make such good international marriages as were habitual with the Toulouse-Lautrecs.

You park your car on the brow of the plateau and descend the drive to a tiny, intimate valley; water at the bottom; a planned wood on a rounded slope opposite; and a long landscape stretching away to the right of it. A little above the water, to the left, is the warm-grey château. The mediaeval towers at three corners were re-costumed in the seventeenth century with typical upward-sweeping cupolas, like new hats confected from fish-scale slates. Into the walls which link them the varied windows are set with the irregularity of a family conversation, making it somehow a lovable and private place. The enclosing hill and the woods beyond give it almost a cloistered feel, where speed is worse than unimportant since it might cost you a memory.

As you enter the courtyard the house is on the left with the stables opposite. These were a most important part of the family's life, since hunting and horsemanship were essential ploys. Before his accident Toulouse-Lautrec was already an accomplished and courageous rider, but judged too young as yet to join the '*meute*' —to follow the hounds in dangerous, broken country. So from an upper window he used as a small boy to look down on the jingling bustle, as his grandfather, his father and his uncles swung themselves into the saddle; unconsciously he registered every movement of the horses. Three-quarters of a painter's gift is the specific, not generalised memory of a momentary attitude, whether the subject be waves, skies or horses. The unforgetting eye of childhood recorded for Henri the delicate, decisive movement of a trotter's fetlock as surely as the bolder muscles of a hunter; and he had disciplined his hand to obey his memory's instructions. The evidence for all this is in the museum at Albi. But think of the iron quality, founded on suffering and disappointment, which enabled him to describe in paint the joys of which he was bereft for ever, the hunter he would never seat, the spanking equipage he never would drive.

The entrance to the house is unpretentious. No extravagant hall receives you, but a well proportioned staircase with plain quadripartite vaulting outlined rather strikingly in black. It leads you to the salon, where Aubusson carpets cover the floor and the walls are hung with tapestried scenes from the triumphs of Alexander the Great. A fine flash of furniture illustrates the styles of Louis XIV, XV, and XVI. The chimney-piece carved with the family coat of arms in the sixteenth-century manner pulls the room to a focus. Just off to the right is the private oratory: still, small, white, dignified, with the sword of Lafayette reposing in it. Here is the genius of the place, where yet lives a branch of the family which once ruled Provence and Languedoc, which has connections with the old royal families of Europe. This house has the quietness of certainty.

There is more to see. Verdure tapestries in the salle-à-manger; court dresses which go back to the seventeenth century; more furniture; more porcelain; and one thing that struck me dead because it belonged so completely to its period. It was a christening present to a member of the family from the Bonapartist King of Holland, Louis Napoleon. He looked ahead to the days when the infant girl would be entertaining on a large scale and so gave her a most elaborate table-centre, which would have been an ornament if you had at least twenty-four people to dine. My memory describes it to me as in length perhaps six feet, oval ended, and surrounded by an elaborate raised ormolu edge. Its pretty ormolu feet support a floor of mirror. When properly dressed it must have been seductive. For on this bright surface were alabaster urns for flowers, obelisques and delicate temples in the same cool alabaster. Picture beneath the yellow candle light the brilliant gilt frame to the milky alabaster which set off the pink or red roses or camellias—and all played back to you in a cold, thoughtless echo by the mirror.

And there is more to see. For in this house you get a clue to the genius of the greater painter, only so recently accepted, which the popular books and films scarcely touch. In the upper rooms you see not only sketches (or reproductions) of his own work, but original work by three generations of his family and talented amateur work at that. When his father, his grandfather and his uncles came in from hunting, shooting or coursing, they sat down in the library to sketch or draw portraits in pencil and water-colour. Stretched out on the hearthrug lay the small Henri, drawing with a bit of cold charcoal from the fire. There was nothing in his home inimical to the practice of the arts.

If you are fortunate, as I have twice been, to be taken round this house of remarkable memories by the painter's cousin, the Comtesse du Bosc, you will win an insight into Toulouse-Lautrec's psychology which you will not touch elsewhere. For this is one of the increasingly rare houses, in England or abroad, where you know that according to the moment you will be equally correct in very old clothes or in a breastplate of diamonds or decorations. This classlessness of upbringing (which carries either from the highest or simplest class because it is unconscious) is an essential in the understanding of the painter's tragedy. Alcoholism touched his body, but never the wit of his hand or eye. The malicious drawings (which are only shown in repro-ductions) in the orangerie prove the physical level at which he was able to make a drawing on a wall. This was reinforced to me by Mademoiselle du Bosc's statement that at the age of five (the last visit to du Bosc before his death) she could not understand why 'the little boy' would not play with her. Yet the orangerie drawings are exactly parallel with the sketches he used to make on the table-cloths of the *boîtes de nuit* which he frequented in Paris. There is a phrase in Juvenal (I think) about the writer's 'itch to write' (cacoethes scribendi). Lautrec had the *cacoethes pingendi'*. He could not leave a plain surface alone—whether it was the walls of his father's orangerie or Parisian table-cloths. His hand must move, must describe. This too, which you see here in miniature, is a clue to the immense variety of his subjects to be seen at the Albi Museum.

In the woods beyond the house are still the little rides, planned as a small Bois de Boulogne, where Lautrec and his cousins used to drive their pony carriages; the water where they used to fish with cormorants, aping his father's passion for falconry; the kennels where lived the hounds of which they hoped one day to be the masters. Psychologists and educationists argue on the formative force of home-life and environment on a child's character. They would find an outstanding piece of case history if they went to the Château du Bosc, provided that they cleared their minds of the vulgar and inaccurate prejudice against Henri's father.

One might call the upper rooms a reliquary; for they enshrine the memories of the painter's childhood, piously guarded in what was his mother's bedroom. Her room is beautiful in its own right, windows in two walls lighting it happily; the alcove with her great bed; choice wall-lights and mirrors with grisaille panels of savages above them like those in the Petit Trianon. There are her wedding clothes and the veil of exquisite lace; the tallboy in which she preserved her son's letters. There are, too, the relics of his infancy: his christening robe, a relic descended from the seventeenth century; the cradle with its blue hangings; his English baby clothes, very chic in those days when English nannies were *de rigueur* in a good French family; his toys, his Punch and Judy show, which he worked himself. A small piece of furniture is there which one knows from earlier pictures but is long since out of use. It is a baby's walking ring, made of two circular shelves of wood separated from one another by four slim uprights of turned wood, supporting the upper shelf. The whole was set on casters; you put the child within the magic circle, and he could then learn to walk, pushing himself around the room without risk of a fall. Henri had to use it again after his accident. His little rush-bottomed chair is there with drawings scattered around it after the way of an impulsive child, eager to start the next one; his child's paint-box—quite a complicated one—and palette, all very professional looking. Horses predominate as a theme.

In a small gallery nearby are the personal sketches he made at many different visits of relations staying in the house, remarkable for their bite, their character and their wit. One drawing represents his grandmother, a keen-eyed old lady with her lips just twitching in amusement at some witticism. Another shows the curé with his improbable nose, to whom Lautrec was devoted; a not quite favourite male cousin is a frequent and silently mocked subject. A true perspective of his environment at home may be found in the sketches by the two generations of his predecessors; for instance a spirited pencil drawing by his father of young Henri cantering. However much they may reasonably have regretted the alcoholism born partly of his fate as a child of two first-cousins but also of the deprivation of so much that he could normally have expected from life, they never for a moment indicated any disapproval of painting as such. Why should Toulouse-Lautrec otherwise have gone year after year to stay at a house which some writers have tried to suggest was hostile to him?

* * *

If, on the other hand, you decide to go from Rodez through Millau to Montpellier, you will start out as for du Bosc along N.88 and after a few kilometres turn left down N.111 away from the old road to Albi. The quality of the 'vin compris' wine round Rodez should not have led you to expect vine-clad slopes bordering your way; and certainly you do not find them. It is a harsh upland scenery that you encounter, though I can imagine it scented in the right season with the sharp smell of box and arbutus, with the sweetness of wild thyme; crushed bracken and juniper for lower notes in the later scale of smell. The horizons are wide and unkempt; you pass great desolate mountain lakes or tarns, to which you feel no animal has descended for centuries to drink.

When you are over the pass of about 3,000 feet beyond Viarouge you fall into a different landscape, say rather a different geology. For the hills are full of exclamations. The strata of their rocks may be horizontal, but they split vertically. The result is a series of sheer cliff faces with a trail of screes and debris at their feet; and the same thing may take place again a few hundred feet below, till you come to see the scene as a garden of rock once terraced by a giant and then left unplanted in perpetuity. For there seems little vegetation, and one does not quite know how life is maintained.

Below this hostile country with its crenellated, turreted outlines, the road twists gradually at first and then hurriedly down
to pasture level, to deciduous trees, to cattle land. At the bottom
of the valley on the uproarious Tarn lies the old centre of Millau,
one of those places which can never die since it is the natural
meeting place of trails from all sorts of remote valleys and hills.
As is the fate of such places, it has been the object of countless
attacks which have destroyed most of the evidence of its antiquity.
For two thousand years carts have rumbled through the market
place transporting Roquefort cheese to more and more distant
places; today more wheels turn beneath loads of the finest gloves
for the Paris market. Millau is not worth visiting for its
antiquities; but you can at least eat there.

The *Hôtel et Restaurant du Commerce* has a deservedly wide
reputation in the district, and Michelin admits that its *specialités*
are worth recording. To judge the relative degrees of magic in
various *pâtés de foie gras* eaten over the length and breadth of
France, to distinguish which *truite meunière* is the cleanest cooked
and yet truly *meunière* requires a gastronomic memory to which
I do not lay claim. If you were to cite with certainty where you
had found the very best example of either dish, you would have
to be the equivalent of old Sir Campbell Dodgson of the Print
Room in the British Museum, who could tell you off-hand, not
only which were the best states of a sixteenth-century print or a
Rembrandt etching, but also which museums had the best
impressions.

Instead let me tell you of another speciality, which I have met
nowhere else in my French journeys. It is sucking lamb, or more
exactly, *Côte de Regord, Tante Elise*. With a gusto, which I find
almost cannibal, I have eaten sucking pig and sucking calf, and
the Roman abaccio, about which I generally concluded that it
should never have survived to maturity anyhow. Before the last
war I knew the *Cochon au Lait* near St. Sulpice where they served
their admirable dish with kasha. I knew, too, just before the revolution against the Lerroux Government one of the last sucking-
pigs ever served by the redoubtable *Casa Bottin* in Madrid, something which as a dish I have found worth remembering as standard

for over twenty years. And then I landed up at this one-cheese, one-glove town, Millau, to find something which surpasses them all.

You do not actually masticate their sucking lamb. It enters the mouth and once or twice the 'ponderous and marble jaws' may close on it; but that is not a frequent necessity. If you call this delicate thing meat, it is inhaled rather than chewed, with its aides-de-camp, truffles and the lightest madeira sauce, unthickened, based (I only guess) on the small lamb's gravy. And this wonder has been preluded by *Fondants de Volaille*.

The *Commerce* could not take us in so we stayed at the *Moderne*, which was busily modernising itself as so many of the hotels in this part of France are doing, and we did very well—excellently, we should have said but for the *Commerce*—at dinner the following night. During the day we smelt our way out to Roquefort through singular country. You hook away from Millau on a low-numbered road, N.592, a further decline in social status from the previous low of N.111. This small road edges along like a poor relation beside the small resident river. Rocks on the right hand are ready poised to fall on you or cover you in a biblical manner. You branch off to an even lower category road, D.25, just short of Lauras and then from the plain you climb improbably. The street which at last you gain is narrow; parking seems impossible. Take the French manner—park, rev. the engine as you shut it off quite gratuitously, and probably you will be unmolested if you have made enough noise. Then you ring the bell of the nearest important building, and soon you will be on tour in the ancient caves where they make the Roquefort cheese.

We went round with a nice man in a beret, a wise man in a beret, since there is a slight but constant condensation in the caves breeding slow stalactites and damp drips on the ageing head. It is an experience not to be missed even by a person such as myself, who is not wildly thrilled by scientific process or progress. For a start, some of the caves in which the cheeses are matured were arched by the Romans; and since that date, whenever arching for support of the rock has been necessary, precisely the same line of arch has been followed. No one now knows when such or such

an arch was made within five hundred years since below ground
the style is traditional. The structure of the rock is peculiar, as
I have already remarked; it breaks vertically. As a result there is
always a faint current of air moving subterraneously through the
faults of the rocks (the *failles*), and through the '*fleurines*' (the
tiny cracks between them); these air currents, winter and summer,
keep the cheese at a temperature which varies only between 7 and
8 degrees centigrade.

Charlemagne accepted this cheese in tribute, and its manufac-
ture probably goes on much the same way now as then. It is made
from sheeps' milk, and the milk comes from sheep on the high
pastures and is first cheesed in the local farm houses. After about
two weeks the immature cheese is brought to the depot, from
which it is transferred to the hospital caves. It is at once given an
injection of penicillin and mushroom fungus by a machine with
a hundred needles; in the old days this dose was given by hand,
slowly, needle by needle. After the drastic modern treatment the
cheese sleeps in its hospital for twenty-five days, when it is
removed to another ward and wrapped in lead foil; this process
not only preserves its outward shape, but permits the secondary
drug (*champignon*) to continue its fecundatory work. At this
stage a bad cheese doctor can produce a 'hard, undeveloped,
unprocessed core'—and we can all guess where we go from there.

It is two and a half months before the cheese is considered
barely edible, after lying in its lead-swathed coma in its air-cooled
room. No one in the district would dream of eating one under
six months. Such are the lessons learnt in an old rural industry.
The men of Roquefort went lively in the seventeenth century and
persuaded the Parlement of Toulouse to impose a fine on anyone
who sold his cheese as 'Roquefort' when it had not come from the
district—an early instance in 1666 of '*appelation controlée*'. The
fine was heavy, one thousand livres. In later days the cheese has
required the protection of international copyrights and obtained
it. Even the busy bees on its wrapping papers are endlessly
patented from country to country.

Isolation is something almost tangible, and you find it here.
Life is extremely hard. You see the sun and feel its warmth only

for six months in the year, and then the sun may be so strong as to send you breathless. Probably you live most safely, air-conditioned in the caves though never really warm. And you would miss, too, the extraordinary view down from your mountain ledge on to fields and valleys often half hidden by mist where men lead the normal life of cultivation, the setting of bulls to stud, the mutation of crops. Up here in a thin enduring wind you do not even know which sheep produced the milk from which you make your living.

*   *   *

As you move south-eastwards towards Montpellier from Millau along N.9, sizable hills appear on the left, the outskirts of the Cevennes. If you have plenty of time on your hands, you can turn off after the village of La-Cavallerie (N.99) making east over hills and dipping down and climbing up steep valleys twisting in the direction of Le Vigan and Ganges. From the latter (which you pronounce in the French and not in the Indian manner) you can turn south to Montpellier, following the valley of the Hérault at times in a close picturesque huddle.

But this piece of country is explored the better from Montpellier itself. You do not miss the gorge of the Hérault (which gives its name to the department) coming from the south but you approach it across the fine chain of the Garrigues hills along N.586, striking at intervals rocky drama. If you care for spectacular scenery, go through Ganges—where you can feed well enough—on N.99 and turn south-west towards St. Maurice and the astonishing Cirque de Navacelles. And if you are still inclined for landscape excitement, you can make a circular tour of it, up the Gorge of the Vis to the early church of St. Guilhem le Désert, solitary and antique.

The course of the small river Vis could be compared either with the chart of a barograph in bad weather or with the shaky handwriting of a very old man, so many are the twists and wriggles of it. It flows northwards into the Hérault near Ganges and squints its way through high piled hills in a miniature gorge. It is not, of course, comparable to the dramatic splendours of the

Gorges du Tarn; consequently it is in no way oppressive. At the start, the road sticks to river level, and it is the hills which climb above you till they leave only a slit of blue sky above the concentrating wealth of the tree-ridden cliffs. Suddenly you hear the river change the note of its brisk chatter to something more powerful, richer in range and harmonies. A waterfall; and the river has changed its level with the same abruptness with which we can change our minds. Now the ascent begins, and your road is laced to the breasts of the hills. You admire the skill of the French engineers, as you slip round the hips of an impassable rock to find that now the precipice is on your right and not your left-hand side, and so your thoughts for the time have left the river.

And so the steady, tortuous climb goes on till you feel yourself swinging and swaying in the upper air. The air is bright in your lungs. You are seemingly above even bird-line, and you look down on isolated peaks which were notable before. In a haze below you lies the world of the plough, the divisions and sub-divisions of its society expunged by height and distance. For a short moment you feel slightly godlike—and then you are over the watershed of dreams. The notable peak on which you have just looked down is soon above you, commanding you from a different angle, once more in the ascendant, tough, nubbly, awkward.

You reach the hamlet of St. Martin and turn right for the Cirque de Navacelles. Whoever first told me to go there had warned me that you could not go the whole way by car. This indeed proved almost true. As the road began to dwindle into a track, notices sprang to life on the stone walls. 'Car Park'; 'Cars stop here'; 'No dogs beyond this point'; and then 'DANGER'. Even the lettering of the word seemed to hint melodrama—how many adventurers had previously fallen down the mountain-side into the valley below?

Not a word of truth in it; I believe you could have driven to the valley's floor; but it did make a very good build-up for the theatrical sequence to follow. From the point at which you are supposed to have abandoned your dog, you walk down a steepish hill. The further you descend the more cars you will have passed which have been parked much nearer the objective than yours. Then you come to a hairpin bend. A little farther down and you have this surprising panorama, the Cirque de Navacelles.

Imagine a torso with the shoulders curved slightly forward. They form the curve at the end of the Cirque, this vast high curve which encloses a deep valley watered by a noisy river. The tops of the shoulders are hard rock polished smooth by wind and weather. What you might call the arms growing forwards from the shoulders enclose the length of the valley, jutting out and pulling back as if echoing some previous course of the stream. Isolated spots of ilex, may and box do not bring any true sense of well-being. For however splendid is the sight before you, ever-present is the sense of upheaval and destruction stimulated by the rocks themselves.

They belong, I presume, to the same formation as the rocks around Millau, stratified horizontally but split by frost and weather, or by some sterner force. I was reminded of a passage in *The Silent World* describing how in very deep dives you pass through barriers of water which seem stiffer, more solid than the rest, and that this will recur at intervals. In the same way on this mountain-side you will see how stronger belts of rock have defied the agencies which forced the rest to split. And so at the curve and along the sides of this remarkable valley the surface varies from cliff face to scree, like the tiers of a theatre, from high light to half tone, until the scree has grated its way down to the edge of the valley bed, there to be slowly pulverised by the attrition of nature into something like soil.

For the most part the rocks have weathered grey, but where they have been newly split they show a brilliant yellow. Certainly in late spring the colour is extremely varied. Plants and shrubs are everywhere in blossom. Yellow saxifrage, wild thyme in quantity, white flowers from may to some kind of arbutus, asphodels with lilies springing to follow them and much that was nameless to my untutored eye. In this paradise of green leaf and colour the white blossom turns almost to the faint green of a young guelder rose.

*   *   *

And so you can wind your way back to Montpellier by devious country and by narrow roads, a country which for all its geological movement in the past seems somehow to have stopped thinking. You drive through a pulseless air. The soil, it is true, produces evergreen trees and crops of a kind, but without enthusiasm; the wide landscapes compose badly. Many centuries ago in the first ages of monastic retreats from the abominable world, this countryside must have seemed even bleaker, with scarcely a vestige of cultivation in the uplands. In those days the descent from these hills, past what is now the pretty church of St. Jean des Fos, to the triangle valley sheltered by precipitous cliffs topped by a ruined castle and fronting on the swift river Verdus, must have seemed a rich and sequestered paradise. I do not remember seeing such earth elsewhere; it varies from yellow to orange. The old abbey's name confirms what I have tried to describe to you. It is St. Guilhem le Désert.

This secret place does not open its arms to welcome you; rather you must hover around it and 'mark well its bulwarks' before you try to come to terms with the scatter of ancient little houses which clutter the approach. You have to work your way round to the back of the tiny relic of a village to gain access to the church. The abbey was founded by William Duke of Aquitaine, rudely called 'Short-nose', who died there in 812, a ruler of sufficient virtue to be canonised; in a secular way he is remembered as an ancestor of the Princes of Orange.

His church is finer than one would expect in so remote a setting and has about it a certain stimulating brusqueness of character. Principally it goes back to the eleventh century, though the transepts and the belfry are later. The nave of four bays has a high cross-banded, barrel-vaulted roof, of which the weight is carried by the supporting aisles. Set in the rough-hewn stone wall above the nave arches are round-arched windows. There was trouble, obviously, over the acoustics of the place, since one sees where a stone has here and there been omitted to break the wave-length of the voice and so to stop the echo. The charms are on the whole charms of detail. Apses enriched with blind arcading seal the nave and aisles. The north chapel is treated as a sort of Musée Lapidaire and contains plenty that is of interest. There is an early altar, said improbably to have been St. Guilhem's, made of marble inlaid with coloured glass. Early sarcophagi may well have been the tombs, as is claimed, of the saint's sisters. Outside the remains of the monastic buildings provide a nice puzzle for the specialist. What remains most with me is that the abbey was luminous to an unexpected degree for its date; and I formed an attachment to a hand raised in blessing, a sculptured boss in the vaulting of the north transept. Emerging at length from this silent place, we were back to the water-music of the Verdus racing down its gorge.

Three gorges in a day: stupefying or mesmeric as sound; an enticement to the eye by the multiplicity of curve and colour in the water; as an emblem of the sheer power of natural force quite alarming. Nothing we could do would stop it.

* * *

Among the less frequent pleasures of life is the magic moment which turns duty into an excitement. This sounds faintly hearty unless I refine upon it. 'Don't you think it would be nice if you called on Mrs. So-and-So this afternoon?' my mother might ask in the days when one still did 'call' on people. It was not a natural sport for a boy of nineteen or twenty to 'call' on someone who couldn't be less than fifty and whose friends would be as old or older. More often than not, however, I should be won over by their gifted conversation and beautiful manners into finding myself happy and fondly imagining that I had managed to talk quite well. They even taught me to learn when to leave, and so got me over a major social hurdle.

My experience at Montpellier fell into this class. I went there, as I have explained, at the gentle instance of Vivian Rowe, with my ears the least bit laid back—and I fell in love with the place. Its colour, pace and bustle are Southern, but not even as we crossed the busy Place de la Comédie did we feel the same fear for life and limb as in the Place du Capitole at Toulouse. The side streets are narrow, populated, ancient, and unpaved; but you are not bruised so much. Of course Montpellier is not so large a place,

N

and so perhaps may be more easily pervaded by the quiet of its
university's scholarship. Whatever may be the formula of
Montpellier's love-philtre, it worked on me.

Neglecting its early history, we find it involved in mediaeval
and Huguenot heresies, taking risks all the time for principle's
sake or burning down an inn because people of the wrong party
were staying there. A positive town. One geographical and one
historical feature might not be obvious. For the surrounding
country Montpellier stands relatively high. Northwards it looks
to the Cevennes; southwards over a coast-line fringed with
lagoons; eastwards over the secret lands of Aigues Mortes and the
Camargues, where theoretically the writ of the Comtes de
Toulouse still ran in 1200. It was the eastern outpost of the Kings
of Aragon, who were even greater men in Spain than in France,
beloved of the Popes for their struggles against the Moors, but in
the days of the Albigensian crusade definitely on the make at the
expense of the Comtes de Toulouse. As a reminder of Aragon's
power you can see on a fine day from Montpellier Mont Canigou
and the range of the Pyrenees in the south-west.

The mental instability of mediaeval kings and princes is past
wonder. It is as if they had been badly wired both for direct and
alternating current; switching from one to the other they fused.
Aragon had built by marriage, conquest and inheritance a com-
pact and forceful kingdom which spilt over the Pyrenees from
Spain as far as Montpellier. What did James 'the Conqueror' do
but switch to A.C.? He split his kingdom between his two sons.
The younger son inevitably lost the internecine war, of which we
shall find traces at Perpignan and in the last desperate fling for
independence sold Montpellier to France to get the cash to pay
his mercenaries (1349).

So Aragon lost their strong eastern promontory, and the
French began their three-centuries tortoise creep to win the
Pyrenees as their frontier. How much wiser if Aragon had
followed the English principle of throwing younger sons out of
the nest.

*   *   *

There are two controlling features in the plan of Montpellier; the detail needs a map. The main axis is east to west and is pinned at either end to an eighteenth-century feature; at the east end to the Champs de Mars and the Esplanade, tree-sheltered havens, and at the west to the Château d'Eau, a monument of delicate grace. A ribbon of boulevards, ghosts of demolished city walls, runs round between them in a loose circle and contains an abnormally rich treasure of domestic architecture, of which the sober, even shabby façades give scarcely a hint. Sometimes the local noblemen—and this is one of the cities where the county aristocracy had their town houses—or the provincial administrator could not resist a fine ironwork balcony or an elaborate doorway as a rose in his buttonhole; but this was rare. The good effects were reserved for the guests as they entered the ample courtyard and ascended the gracious staircase.

In a city so rich in architecture of such diverse periods, it takes days to scratch the surface. For a brief view, you find the *Guide Pratique des Vieux Hôtels de Montpellier* (120 fr.) invaluable. But if you are really in a rush from the Côte d'Azur to the Côte Vermeille or the Costa Brava, then take your pick from any of these nine streets. No lover of Montpellier will produce the same list; nor will he have space for a fine balcony, even if a dark Juliet were to lean over it under the moon.

Rue du Cannau is full of good things, particularly Nos. 3 and 6. Rue Fournarie No. 1 (Hôtel Solas) was latterly the home of the Valerys, where the poet often stayed. The early seventeenth-century doorway is violent with its exciting bosses; peep through to the elegant staircase which replaced an earlier spiral. No. 3 is a very good house, too.

Rue Eugène Lisbonne has the Hôtel Aures, ostensibly a charming eighteenth-century house, where lately they have discovered wonderful mediaeval columns and vaulted cellars overlaid in the age of reason. Hôtel Montcalm, Place du Sauvage, was the family house of the gallant defender of Quebec. Rue des Trésoriers de la Bourse, No. 4, Hôtel de Rodez, has applied an eighteenth-century costume of immense quality to mediaeval bones. For there is a good deal of fifteenth- and sixteenth-century work left in

Montpellier sometimes incorporated in a later building. No. 5 of Rue des Trésoriers de la France shows a splendid staircase of this kind, built for Jaques Coeur, whose house at Dijon is world famous.

In the Embouque d'Or No. 2, Hôtel St. André is a splendid piece of swagger; in the Rue de l'Aiguillière you may take your choice, but don't miss No. 1. For an enchanting curiosity, really a sheer piece of architect's vanity which obviously appealed to the people of the city since it had its imitators, turn to the short Rue du Palais No. 6, the Hôtel Sarret. Imagine that common object, the right angle made by the corner of a building on the street. The architect of the Hôtel Sarret was not content with this simple obvious solution. Instead, between the first floor and the ground he cut back the stonework and had it hollowed and carved into the form of a vast shell, so that apparently the upper floors are supported on vacancy. Yet the shell-form is so beautifully executed that it stops one's mind from arguing about this defiance of established architectural practice. No doubt in his day he was the devil of an angry young man, but he certainly had good manners.

From bravado to humility. No. 9 Rue des Trésoriers de France is not of importance except on August 16th, when the devout visit the miraculous well of St. Roch, a native of Montpellier. St. Roch left on a pilgrimage to Rome, from which he was deflected to help in curing or nursing those suffering from the plague; he went from town to town, till in the long run he fell a victim to it himself. Quite properly he was cast without the walls, where his faithful dog (a mongrel in every representation I know) licked his sores and filched him bread from the bakers until he recovered enough strength to regain Montpellier. His cousins, who wanted his share of the inheritance, declined to recognise him; so he was cast into jail as a vagrant and died there. What interests me about this type of story is that the virtue of the dog is recognised in so far as it is fulfilling a feudal duty—looking after his master. Once his master is dead, the dog has no further social or emotional value. No one knows what happened to that admirable animal, and I fear that it perished ignominiously. Such is often the fate of the second in command.

*   *   *

And so at last we come to the two jewelled pins which secure the ribbon round this rag-box of noble houses. Like Montauban, like Nîmes, Montpellier was a Huguenot stronghold. After the end of the religious wars it recovered its prosperity as its architecture shows; its dominance in the wine trade (still maintained) and the opening of the new port at Sète and of the Canal du Midi favoured the place. Then the city was hit hard by the revocation of the Edict of Nantes; and Louis XIV, to rub salt into the wound for the Huguenots, set up a triumphal arch, to remind them not only of his victories but of his edict, and ordered an equestrian statue as well.

This stark royal insult was absorbed later into a most lovely piece of civil design. The expanding town needed a better water supply, which was provided in the most open-handed manner. Fifteen kilometres of aqueduct carried the water to the highest point of the town for dispersal, and as if to acclaim its arrival a temple, a Château d'Eau, formed the centre of an elaborate layout of which Louis le Grand's insult was reduced to a subsidiary part. The architect, d'Aviler, set his temple on the sky-line and surrounded it with lawns of water controlled and intersected by balustrading. A drop in the level, faced with stone so laid as to make a surface of broken light, leads to another field of water. Interspersed statuary joins at intervals in the general thanksgiving for the arrival of the aqueduct at Montpellier.

The scene breathes tranquillity. The Château d'Eau itself is perfect in proportion. Quadrilateral in plan, it suggests from some angles a hexagon by the recession of the two sides. Coupled Corinthian columns surge up to support a great classical entablature and to contain open arches with carved festoons above. From whatever angle you look at this lovely thing, perspective is always enlivening your eye. No photograph I have found does justice to it because it cannot express what the physical eye sees—the ever-changing colour perspective of stone in relation to mediterranean sky, which the Greeks understood—and so did M. d'Aviler.

If you like that kind of thing, you can walk down to the Jardins des Plantes, the sort of place which to an unskilled man like me can be effortlessly pretty. Botanical ignorance forbids me to praise

or blame but leaves me free to enjoy. Actually this is one of the
earliest Botanic gardens in France, founded by Henri IV just
before the time when John Tradescant was bringing in odd plants
from America and trying to foster them at Oxford.

Over your right shoulder lie the Cathedral and the School of
Medicine. The cathedral with its three square ornamented towers
of the nineteenth century, their stone as hard as a money-lender,
did not add all the pleasure to my life that I had hoped for. Certainly the nave of six bays is dignified; it was built between 1364
and 1369 with the support of Pope Urban V as an abbey church;
but the bogus transepts are common as a village pageant. We
must forgive these errors, which are partly a record of Montpellier's history. The Catholic League had broken up the cathedral in 1589, and by the time the commercial prosperity had
returned which might have repaired the damage suitably, the last
spark of faith had flickered out with the steady exodus of the
Huguenots. The devout Catholic nobles preferred to spend their
money on their parish church, Notre Dame des Tables, which
they intended to coat with marble. But even this effort died away
incomplete. So much for the constructive results of the Catholic
League and Louis XIV's gallicanism.

The grand thing about the cathedral is external: the porch is
a 'baldachin' as at Albi. Its height is the height of the nave, and
it is supported at the outer end by two thick circular pillars of
massive strength; sharp cones rather than pinnacles surmount
them and cut the blue sky. Hung high between the cathedral wall
and these two piers are the sharp pointed arches, linked by Gothic
vaults. It is a fantastic sight, unparalleled, this canopy of stone.

As you climb the gentle slope to the cathedral you are conscious of an ancient building with averted eyes—the eyes of a
monk disregarding the world. This, too, dates back to the same
period as the nave and has in its various stages of life been monastic premises, then with additions the episcopal palace, and
finally the headquarters of the Faculty of Medicine for which
Montpellier University has been famous since 1200, the first
indeed where dissection was allowed—one corpse a year. Here
in their great hall, where the annual prizes are given, are the

original or copied portraits of the great doctors who passed through the school which still maintains its place today. The famous library was closed when I was there out of term time; but they showed me Rabelais's gown or (muttering under their breath) at least an old one of the same pattern. This I thought singularly honest.

There is hardly a subject you cannot study at the University of Montpellier. Its first pre-eminence was in medicine, an imaginative feature for the thirteenth century, when the Kings of Aragon were still running on D.C. Still on the same circuit, they installed a faculty of law, so that they had a posse of trained men who could wrangle their causes in the papal curia. So the thing grew up, faculty by faculty, courtyard by cloister, century by century in architecture, the libraries and the lecture rooms above the supporting arcades under which you walked and argued. The valuable principle of living in College seems to be the invention of Oxford and Cambridge; it localised arguments to rooms, and perhaps in consequence we have never had the recurrent rash of 'students' riots' which have pock-marked European history for better rather than for worse.

Now, the last pin to the ribbon, the eastern pin. A museum, and an esplanade of trees by a lake, a pin with two stories. Museums are not everyone's cup of tea; but the Musée Fabre must be mentioned as one of the best outside Paris. It was founded by a native of the city, Xavier François Fabre, himself a well enough known painter in the manner of David, who had the good fortune to meet the Countess of Albany, formerly the disappointed wife of the Young Pretender, when her poet lover, Alfieri, had just died. She and Fabre lived together in Florence till her death in 1824, when she bequeathed her estates to him, which included a remarkable series of fine Italian and Spanish pictures.

Fabre's undoubted gift as a second class painter suggests that he was worldly, neat-handed and chic. And he set about the conquest of Montpellier and a barony with his late mistress's collection as his ace of trumps. He played his hand so well that his conditions were accepted; the museum was to be an isolated building and ground was to be bought against future expansion;

his word was to be law in matters of hanging; meanwhile, he was
to have a flat in the building and full use of the building at any
time convenient to himself. He died there in 1837.

A year earlier his bequest had already born fruit. In 1836
M. Valedu presented a valuable collection of Dutch and Flemish
pictures. A generation later, in 1868 and 1876, outstanding gifts
were made by Alfred Bruyas from his collection of nineteenth-
century painters. He was a strange type. The son of a rich banker,
he was a consumptive and a narcissist; he preferred, for instance,
to commission his own portrait from a painter rather than the
landscape or still life which might have given the artist more
pleasure. And so his long face, his soft beard and brooding eyes
pursue you as you contemplate the Géricaults, Delacroix, Manets
and above all the Courbets.

Courbet, whose work I first came to know at old Percy
Turner's wonderful *Independent Gallery* in the early twenties, is
now undervalued: for two reasons, I think. Too much realism,
and an essentially vulgar mind. Here in the scene of *Le Rencontre*
Courbet paints himself meeting his patron, Bruyas, at Montpellier;
he has just arrived in shirt sleeves with his pack on his back. Out
juts his splendid black Assyrian beard at a theatrical angle that
would be intolerable on any stage. He, '*Le Maître d'Ornans*', generously proffers his hand to the patron who was going to pay his
keep for the next month or two. A true republican, this obligation
cost him no heart-burn. Bruyas's servant stands behind, his hat
doffed in reverence before the supreme republican being. Even
the family dog stands to attention. Such was Courbet's record of
his arrival; as paint, magnificent; as egotism, unsurpassed.

This brilliant painter, a stupid, boastful Franche-comté peasant
who had to learn his limitations the hard way, is splendidly represented at Montpellier. He finished unhappily in exile for his part
in the Commune of 1871 when supposedly he was connected
with the destruction of the Vendôme Column. He was sued for
wanton damage to the property of Paris, estimated at 323,091
francs, 68 centimes. Not unnaturally he fled to Switzerland. Yet,
however regrettable as a character, he had the real intelligence to
say: '*La peinture ne peut, sans tomber dans l'abstraction, laisser*

dominer un côté partiel de l'art; soit le dessin, soit la couleur, soit la composition'. A great prophet. ('Without falling into the abstract, painting cannot allow one side of the art to predominate, whether it be drawing, colour or composition.')

The city has kept the collection going with purchases and gifts so that the list of names runs down to Marquet and later. The gallery is in fact a beautifully select assemblage, including a witty terracotta portrait of Voltaire by Houdon, so penetrating that it almost relieves you of the necessity to read even one of the author's works. And Montpellier does not consider its duty done, when it has provided us with all this intellectual food. It has its restaurants, too, which are far from negligible. How I should love to eat again at the Brasserie Lorraine in the Rue Maguelone, and though this place may once have been low as a brasserie, it is so no longer. Francis Toye, gourmet and musician, once promised to cook me a guinea-fowl that I really should like. The bird was indeed beautifully cooked, but it remained a guinea-fowl for me. But let the chef at the Lorraine get his hands on one and turn it into a cromeski, then herbs and whites of egg will fly it into the celestial spheres. They do a lot of clever things there; expensively but the lavish portions would do for two English stomachs. Strange that our next lucky strike should have been the Restaurant d'Alsace, of which I can only say that the reception is a little cool, but once you are inside the manners are charming and you leave 'with good capon lined'.

And now if we are taking this extremely devious route and if its objective, the eastern passes of the Pyrenees remains a serious one, we must move westwards towards Perpignan, the French capital of the short-lived Kingdom of Majorca. You have two choices for your westward route, both of which will join at Béziers, where the Catharists were so atrociously massacred. They run on either side of the vast lagoon still known by its Phoenician name, the Bassin du Thau. On the inland route, N.113, you can switch away to flirt with the mediaeval town of Pézenas, where houses of the fifteenth and sixteenth centuries are two a penny, where Molière stayed as a strolling player from 1650 to 1657 (Maison Barbier Cély; a plain house); where they play a form of *pallone* in the Place Gambetta, a game for giants where volleying is all the art.

Or you can follow N.108 which will take you by the town of Sète and by a long isthmus of sand, a campers' and bathers' paradise since the sand is fine, on to the black-avised fortress cathedral of Agde, still terrifying to the intruder. Both Agde and Sète have at least classical origins, if not earlier. To Sète fell the good fortune to be rescued from the centuries of silt and depression in the seventeenth century, and now as an oil port it ranks in Mediterranean France second only to Marseilles. All the great names of the 1600's played their part—Henri IV the begetter, Richelieu, Louis XIV who granted the citizens special privileges, the ubiquitous Vauban, and a man less familiar to the general English reader, Paul Riquet.

The English do not take canals seriously, otherwise they would never have handed them over to a lingering and expensive death in the Ministry of Transport. In fact our first canal was started just a century later than the completion of the first in France, where still the waterways provide state-supervised, tax-free transport for over five hundred million tons of merchandise annually. Paul Riquet built the Canal du Midi from Bordeaux to the Bassin du Thau between 1666 and 1689, a matter of about 150 miles, rising and falling through 119 locks, a tremendous enterprise for the date. It only cost a million and odd francs.

Slightly earlier, royal enterprise had started the resurrection of Sète as a port. Sitting at the entrance of the lagoon into which pour the Canal du Midi and the canal from Arles, Sète has a sort of mermaid attraction like seaweed waving at low level. In the lagoon are oyster beds and mussel beds. Nearby they make that welcome apéritif, Dubonnet. In the old port they still conduct the water-jousts from rowed galleys as they used to do in the seventeenth century—the white boat against the blue, the spearman standing with his lance in rest and his shield on a platform high up above the stern of the boat. This will be on the first Monday after August 25th. It is a scrap-book of a place: the sands; the new casino; the Cimitière Marin on the hill-side, Paul Valéry's last resting place and the theme of one of his greatest poems.

I find it hard to rise to the point of emotion which makes burial in a certain place important. By the hour of burial my eyes will have been well closed; physically I shall look out over nothing. Yet the men of Sète, Valéry among them, prize the right to burial on this lovely hill-side, scarred by bad taste and the loud cries of monumental Carrara marble. But to a man still living a church-yard can be a Gray's *Elegy*; and one phrase of Valéry's threw me back to a little known Constable of Polstead Churchyard in Essex. A golden light silently touched the white sheep browsing in the foreground and lit the tombstones beyond to the same warm brilliance. '*Le blanc troupeau de mes tranquilles tombes*'— Valéry's phrase—was painted by Constable that June evening, I thought.

Away to Béziers, away to the honey of Roman Narbonne, away to flirt with the skirts of the white wine Corbières moun-tains and to turn south to Perpignan, the French key to Spain, the capital of Catalan France.

IX

To Perpignan

I HAD looked forward to seeing Narbonne. Odd Latin tags about 'pulcherrima Narbo', Hannibal's armies and other classical sundries from my youth predisposed me to the place. I was disappointed. I knew the choir of the cathedral (but no other part) by photograph and it looked good. So it was—but what of the rest, dying away into a fading effort at completion in the eighteenth century. Roman remains in museums are not the equals even of broken aqueducts. The map showed water flowing through the place; it proved a stagnant canal. I had read how the jolly, lovable Narbonnais flocked to their splendid cafés beneath the plane trees of the Cours de la République, where all was gaiety and southern merriment. Maybe it was there, but against a style of sweaty shirt-sleeves and bulging, ill-cut trousers: and I bet they had grit in their shoes. At my low of depression I ran into Demas putting the odd bit of polish on his gold brick. I was even glad to see the old scamp, whom I had missed for some time, so I offered him a glass of wine which was served in dirty glasses. He asked me where I was going.

'To Perpignan,' I told him. 'And the sooner I am there the better I shall be pleased. I can't think why, but I don't care for this place.'

'Not for Narbonne? But, of course, you're getting on now—not allowed to eat honey? And your wife doesn't like the noise? It comes to us all. No, I can see you'd be better out of this place, and I can tell you of a charming spot, a Benedictine abbey; quite remote in its way and yet only a kilometre or two off N.613. You turn aside somewhere or another—to the left, I think, yes, twice to the left.'

And the dear old rogue vanished, glass of wine, gold brick and all.

Thus we came to the Abbey of Fontfroide, the Cold Spring,

accurately instructed by Demas. A needle of anticipation kept
pricking me as we drove through uninteresting country, which
steadily deteriorated to stonier ground, to stones, to rocks on
which myrtles eked out some kind of a peasant living; moderate
rocky hills rose in the distance. It was hot and still; but for the
orchestra of the cicadas it would have been silent; and silent it
could abruptly become when the shadow of a cloud fell across the
landscape and stilled the insects like a conductor's hand. From
this relative desolation you round a corner into a new world,
where monks have planted and cultivated for more than nine
centuries. The warm shape of cypresses, the strong growth of
pines and umbrella trees, roses and flowering shrubs create a new
world still impregnated with stones. And a sharp ear will catch
the sound of 'The Cold Spring'. The water which gives life to
desolation.

The valley in which the large abbey stands was first tamed by
the Benedictines, who were naturally suppressed by the large-
hearted hand of the revolution in 1791. Later the Cistercians tried
to take it over; but the work of repair proved too costly and it
was bought by a rich, imaginative man, Monsieur Fayet, who not
only concentrated on the conservation of the place, but installed
a school of commendable stained-glass workers under Brughstal,
and purchased from time to time pieces of local statuary suitable
in style to the place. Though there is, as in so many old monasteries, a fair amount of supplementary seventeenth-century
work—and it is by a grand courtyard of this period that we enter
—one goes to Fontfroide primarily for the church, the cloisters,
and the Salle Capitulaire mainly of the twelfth and thirteenth
centuries.

An unusual feature, which gives a key to the architecture of
this secret place is the use of the circle. Below the eaves of the
tower is a great, plain quatrefoil window, four circles in elision.
In the cloister the space above the coupled columns and arches is
filled by round, blind circles. The upper part of the tracery of the
central window above the arch to the apse contains five circles.
In the Salle Capitulaire families of round arches, half-circles, rise
from columns set on bases of varying levels grouped singly or in

fives, creating almost an uncanny sequence of shadows. This is said to be Mosarabic work, the design of Spanish Christian builders whose lives the Moors spared on account of their skill. The capitals attest the extent to which they had adopted the style of their conquerors, who still left them their faith in exchange for their skill. And so it has a slightly secret society air; beautiful, yes; but creepy. I am still a little haunted by the blind eyes of the cloister. Before you know anything of the existence of the *Salle des Morts* where the vigils were sustained, which you see late on the tour, you sense a shrouding of the atmosphere. The beauty of the restoration conceals at first that this is a city of the dead. There are no monks to kneel and pray. How sad that the well-intentioned, well-designed effects of Monsieur Fayet who had been so tactful a restorer missed faith by a hair's breadth.

There is no road on to anywhere from Fontfroide; it is the end of its local world. You must go back to Narbonne, speculating over Demas—had he just given himself a good laugh or had he done you a good turn—in order to regain the road to Perpignan. For with Perpignan, as at Foix we approach journey's end, since these two cities hold the keys to the eastern approaches to Spain. Yet Foix must bow to Perpignan. At its best it was no more than the stronghold of a count who was not originally even a tenant in chief of the French King. But for sixty-three years Perpignan was the capital of an ephemeral kingdom, and has never forgotten it. It is still the capital of the old province of Rousillon, the red land, which still has its own speech, Catalan, and which still has a written language in use today; still spiritually related to the Catalans across the border in Spain and to the émigrés from the Franco régime who brought back into French Catalonia their national dance, the Sardane. Such is their regionality, that I think of an old man who told me that, yes, he had fought in the first war for France, 'though he was a Catalan'. Clearly it had been a matter of courtesy between one gentleman and another.

Perhaps it was chance that determined my affection for Perpignan. We were unlucky in our first hotel—not because it was a bad hotel, but because it was so close to a carillon that even the deaf would have to hear it. During that sleepless night there had, on average, been no more than twenty-nine silent minutes to the hour.

We made a fortunate change to an old-fashioned hotel, La Loge. Why it is not in Michelin heaven knows. In the middle of the city it is an island of silence. You cannot, for instance, drive a car up to it, though you can get near to it and they carry your bags; it dwells round an inner courtyard, a well of quiet. Madame la Patronne has caught something of this note. Her diction had the timelessness of exactitude; '*très calme*', '*très tranquille*' were phrases of three and four syllables, not of two or three. One felt a curtsy in her voice as she pronounced correctly each final sonant 'E'. She was the same on the telephone. The words came out at an even rate of syllables to the minute as if her voice were 'verbo-statically' controlled, if such a thing could be. We have been happy and comfortable there more than once in an old-fashioned way. The water is hot; the coffee strong; and we were at the very heart of the city, as we shall see; in Perpignan 'La Loge' does not mean a box at the theatre as it would in Paris; it means something a good deal older.

*   *   *

Every capital city has a history which will tell the story of its country, particularly when you are dealing with fractional French history as in Rousillon. In Perpignan one learns the story from civil rather than from ecclesiastical buildings since here, by comparison with Cahors, Toulouse or Albi, bishops were not a gilt-edged security. On a slight eminence above the town, which lies near the sea in a wide plain, is the royal palace, the castle, the citadel, as it has been called at different times. The approach to it is really rather daunting—squalid buildings and wanton ruins made by Germans in retreat. Shrug them off your shoulders as you dive into waves of imagination from the past.

Imagination you need, though the Ministère des Beaux Arts gives increasing help by clearing away the debris of a hundred and fifty years of military occupation, during which the great vaulted mediaeval halls were sliced into three storeys of soldiers' dormitories. The old boy who took us round had done his military service there in 1908, and remembered every detail. The high spot of his life was the banquet of 28th June 1954, held in the newly restored hall of the kings of Majorca, where the original vaulting, the ancient corbels, fireplaces, tiles, rose windows and pointed windows had at last been exhumed from their sacrilegious, military grave. The hall that night was lit with torches; sarabandes were played; sardanes were danced; Catalan songs were sung. For the Catalan recruit of 1908, privileged to pass his service in the palace of the old kings of his old nation, this night has paid for all and has irradiated each succeeding day. It is quite a beautiful experience to meet an utterly contented old man who knows why he is contented. The only shadow on his brow was cast by fear that he might not live to see the complete restoration of the palace.

Now to be slightly more serious, though the happiness of an old man is serious enough after all. As was explained in the Montpellier chapter, James I, 'the Conqueror', of Aragon started this royal palace in 1284 and then by his ridiculous will bequeathed it together with Majorca, Rousillon, Montpellier—and anything he could lay claim to north of the Pyrenees to his youngest son, who became James I of the Kingdom of Majorca with dual capitals on the island of Majorca and at Perpignan. In no time big brother Peter III of Aragon was after little brother and by a *coup de main* captured the palace from which young James escaped ignominiously by the sewers.

Young James got control again and the mediaeval palace, the remains of which we see today, was largely his creation, a place designed for high entertainment, for dancing and song and poetry, for all that the flower of the Middle Ages considered valuable. And it is singular, this impress from the first inception; an air of hospitality, a happy place for meetings and negotiations. Schismatic Popes and Emperors consorted thither to solve their difficulties or to increase them.

So first one is aware of this central mediaeval block, which gradually is being disengaged from the unperceptive coatings of the past. The central courtyard is a wonderful thing. As you enter it over rather an unappetising footbridge, which replaces the old drawbridge, you stand under a nobly arched colonnade. Wide

Perpignan: La Loge

(*below*) the ancient chapel of the kings of Majorca

Perpignan: the ritual *Procession de la Sanch*

arms of masonry tattooed with Gothic windows stretch out on either side. They are built of the local material, a mixture of brick and water-worn, rounded pebbles from the river Tet, with stone dressings—a surface which is kind to the eye in strong light. What confronts you is unforgettable, since the restoration is so honest as to be undisturbing.

A matter of two storeys, behind which rises a square ecclesiastical tower with a rose window surmounted by twin houses for two bells faintly recalling the Toulouse manner. But this is only the first focus. On either side of the court a flight of steps, supported on arches of unclassified curve, lead to a first-floor loggia. This loggia in its turn is supported by a central rounded arch on a broad curve, which is flanked by purely bucolic arches: I don't believe there is a technical word, even if I wanted to use it, to describe these differing curves, which produce harmony out of discord.

This central space houses two chapels one above the other. The lower is the Chapelle St. Magdalene, a tiny, round-arched place, a place of intimate worship. Slightly later, above it, is the Chapelle Royale with its façade dressed in local marbles. This again has its own atmosphere; traces of early painting have the quality of a half-remembered dream; in the small space are five radiating pointed arches; conical niches recall Majorcan technique and remind you in whose private chapel you are at prayer. There is the aumbry; there is the stone basin in which the priest could wash his hands, the western rose window and some glowing glass of the fourteenth century. Out behind all this is a huddled courtyard, where an ancient olive-press concealed an escape route.

Slightly oriental is the fact that the kings and queens of the short-lived Majorcan kingdom came from opposite wings of the Palace to their chapel and heard Mass from different balconies. This also explains the exterior ramps to the first-floor chapel and loggia, which conducted the courtiers to worship by the same geographical sex-differentiation as their rulers. From that point they went on jointly for the appropriate feast in the Salle des Rois de Majorque.

In this room you can unlace your imagination. From a single

o

original window, of twin Gothic lights set back from the wall with
seats in its embrasure the whole design was deduced with a little
additional help. It is a great feat of intelligent restoration. Under
skin of Napoleonic plaster were found hints of fireplace
mouldings sufficient to show the experts how the great room had
been arranged hundreds of years ago. As you see it now, it is
invigorating with the true pulse of life. It conveys a sense of
luxury well used, the monument of a brief kingship. It was here
that my old guide's *'grand festin'* took place in the memorable
June of 1954.

'The garlands wither on your brow.' Soon for Perpignan its
palace would wither to the status of a governor's castle, and finally
into the citadel of a fortified provincial town. After the disappear-
ance of the Kingdom of Majorca (1344), the kings of Aragon still
respected it. But when in the persons of King Ferdinand of
Aragon and Queen Isabella of Castile, Aragon became Spain,
Perpignan was, alas, no longer a court card. It retained technically
its civic constitution, its elected consuls who could represent the
town against the governor; Charles V, Holy Roman Emperor and
King of Spain, wielder of enormous power until he distilled himself into a monastery, recognised the old palace by some additional
building. But from his time for about a century the town just
bickered against its military governors, while France and Spain
were so frequently at war; and it bickered against governors who
might be Spanish or Italian or Greek, but never, never a man of
Rousillon. These Catalans came to hate the Spanish as much as
their cousins down in Barcelona still do. Is it not strange that of
all the European colonising powers Spain has lost the greatest
part of its achievement? What can it show comparable in history
to, say Goa, still loyal to Portugal despite the heteroclite wooings
of Nehru.

The final mistake was made by the Marques de la Rena,
governor in 1640, who trained guns on the city. After that
Catalan Perpignan hoped no more from Spain, but leaned to
France of which from 1659 she was with the rest of Rousillon
made a part politically. Steadily, and on the whole tactfully, the
French have tried to gallicise this younger child of their kingdom.

Vauban's lovely work at the old Majorca Palace is evidence; the rest of his work, the splendid moats and ramparts aligned with a faithful mathematical beauty were pulled down and his moats were glossed over early this century. But how could either the Spanish or the French school absorb such an individuality in painting or sculpture as Catalan Art? How fortunate were the Basques in offering to the alien races with which they have had to deal no similar artistic, no similar spiritual problem; at any moment they could wrap round themselves the dark, impenetrable cloak of their language. But, as we search through the wide plains and uplands, mountains indeed, of Rousillon, we shall find individuality persistent from the tenth century onwards.

*   *   *

As recently as 1904 Perpignan was still encircled with the walls which Vauban had redesigned in the late seventeenth century. Now apart from the citadel only one fragment survives, the Castillet. This is a fort of most striking design and colour. From the outer angles of the central square wings project, of which only the sides facing inwards have windows for cross-fire; their outer flanks are blind unscalable masonry. These walls are crowned by battlements and machicolations of the strangest form; so long are they that they seem to hang down like tresses of hair. Above all this rises an hexagonal watch-tower, machicolated in the same manner, surmounted by a dome. It is all built of a rose-coloured brick, very violent in the sun; and the bright stone corbels which support the brick machicolations give the effect of a jewelled necklace of precious stones. It was built in the fourteenth century to guard the crossing of the river Basse; and under a brief French occupation towards the end of the fifteenth century the gateway, the Porte Notre Dame, was tacked on to it. You can climb to the roof by a spiral stair past the offices of the Syndicat d'Initiative and other municipal departments and enjoy the wide scene from the blue Mediterranean to the distant snow-capped mass of Mont Canigou, which seems to be the omnipresent tutelary god of Rousillon landscape.

However much one may regret the old ramparts, one must at

least admit that the modern approach across the river to the old
town has been handsomely laid out. To the left of the Place de la
Victoire which confronts the Castillet are fine avenues of planes.
To the right is the Place Arago, gay with municipal flowers at the
foot of the statue to the great astronomer, a native of these parts.
He was a man of remarkable intelligence, François Arago, so
brilliant in his day that he was made a member of the Académie
des Sciences at the age of twenty-three, and achieved a European
reputation. But he could not keep his fingers out of politics and,
at the expulsion of Louis Philippe in 1848, joined the provisional
government and became Minister of War. He refused to take the
oath of allegiance to Napoleon III as Emperor, and died a year
later—a typically intractable Catalan.

Let us go in by the Porte Notre Dame and up the Rue des
Marchands and the Rue l'Argenterie, which is the lively shopping
street, too lively indeed for window-shopping since old ladies
with outworks of shopping baskets will soon make the place too
hot for loiterers. I never could analyse my attitude to this Perpignan crowd, which so imperturbably made its juggernaut way
up and down the hill. Being pushed around has never had any
appeal for me at all; but in Perpignan I never minded it. Perhaps
it was the inevitability of the process; the narrow street provided
no other solution, indeed made it seem quite a reasonable
method; and, surely, what is reasonable cannot be interpreted as
impolite. A turning to the left frees you from this hurly-burly
and leads you to the Place Gambetta with its seventeenth-
century houses dominated at the upper end by the Cathedral of
St. Jean.

The west front frankly disappointed me. It is set between two
projections which look as though they had been designed to
carry towers; indeed the right-hand one was crowned as an after-
thought with a white stone clock tower, surmounted by a most
elaborate piece of baroque ironwork, the cage from which the
bell is hung, beautiful in itself but quite inappropriate here. While
these near-towers are built of multicoloured stone with a little
brick as well, the centre is made principally from the local pebbles
interlined with courses of brick; sometimes there are brick tiles set

in a herring-bone pattern, which make the place look horribly tweedy; moreover the whole thing is decorated with feigned Gothic arches in brickwork. Of course, the craftsmanship of it is wonderful—but so is that of a chef who overdecorates the meats on the cold table. To complete your confusion, on the delightful classical porch is set a bright white marble statue of St. John the Baptist by Maillol. Like the iron bellcage it is, in its own right, a fine thing; but, oh! to see it anywhere else.

Now the worst is over. Once you are inside a rich peace settles upon you. Though the church as we see it is still Gothic in form, even in the fifteenth century the architects in this part of France hankered after the old breadth of the classical. So the span here is very wide in proportion to the height, about sixty feet in width against a tall seventy high. The length is noble, over two hundred and fifty feet. Lateral chapels run down the north and south walls, so that they support the span as the columns of an aisle would do. They also provide a rather low, warm light to the nave from their high placed windows, and this soft infusion adds to the sense of peace which overcame me on every visit. Nor have the architects exhausted their skill even now. This cathedral, which was completed in the very early sixteenth century, glows with the luminosity of gilding in the dark side chapels. In them and at the high altar you find wonderful examples of the individualist Catalan sculptor's polychrome work, set in great architectural frames. Some, rescued from decaying monasteries like St. Martin de Canigou, may run back as far as the fourteenth century.

I found all this detail a source of fascination and stimulus. The altar of St. Peter's chapel is ornamented with all the refinement of the late fifteenth-century carving; it contains a Pieta in which, as Christ's body lies across her knees, the Virgin grips his left wrist tightly, clinging to it as if it alone were the present, though you can see from her down-drawn lips that her thoughts are years away. The famous organ loft of 1504 arrests you as you turn to go out and elsewhere you find its Catalan painted shutters— Salome's serpentining figure and the dubious courtiers, wondering whose turn it might be next: the font, white marble of an antique simplicity, perhaps as old as the eleventh century. These things and others like them, too many to name, constitute the richness of the cathedral. But there are two other statues which must be mentioned. Both are in chapels adjoining the cathedral and are valuable apart from their artistic significance for their local associations. The chapel of Notre Dame del Correch (of the stream)—the oldest part of the cathedral—still retains its early apse which enshrines the ancient statue of the Virgin and Child, an object of long veneration in the city. She is a happy mother and her child's hand is gaily raised in blessing; it is radiant. The other pole of the emotions is reached in the incredible wooden Crucifix, known as Le Dévot Christ, which you find in a back-street chapel on what used to be abbey ground, now mainly occupied by warehouses and light industry. Can one speak of 'stylised realism'? It seems a beastly piece of jargon; and yet I do not quite know how else to describe this carving which evokes so profound a sense of physical suffering without attempting exact delineation. Indeed the thing is done by exaggeration, one would say in an intuitive mood; yet the individual details—the appalling strain from the weight of the crucified body on the muscles of the arms, the chest, the neck, the stomach—are all starkly in proportion with each other, and as a result there is no more exaggeration than in a change of key in music. It is a sacrificial figure, Le Dévot Christ. We shall meet this statue again, since it is part of the ritual life of Perpignan.

*   *   *

The oldest parish church in Perpignan is that of St. Jacques on the eastern edge of the town, of which the inhabitants are called 'Hortolans', market gardeners, the dialect name being derived from the Latin, *hortus*. It is an odd neighbourhood, entirely individual in providing an atmosphere faintly Moorish, faintly Spanish, unlike anything else I saw in Rousillon. The manner of life suggests that in the marrow of the people is a nomadic core; you could call them gipsy-eyed or Bedouin-eyed; but they stay on the spot in shacks which look permanently temporary. It is from this church, so rich in symbolism, so rich in relics, sculptures and altar pieces, that the ritual procession of Jeudi Saint (Maundy Thursday) starts. This is the *Procession de la Sanch*, which illustrates the Tragedia Sancta of Christ's passion.

There are two strands to the story of this procession, which (so people tell me who have seen both) is the nearest rival to the renowned Good Friday procession at Seville; both belong to the same instinct. In the first place, one must think back to the time when secular plays barely existed, when entertainment was scarce and the void was filled for the people as a whole by the dramatisation of episodes from the life of Christ or the life of saints. It was St. Vincent Ferrer, the Spanish Dominican preacher, in the fifteenth century, who founded confraternities for the practice of religious discipline which included the accompaniment to the scaffold or block of those condemned to death. These men were the 'Penitents', and wore for this purpose black robes and a tall black hood, as high as the old silver candle-extinguishers, slitted for eyes only, leaving the man within anonymous, a vehicle of prayer. This special contribution of St. Vincent Ferrer is the second twist in the thread; for at Perpignan the Confraternity of St. Jacques came to elaborate with other confraternities a procession of Penitents to accompany in spirit the body of our Lord on His pilgrimage to Calvary and to enact the sequence of His Passion. In the old days two and three hundred years ago it was nothing to have 8,500 verses declaimed in the single night from dark to dawn, as the procession halted on its way round the city. In the sixteenth and seventeenth century the ritual was invaded by the Flagellants. As the hooded men walked round the city chanting by torchlight, they would whip one another with thongs in which nails were embedded till the blood ran, in memory of the Flagellation of Christ. This was a favourite exercise of the pervert, Henri III. The devout of Perpignan were much addicted to this sexual peculiarity and persisted in it until a royal governor in the 1700's forbade it. The Consuls of the town protested. The governor replied with cynical wisdom: 'Continue the practice, then. But on one condition—that you will adopt every child born nine months after the Procession of La Sanch.' The idea was never heard of again.

As one sees it today, La Sanch is something far greater than a

local procession, since it is joined by confraternities from neighbouring towns and villages. This year (1957) one contingent
came even from the remote mountains of the Cerdagne, the little
village of Sonto, bringing its processional crucifix, on one face of
which is Christ crucified and on the other the Virgin at Calvary. It
is impossible to give a detailed description of everything which
passed before our eyes that night, since no fewer than seventy-
five individual sections formed the whole, concluding with
'Groupe de Scouts'. Where we stood penned in the crowd in the
heart of the city above the Castillet, we were caught into a rapture
of emotion which was religiously natural, even though we could
not follow the Catalan songs and dirges, goigs and coblas, nor all
the Latin prayers, recited in an accent not prevalent at school. It
is the sort of thing which is anathema to most Protestants—
sculptured Madonnas clothed in black, carved episodes from the
Passion, the emblems of the Passion and so on all carried in procession; graven images, idolatry in short. Yet if you open your
mind to the theme without worrying about the dogma for once
(as if you were a mediaeval English soldier of fortune down here,
say, in the fifteenth century), your head will join with the rest and
bow as if a wind had passed over the cornfield. Dull must he be of
mind who can resist this imagery. Ruskin was Protestant enough,
God knows, and yet he could take the Italians primitives and all
the things for which he would have condemned the Catholic
church of his own day.

Three strokes from the clock tower of St. Jacques. Three
strokes from the iron bell carried by the leader of the procession,
the 'Regidor', clad in scarlet robes and hooded in scarlet. Behind
him is a group of drummers, 'black-stoled, black-hooded as a
dream'; even their drums are draped in black and to this muted
music now slow movement begins. They prelude the great processional cross, which is accompanied by a choir of children from
all the parishes of Perpignan, learning at this relatively early age
their local litanies. A group of three, black-hooded again; one
carries a tall triangle formed by a ladder, the lances and a cross-
piece supporting the other emblems of the Passion. Immediately
behind follows the banner of another ancient parish, La Réal.

The movement halts intermittently in the town at places roughly equivalent to Stations of the Cross, where songs are chanted and prayers are made; but with this difference. This ceremony commemorated not only the Passion and its story but *Mater Dolorosa*, the Virgin of the Sorrows. And so we come in the procession to what are called '*Les Mistéris*', a word which stems from mediaeval and classical thought. Both ideas carry the idea of initiation, sometimes to a craft, sometimes to a religion or to a religious sect or order. In the Perpignan procession the villages and confraternities bring out the emblems of their 'mystery', usually painted sculpture, set on a carriage bedded with flowers. St. Jacques is particularly rich in these endowments, and from the church are borne the '*Mistéri de l'Hort*'—the scene on the Mount of Olives; the Ecce Homo; St. Veronica, whose image is drawn by young women dressed in black set off by white mantillas of a modest kind, and bearing staves as they walk. The statue of the saint holds in her hands a representation of the cloth with which she wiped Christ's face on his way to Calvary. Then there would be the mourning Virgins, clad in black, with the heart pierced by the seven arrows of the seven sorrows embroidered on the breast. The Virgin at the Calvary comes from Millas, an ancient town; a crucifix from the church of St. Matthew is carried by women wearing Catalan bonnets. Borne over the city on the wind by loud speakers are the chants, the hymns, the prayers; the atmosphere is concentrated and the crowd is still. Last of all the 'Bed of Christ' passes, a crucifix carried on a palanquin of black velvet and silver embroidery, recumbent, carried as ever by the hooded men of the black fraternity of St. Jacques.

There are two crises of emotion. Remember that one original function of the Penitents was to accompany and to pray for those condemned to death. Suddenly massed choirs break into the acrid, heart-rending *Miserere des Pendus*; after the long contemplation of Christ's sacrifice the crowd is literally shocked into a catch of the breath by this piercing dirge. From the origin of this devout procession in the religious plays of the mediaeval age the essential dramatic touch has not been lost.

And so to the last high moment, after which the procession

fades its way back to the church of St. Jacques. The Mistéris and the hooded men who have drawn or borne them through the city, the 'Caparutxes' as they are called in Catalan, have arrived in the square before the cathedral which we have already visited. There to receive them is the poignant statue of 'Le Dévot Christ', the Christ who has taken away the sins of the world on the Good Friday of which the dawn is breaking. And as the Penitents reach on their return journey, by the Rue de la Barre, de l'Argenterie, Place Rigaud and the rest, to the ancient church of St. James, the hooded men replace their holy mysteries. The church smells of candle fat, incense, humanity. The earlier brilliance of the massed candles is paling in the April light which, in recompense touches up this strange, candle-snuffer shape of the high hoods, a symbol to me of death.

Not all of this did I see, since it was difficult to flit knowingly from right place to right place, not being a journalist with a camera and a schedule laid down. I was directed for certain elucidations to the chemist who may have headed the committee which arranged this year's procession (for there is a plan and a post-mortem on the ceremony annually). His personality was remarkable for its entire serenity. As he served his customers (and he knew what was wrong or likely to be wrong with each of them), he would return to the thread of my questions as if there had been no interruption. If you had met his face finely sculptured in fourteenth-century stone or marble, you would have marvelled at its spirituality. This was Monsieur Deloncle of 2, Rue Lucien, a christian and a royalist who endorsed a phrase I heard in a restaurant at Tulle when the Queen's speech was broadcast from the state banquet: '*Voila une voix fraiche et naturelle, à laquelle on peut se fier.*'

* * *

The history of this town, so far as I have been able to show it to you, the Catalan nature of its individual procession, of its carved altars in the cathedral and St. Jacques, the resurrecting splendours of the royal palace may, I hope, have led you to expect something more. Old houses from the early sixteenth century, of course, with their arcaded courtyards; here and there a graceful staircase; a Renaissance window. But these details are for the amateurs of architectural hide-and-seek.

As I described the busy streets from the Castillet, up which the procession winds its way, I kept your eyes and mine temporarily diverted from the Rue de la Loge, which bears off to the right. This is a street which is not a street; stout posts of stone linked by bronze chains interdict all wheeled traffic; yet 'wayfarers though fools, shall not err therein'. It is from very old days the administrative centre of Perpignan.

The name itself is a French corruption of the original Spanish or Catalan name, La Lonja, the exchange. For it was here that the shipping business was done, the contracts made, the cases of maritime law decided. The trade must already have been considerable before 1397 when the enchanting Loge de Mer was begun. The architect was concerned to express a proud dignity; and his plan has struck many as Venetian by origin, though this has never been proved. It is built on a corner site, two pointed arches fronting on the Rue des Marchands, and four ogee arches on the Rue de la Loge, slightly taller. They demarcated a covered space for walking, talking and striking bargains, the same sort of thing as you find in an old-fashioned Corn Exchange in an English county town. And this space is most beautifully vaulted, hexagonal piers supporting the spring of pure Gothic arches very much in the manner of the Salle Capitulaire of the cathedral. This front is later in date, as the carved date 1540 shows. Above is another flamboyant store lighted by decorative windows in rectangular frames. Those on the later front are again of ogee form and at first set in pairs coupled within the frame; then suddenly they sprint off in a sequence of three pairs, all close-coupled, a most spirited effect. From a pole at the corner hangs the bronze model of a caravelle in full sail, the building's insignia. Gargoyles abound and a fretted parapet seals the brilliant design. Nowadays the place has been converted into a popular café with questionable tracery and stained glass filling in the old open arches of the ground floor. Vulgar globe lights on tall standards stand like commissionaires outside it. But in a sense the busy café life reminds one of the

active throng which has always moved beneath those splendid
arches.

The Rue de la Loge is paved; and the continuous flow of
façades of the sixteenth and seventeenth centuries give it the air
of a Venetian Campo. Here we contemplate well-housed official-
dom, the Hôtel de Ville with its nobly arcaded courtyard and the
fine sculpture by Maillol. *La Pensée*, contrasting with the pinks
and greys of the local marble. The taste for gargoyles hung on in
Perpignan later than in northern France; and though the courtyard arches are classical in form, yet guardian gargoyles are set in
the corners and centres of the walls. The exterior has been refaced
and the windows fairly tactfully restored; two well-modelled forearms in bronze project to carry standards on official occasions.
Beyond the Hôtel de Ville is yet another civic building of fine
character, the Palais de la Députation. In pre-revolutionary days
representatives of the local towns used to gather for their discus-
sions, entering by the great round-arched porch.

On the opposite side are more cafés and restaurants and good-
class shops. But it is not with these that my happiest memories
are linked. At night time, when all the lamps are lit and the cafés
brilliant, the big paving stones come alive with lights and shadows
and echo the feet of strolling men and girls, the high-heeled click
and the male shoe or espadrille making their own pattern of sound
in a slow complicated rhythm. For it is in this square that the
'Easter Parade' takes place nightly in fine summer weather.

We were dining there one early summer evening, and dining
well, I am glad to say, at the Café Glacier de la Loge—something
to do with soupe de poisson and Crochette de rognons if I remember right—and we became conscious over our brandy of a small
platform to the left of our table. Men of ages varying from sixty
to sixteen began to gather behind it outside another café; another
cast of the eye suggested that they were unpacking musical instruments. 'Good God!' I thought, 'here is the town band ready to
blow our heads off. Why didn't we dine on the Place Arago or by
the cathedral.' You can see, I was all set for a nasty night; and only
the quality of that particular brandy kept us seated for the necessary minutes in which a decision can be reversed.

I was in fact right. The town band it was. But such a town band as I had never heard before. The musicians arrived severally. They tuned up, not in an opera house Persian carpet of sound where the high-lights of the violins contrast with the purple of cellos, the maroons of double-basses and drums. No, these men tuned up in échelon as it were, each introducing his instrument to the assembled public; and very strange instruments indeed they were by shape and sound. One made a noise like a major pig-killing operation; at a lower range equally piercing sounds were tested out by breath, string and drum. I realised that I was due to listen to the funniest town band on earth, a scream obviously; and I broke into spasms of loud laughter.

Then the band went into action and, like Henry I, we never smiled again. The tuning up had been something like a bird's love-call, an incitement to dance. A steadily pulsing rhythm took over; repetitive; deriving its force from variations of pitch, orchestration and sheer drive. It is fantastic how many shades of feeling could be pinned on one rhythm, which persisted throughout in two-four time.

'Ta/Rum ta ta/ta Rum ta ta/ta tiddle dah' it seems to go.

Within a few minutes three or four will be drawn by the itch of their toes to start dancing; three or four girls or men, since it is not a matter of finding a partner of the opposite sex to dance. You join the ring and you do so by joining hands, since all the dancing is done in a circle, with hands linked in set, symbolical positions. As space in the square grows short and as the desire for dancing increases, an inner circle of dancers will form within the first ring. In the Rue de la Loge I have several times seen three sets of three concentric circles, as often as not with children in the centre picking up the steps as best they might. And you will often see in a corner a few girls of five or six, white frocked, their black hair tied with a white or pink bow—a rare boy to keep them company, trying to foot it featly. But for the most part this is beyond a small child's stumbling scope and has much the same effect as infant singing, breathy and tremolo.

The dance has the Spanish tradition of rigidity for hips, neck, head; the eyes expressionless; impersonal. I remember seeing one girl several times, black hair, not a beauty but for a slim figure, whose grey eyes never flickered from their level. Only the movement of the feet, the slim legs, and the position of the hands tell one the emotion of the minute. The dancer does not change his ground except in a rush at the end of one section and then only by thirty degrees, like the sudden ripple of wind on a willow. The feet slide to the slipped rhythm, toes barely kissing the ground. Then there is a moment of syncopation played by the ankle; an increase of excitement in the orchestration—and the leap, which for dignity's sake never is quite a leap; it is a leap with a back-kick, which for all its drive leaves the head still Spanishly rigid. I had never believed that arrested movement could be so beautiful. The last chord, and all the linked hands shoot out to the centre of the circle and the handclasps dissolve. The dance is over. The dancers go back to their own café table without a word to the other man or woman whose hand they have held, whose rhythm they have shared for the last fifteen minutes.

This sudden, dispassionate dispersal of the sexes reminds me faintly of village hall dances in my Midland youth. But here, in Catalan France, we are up against something very much older. For this dance, the Sardane, the spring dance of fertility, some authorities claim at least Greek origins; indeed the Greeks had colonies along this coast down to Barcelona; and one finds on Greek vases figures dancing, their hands linked very much in the attitudes of the Sardane. I have seen in reproduction illuminated manuscripts of the fifteenth century which clearly show musical instruments identical with those played today, those strangely pitched flutes and horns, the bumble-buzz of the double bass. Old prints by engravers of the neighbourhood depict the same dance in eighteenth-century village settings with the same instruments. It was in the nineteenth century that the old folk tunes were codified and orchestrated, as their make-up still implies to the ear. Casals told me that no Catalan composer worthy of the name had failed to write at least one Sardane; his name is not among the failures.

While in Spanish Catalonia with Barcelona as its old capital the dance has had a continuous history, in France it had declined in popularity by the time of the Spanish civil wars of the 1930's. As the Spanish Catalans crossed the mountains they did not, like the Jews of the dispersion, hang up their harps but nostalgically played their open-air music outside the villages wherever there was a flat space suitable for dancing. The French hearts and toes were quick to respond, and now the popularity of the dance is pretty general. On festival days, as I saw it done at Perpignan on the evening of Easter Sunday, there is a lavish use of local costume; there is formality and a perfection of the ensemble. Yet in my heart of hearts I preferred the amateur performances of the summer. Then I was there for the pleasure of watching and comparing the individual dancers, in an aimless way dissecting their characters so far as I could imagine them—the slim, grey-eyed girl; a white-haired man of about sixty whose feet never betrayed him; another much younger, reddish-haired, whose hands were eloquent; the show-off piece who always leapt too high; an immature girl of fourteen or fifteen whose feet never seemed to touch the pavement. It was a pageant for fifteen minutes which you could drape out to your own taste, just as on Jeudi Saint the houses were draped with fine carpets, rugs and velvets; an eddy rather than a whirlpool above which like a cloud of mosquitoes they danced to a self-devised musical pattern, flying and falling in air.

X

Rousillon, the Red Land

MAPS of mountainous districts have presented me often with a difficulty or a grumble of some kind. If you consider, for instance, the Eastern Pyrenees on a map of France which shows the heights in what draper's language calls a four-colour range, you conclude that the whole thing, an area of several thousand square miles, is high or sometimes very high, and you wonder how on earth people communicated with one another. Clearly you need something with larger scale, and perhaps some kind friend, seeing that you have made no progress with the colour effects, puts into your hand a departmental map or maps of the district, all beautifully contoured. You follow these spider-lines as they swoop and whirl like the sea at high tide over hidden rocks, as they thicken close together and drift apart, and after an hour of study you overhear yourself muttering 'this will take me an awful lot of time'.

It is all a matter of rivers in the Pyrenees. From Perpignan, disregarding N.9 by which we came in from Narbonne, there are four main exits each following river valleys once you are out of the plain. The one that runs east to west, roughly through Quillan to Foix along N. 117, starts up the valley of the Agly, then turns right to follow the Maury, after which it has a rather difficult time with mountains and a pass before making Quillan. This country is called the Fenouillet. It is a dry, hard country, lying at the foot of the Corbières mountains. Some of the villages are connected by overhead cable to the fine marble quarries, from which the slabs swing down still in their variegated colours. There is inevitably the good romanesque church like St. Paul de Fenouillet; the romantic wreck of the triangular castle of Puy-laurens. And from that, if you like a cross-country route, you can travel to the Prades road by gorges and rock-strewn valleys, through feudal France and through frontier France for centuries

The Abbey of St. Michel de Cuxa at Prades

The North Portal
of the Abbey Church
of St. Michel de Cuxa
at Prades

The Cathedral at Elne:
detail from a capital
in the cloisters,
showing the Annunciation
and the Visitation

before the Treaty of the Pyrenees, recorded in such names as Montfort and, further to the east, Latour de France.

Next is the valley of the Tet (pronounced 'Tett'), which flows north-east from the mountains to Perpignan and the sea, escorting N.116 along its course of joining Perpignan to Bourg-Madame. The central part of this route is called the Conflent, and has so many happy memories for me that it must always remain my favourite. It is also the home of an individual school of Romanesque sculptors and architects. But this personal preference is no rood stick for another's judgment.

Then there is the second route into Spain (for N.117 is only a matter of lateral communications) which uses the river Tech for its convenience (N.9). And here it is my duty to warn you that you drop the river's 'H' either in reverence or in fun—you call it, intimately, 'Tec'. There is much gaiety in the lower part of the road to the Le Perthus frontier post, but if you turn off it (as we may do) at Le Boulou along N.115 you enter the softly-named Vallespir district. It is a sound suggesting something between 'espoir' (hope) and 'respirer' (to breathe, freely one hopes). Abjure romanticism. The name, as we shall see, means anything but that.

Then comes the last and oldest road, the ancient world's *Via Domitia*, now degraded in French Road Society circles to a mere N.119. Along this conquerors' route—for all the great men travelled from east to west and back on these tracks—unhelped by any river, you slog your way like any legionary up hill and down dale over the steep valleys carved by the sea and by the spate of melting snow from the foothills of the Albères mountains, the eastern outposts of the Pyrenees. For much of the way the Mediterranean lies just below your feet, while to the west hangs as always the snow-capped Guardian God, Mont Canigou. Let us take this as the first of our roads into Spain.

*   *   *

It starts, as all these roads do, straight and unhampered, over the wide, rich plain which spreads round Perpignan. Improved methods of agriculture have made it a most prosperous area.

P

The sun's heat, rivers, streams and irrigation yield several crops
each year, so that every farmer yearly grows different things and
so covers himself against the total loss of a single crop. It surprised me to learn for a fact that Rousillon is the heaviest wine-
producing area in France—heavier than Bordeaux or Burgundy.
Yet the evidence of my eyes supported my reading. For mile
upon mile the vines encompass you. And surprisingly good and
robust their wine is, and it is a pity that we do not learn to drink
Corbières or Rancio at home, their reds which show a kinship
with claret, while their whites—the best again from Corbières
—can be as dry as chablis. Planted in with them are fruit trees of
all kinds though the peach and the apricot perhaps are the
favourites; this practice was developed slowly as the coming of
the railways in the late fifties and sixties opened new markets.
Corn, vegetables and maize—for animal not human consumption—fill in the bill. Any Englishman is trained to defend the
flavour of the English hot-house peach as the finest in the world.
But in the fields of Rousillon is a rival to be considered an
honest challenger; you can almost blow the skin off the flesh of
a Rousillon peach. And as for their apricots . . .

Amid this wealth of growing things, which on the flat plain
are quite uninteresting companions, with mountain line to the
right and the blue Albères in front of you, you drive uneventfully
until you see a small town on an eminence, capped by noble
church towers. This is Elne, said to derive its name from the
memory that St. Helena stayed there. That the place was called
Castrum Helenae there is no doubt and one can still see the sub-
stratum of Gallo-Roman walls beneath the remains of the Gothic
fortifications. The town itself however is notable not for civil
or military building, but for the old cathedral whose striking
towers you have seen and for the cloisters of which the earliest
portion comes within sight of Moissac's perfection.

The west end with its two towers presents a fortress face, and
the lower part of the walls of the north-west tower is sloped
inwards, as at Albi, to frustrate attacks by scaling ladders; its
upper part was completed in brick at a later date. Its southern
brother, however, allows more to the graces. It is the taller of

the two and there is space for three tiers of blind round arcades; above them are two more storeys similar but for the piercing of the central arches, dark jewels. The broad battlements make a splendid crown of defiance.

This tower is typical of many others you will see later in this region in the decorative use of windows in tiers. The interior has quality as well; for its high barrel-vaulted nave dates back to the eleventh- and twelfth-century Catalan style—cross-banded and supported by lateral chapels though plain in itself. Each aisle finishes in an apse in which is set a round window giving a surprising, almost too surprising shaft of light. The cathedral was consecrated in 1065; but the quadripartite and sexpartite vaulting of the side aisles shows them to have been either later additions or, more probably, modifications due perhaps to damage during the capture of the town by Philippe III in 1285.

Impressive though the general effect is, the side chapels offer more of an unusual interest. Their carved bosses might be an early search for the idea of pendentives. There is a fine twelfth-century tomb of a bishop, and in the chapel of St. Agnes a wonderful altarpiece, carved and painted by an artist who had obviously learnt his technique in Barcelona. The colour of the panels depicting the Miracles of St. Michael is still remarkably fresh and vivid. There is much more beside; but I can only mention one piece which would serve as an exhibit in 'Animal, Vegetable or Mineral' on T.V. It is the font. In form it is like a straight-sided goblet set on rather a short stem. It is of white marble, almost toned to gold by the patina of the ages. The robes of officiating priests brushing against it through centuries of baptisms, the cloths of cleaners and the dust of time have worked this alchemy. The interior is carved into nine grooves, broad and deep at the rim, but slimming and shallower in cut to meet in the base of the bowl. The outside is most beautifully ornamented with acanthus leaves, growing alternately upwards and downwards. It has the satisfying excellence of beautiful material finely used with proportions of indefinable rightness. And no one is sure when it was made. Some authorities say it is

Gallo-Roman, perhaps sixth century; others take it for authentic
Roman; a third party has put it earlier still. Precision on this date
does not affect its wonderful quality; but I, for one, should dearly
like to know which period was honoured by the creator of this
admirable thing.

The glory of Elne is the cloister, begun about a century later
than the cathedral itself. The rhythm is rich. At each corner
stands a square, massive pier. Each side is trisected by rectangular
piers between which pairs of arches are carried on twin columns;
the piers are coupled to the cloister wall or to one another by
round or pointed arches. One forgets the horticultural hugger-
mugger in the centre as one looks across to the opposite wall,
decorated by that simple method which the old Venetians understood so well—the right choice of variegated marbles. The
surface above the arches is patterned by setting the veined
marbles from the Corbières mountains at different angles, a
patchwork effect, soft, 'counterchanged' if it were heraldry. The
old cathedral wall rises above and behind it, built of waterworn
pebbles.

The cloister arcades vary considerably in date and in quality.
They descend architecturally from monasteries, we shall see
later (St. Michel de Cuxa and Serrabone and St. Martin de
Canigou), and form part of an architectural group peculiar to
this part of France. If you are lucky enough to see Elne before
the others, you will draw full pleasure from it; otherwise one
could be tempted to say that in some respects it is not quite so
fine, if one is to be really critical. Let us leave considerations of
the capitals until later, and allow our eyes to pass leisurely over
the funerary inscriptions from the twelfth to the fourteenth
centuries which decorate the cloister walls, recalling memories
of bishops, priests, and an occasional eminent townsman. Here
is a pleasant sample from 1186.

> Here lies Guillaume Jorda, pastor of the flock of Elne, bewept by
> young and old. He was the honour of this city and of the world,
> which beweep him together. He died on the eve of the Assumption
> of Our Omnipotent Mother, seven years twice deducted from twelve
> hundred.

On the 30th June 1602, poor Elne, after a thousand years of episcopal eminence, had to yield the pride of its place to forceful, bustling Perpignan. Elne has never recovered from it.

* * *

Further south along this road to Spain lies the siren town of Collioure, which has not sung her songs in vain to painters, among them Matisse in our day. Nor has it changed much since the early nineteenth century, when Baron Taylor commissioned lithographs of it for his endless and invaluable *Voyages pittoresques dans l'ancienne France*. The perfection of its site cannot change. Above the elliptical bay rise two sharp hills; down their steep sides the little houses feel their way to the fishing port below, once an important focus of commerce with Genoa, Venice and Africa. Their roofs are almost purple, and the soil behind them has the brilliant red from which this part of France has been nicknamed La Côte Vermeille. To the left with its walls washed by the sea and keyed to the rocks stands the fawn-coloured mass of the old fort and church, and the domed circular tower beyond. The sea is blue, the sky is blue, many of the house doors are painted blue. It is indeed brilliant as colour.

You can see it to perfection with a drink in your hand from the terrasse of the restaurant La Ballette on the southern hill. Collioure is a dreaming place except in the tourist season, or at night when the anchovy boats (lamparo) go out, or at any week-end. From August 15th to 19th is also an extremely dangerous time unless you go there on purpose. Then is held the riotously festive 'Fêtes de Collioure' in commemoration of their patron saint, St. Vincent.

St. Vincent lived a hermit life on a rock, now unromantically joined to the pier by a causeway but in his day a rock of his own, impossible of access in rough weather. In time the holy man died and a small chapel was built on the place he had sanctified, where they piously buried his bones. Every year these would be fetched by boat and a service held to invoke his blessing on their ships and fishing during the coming season. In modern times the service is still held but no boat is necessary to fetch his bones. This does not prevent an uproarious torchlight procession of boats to the rock and as much jollification on shore as the southern Frenchman can think up—and that is a good deal.

Collioure lost her prosperity in the latter seventeenth century; and though it was thought desirable to modernise the fortifications against the predatory corsairs and Spaniards, Vauban entrusted the work to one of his subordinates. He, himself, had other ideas. A few kilometres further on was a little fishing village, Port Vendres—Portus Veneris, the harbour of Venus, in Roman days—caught his far-seeing eye. Its harbour would take vessels of deeper draught than old Collioure; and Vauban foresaw the days of greater ships and prepared for them by building quays and jetties for the future. Soon Port Vendres eclipsed Collioure and took the lead in prosperity for a hundred or so years. Now they compete at walking pace, both left behind by maritime progress. They differ in that one specialises in fishing for sardines and the other for anchovies.

After this the road continues to climb up and slide down these sharp valleys of incomparable red until you come to the welcoming resort of Banyuls. The sea front is charmingly laid out with masses of flowers and flowering shrubs; somehow the grass is kept going. From the point of 'plage-life' this wide bay with the bright, gay town behind is the most spirited of those I saw along this coast. Banyuls also makes a wine all of its own, a sort of all-purpose wine. The locals drink it as a table wine, or as the equivalent to Dubonnet (I met it first in this character and was delighted by it), or in another strength as a liqueur. I find it impossible to advise on it beyond saying the obvious 'only the best will do'. After my first experience, I searched for it again eagerly; but it was often too sweet for my taste. Still it is a popular wine of the country and you will find it at most cafés and restaurants if you care to make the experiment. If you approve, you are allowed to go over the *caves*.

You climb again. Above the Cap de l'Abeille you get a superb view up and down this splendidly vivacious coast-line. But from this point you twist and slip downhill all the way to the frontier towns of Port Bou (Spanish) and Cerbère (French). There is a

particularly nasty right-angle turn half-way down the steep hill
into Cerbère, which must have undone many an unwary traveller.
The beaches are small but the sands are good. No one takes any
trouble about domestic architecture in a frontier town; there is
no profit in it. If the name 'Cerbère' has any reference to Cer-
berus, then it expresses neatly and briefly the age-old hatred of
the French for Spain.

*   *   *

This rancour seems to have dissipated at Le Perthus, the
terminus of our old friend, N.9. Here all seemed gay amity, and
the little town, bright with restaurants and cafés, slips unchecked
over the frontier. We spent a peaceful, beer-filled hour watching
the cars being customed by smiling officials, whether French or
Spanish. Without let or hindrance we walked into Spain; no one
asked for a passport; no one even looked at us—a disappointment to my wife, I fear. This road from Perpignan is easy until
the last climb to the frontier height, which makes good scenery;
up to that point, soon after N.115 diverges to Céret, near Le
Boulou, you have travelled through pretty, prosperous country,
heavily cultivated, with many a little village around to brighten
the plain.

There are two other episodes, one roughly historical, the
other architectural, which must not be forgotten as one traverses
this road by Le Boulou. After the Napoleonic wars demobilised
troops behaved in a centuries-old manner and took to brigandage.
They were known as Les Trébucaires and no man, no traveller,
no farm was safe from their attentions. At last it was decided to
stamp out this race, which used to hang its victims from an old
oak, the worm-eaten base of which may still be seen. In the long
run they were smoked out, taken to Perpignan and hanged. In
some strangely macabre mood the order was given to take their
death-masks. And today, if you care, you may still see them in
the unlikeliest of places—or is there some cold logic behind the
choice?—the Natural History Museum.

There is nothing macabre about the tiny frescoed church of
St. Martin-en-Fenollar. Though it is only a few hundred yards off

the main road to the right a short three kilometres from Le Boulou, one can easily miss it. Through a screen of poplars it looks no more than a barn, and a small barn at that. But today you can cross the small stream by a foot bridge, walk past an indifferent kitchen-garden, and open the plain door in the plain wall, expecting to see no more than an ancient white-washed place. Instead you see an apsed chamber richly frescoed in the Byzantine manner.

The sequence represents Scenes from the Life of Christ—the Annunciation, His birth; the shepherds, the three Kings. And then we turn to Christ in Glory attended by the Ancients of the Apocalypse and the four Evangelists, while in another part the Virgin is enthroned, supported by angels. These scenes are placed above a dado of festooned drapery and decoration, later in date and now considerably perished. But the frescoes themselves are instinct with life, conveyed by a very simple palette—blue, red, green and black—and by drawing which at moments is severe to the point of brutality. These figures, set upon the walls in stark majesty, are the lineal descendants of the mosaics at Ravenna. There are the Ancients of the Apocalypse with their cups and viols and their queer eastern mitres or cylindrical hats. The horse and camel of the Magi are remarkably drawn. The eyes of saints and prophets which seem to be of onyx are frankly hypnotic. For something on so small a scale this chapel is a place of great power. You can see a copy in the Palais du Chaillot.

*   *   *

At Le Boulou, an unimportant, slightly *gamin* health-resort, we turn off to N.115, the Vallespir and the Aspres. Perhaps we should settle first of all this business of the word 'Vallespir'. It is the valley (val) which leads to the 'Aspres' (espir) which means the high barren ground of the mountain-sides encompassing the head waters of the Tech with peaks running over the 7,000 feet mark. The country of the Vallespir itself has infinite charm, but it leads you on to a nothingness of goat tracks and possibly smugglers' ways. No road leads from it across the Spanish border; so it may be significant that hereabouts for the first time, if I had not been previously unobservant, I saw in quantity the sure-footed mule.

Nothing can be more delightful than our introduction to the valley and its principal town, Céret, a smiling town. Plane trees in the irregular central square, orchards of cherry, peach and apricot set about it and within it. It had aroused visions of the paintable for Dufy, Braque, Picasso and Marquet—to name only a few; and one of them, Jerome Brune, had the idea of starting a museum which has since become one of the most remarkable provincial collections of roughly contemporary painting in France. Variety of soft colour accompanies your amblings round the streets; it is hard to tear oneself away from its very feminine charm.

Then the Tech begins to have trouble with mountains, and rumbles away at their feet while Amélie-les-Bains and Palalda on either side of it stand on cliffs. Indeed I should never be surprised to hear that Palalda had fallen heavily into the river. It has the character for drama, while Amélie-les-Bains (its name proudly changed from 'Bains du Tech' after a visit from the Queen of France) is 'spa' from head to foot. Amélie-les-Bains will cure you of all the rheumatisms, troubles with the joints and so on which you can possibly think up. It is in fact open all the year round, since the great mountain masses of Roc de France, Fort de France and the strong ramparts of Mont Canigou protect it from all uncouth winds. It has the virtues and defects of the bourgeois ideas it represents.

There is a wonderful twisting mountain drive you can take from Palalda over Les Aspres to the Prades road, N.116, a forester's remote, silent world. For the rest the scenery up the valley, even though growing more and more abrupt, has had a lively spice of trees, planes, cork-trees, chestnut; in the narrowing bed of the valley fruit trees still shoot their pure blossom and higher up olive trees wave their silver bouquets in the wind. After Arless-ur-Tech and its Romanesque church and sculpture the pace of the climb and the convolutions of the river's course increase steadily. The mountains are still wooded, but now entirely with evergreens. You ascend the redoubtable Défilé de Baillanouse,

hanging by your ear to the mountain-side. Then suddenly you
come upon the last fortified town with a fortress above it to make
doubly sure, Prats de Mollo. It says something for the quality of
the Spanish light troops even in the late seventeenth century that
France should have taken so much trouble to cover this very
difficult approach from Spain. For when you have passed Prats de
Mollo, nothing is left for you but to reach La Preste, turn round
and come back unless you have a date with the local sanatorium
or a ski run.

But for me, at least, this journey into vacancy was not time
wasted. I saw Mont Canigou from a new side, from which he
appeared to show veins of green granite between and above the
forests of pine. This backview of him is not as dramatic as the side
that faces Prades. Here at Prats de Mollo you are already placed
high; but there is a considerable build up of height to Canigou's
mass—Serre Vernet at 6,000-odd, Pic des Trois Vents over 8,000
and others of the same order, snow-patterned still in late spring.
And then by contrast below Prats de Mollo suddenly spreads a
wide, fertile valley, a green brilliant against the cold rocks to
nourish the garrison. Does 'Prats' derive from the Latin 'prata',
the fields?

Towards the end of the day I left the little fortress and its
Gothic church, its aspiring Catalan altar so rich in gilded carving;
and I left it by the west door of thirteenth-century oak, reinforced
by convoluted bands of wrought iron. Down the straight, narrow,
military streets, past the ill-nourished *Place*. High up above the
little town was yet another seventeenth-century fortress, smiling
in the sun, toothless, barkless, like a very, very old watchdog.

*   *   *

The road from Perpignan to Prades and Bourg-Madame, our
westernmost pass, starts in much the same way as those you have
already traversed to the frontier. For anyone who has the time
there are many small delights in the little villages which sprinkle
the plain. Vinça, for instance, has fine carving in its old church.
Marquizanes is surrounded by circular walls and crowned by a
circular castle. And there is romantic Eus, where on a naturally

strong site church, castle and village fortified themselves with
ferocious granite; the villagers were tough fighters and usually
successful in defence, till in 1793 the Spaniards starved them out
after a long siege. Even so, they would not surrender but escaped
to the mountains for further resistance.

It was hereabouts that old Demas caught up with me again with
something to show me a little off the main road, a jolly place
called Thuir, he said, the home of the famous aperitif, Byrrh. I
was wrong to have attended to him, since the tour of the vast
works (with its own private railway) is conducted purely on the
statistical method, in which everything is larger than the last.
What one sees is cask upon cask and vat upon vat, until you are
shown the largest vat in the world (someone has got to have it
anyhow) which holds one million litres of Byrrh. To such a size
has the business grown since 1866, when the vats were pitiable
little brass-bound things barely large enough to drown a well-
grown child.

Yet the place had a private fascination for me, since one of the
Violet brothers, whose grandfather had invented the drink, had
the idea of indirect publicity for their product. He became a patron
of the arts; had an important building designed to hold the *haute-
couture* business of the celebrated Poiret and an art gallery of
which an old friend of mine, Percy Moore Turner, was a director.
It was at the suggestion of the French government Turner
organised the first comprehensive exhibition in Paris of Aubrey
Beardsley's work, which then had considerable influence upon
French illustrators.

A key collector, a Mr. Pollitt was a recluse who lived in West-
morland. Turner saw him, saw his fine collection and won his
support—but on one condition. Pollitt would lend nothing at all
unless the illustrations to the *Lysistrata* were included. Now this
important series had never been publicly exhibited 'for reasons'
(Turner told me) 'which were obvious the moment you saw
them', though their artistic quality could never be in doubt. But
what of the law in France on such matters as indecent drawings?

International lawyers, French government lawyers, the Chief
of the Paris police all had to be interviewed. In the long run a

written opinion was extracted permitting the exhibition of the *Lysistrata* drawings on the following conditions; they must be shown in a locked room of which Turner must keep the key; Turner must personally question anyone applying to see the drawings and satisfy himself on their motives; if he was satisfied, he could let them in and then lock them in until they asked to come out. The show opened, and soon the six first-floor galleries were thick with the smartest crowd of intelligent Parisians.

It was not long before Turner had his first chic applicant. She satisfied him that she had a serious interest in Beardsley's work and had known of the *Lysistrata* drawings without having seen them; so the door was unlocked. When she had finished, she asked if she might fetch a friend, who had an equally lively interest in Beardsley. To this Turner assented on the condition that she, too, would agree to be questioned. The affair then developed like the nursery story of Alice and the cheeses—everyone who had seen them going back to fetch a friend. All went smoothly until Turner, taking a minute's rest from incessant conversation with visitors to the main exhibition, looked out of the window. Crossing the courtyard, he saw Monsieur Lepine, the chief of the Paris police. Simultaneously Réjane, the famous actress who had played the lead in the *Lysistrata* not long before, made her entrance into the gallery. Here was a double risk since some of the drawings, apart from their indecency, were deliberate and recognisable caricatures of Réjane's cast.

Turner went into the attack, and challenged Monsieur Lepine on the motives of his visit so soon as he had asked to see the locked room. Was he here officially or privately? If privately, what interest had he in Beardsley? A thorough examination. And after all, why not? To have been told that the corresponding official at Scotland Yard in 1906 was a Beardsley enthusiast would, in Belloc's words, 'have made one gasp and stretch one's eyes'. But in Paris the improbable can always be true. Monsieur Lepine, in fact, knew his Beardsley very well, was admitted to join the other three, while, outside the door, Turner strained his ears to catch a reaction. Was that a chuckle? Surely that was a laugh? Then, undoubtedly, laughter; and his heart lifted. Soon after the traffic police called to complain of the traffic blocks extending from the Boulevard Malesherbes (where the gallery was) to the Madeleine. Special police had to be called in to deal with the concourse of carriages.

I remember in the early thirties at, I think, the Warren Galleries, an exhibition of drawings by D. H. Lawrence. They included representations of lavatory pans and similar equipment, which were thought at the time to be very frank and true. No extra police were necessary for traffic control.

*   *   *

Having won our way thus far past the striped carpet of wines knotted with fruit trees on their red ground, with old Canigou coming closer and closer till you can see the strands of his snow-white hair beneath his white cap, let us pass through Prades leaving on one side for the moment the three famous monasteries of St. Michel de Cuxa, St. Martin de Canigou and Serrabone. All this time you will be guided by the talkative river Tet, and as you climb the long pull to the frontier, mountain streams will chatter their way down narrow valleys and ravines to add to its strength. For this reason this district is called Conflent—the place where the rivers flow together, 'confluentes' a better recollection of Latin than the German name, Coblentz. Variety of human and natural beauty are on either side. Just as at Mirepoix, I was arrested by a mediaeval gateway and walls, of which the perimeter had been expanded in the seventeenth century. I was rewarded by far more than walls, since they enshrined antiquity in houses and a church with some remarkable sculpture of the fourteenth and fifteenth centuries, which seemed to me to rise above the provincial class. I liked, too, the Latin inscription to Jacques de Formiguières who died in 1306: 'Whoever shall read this inscription let him pray for the soul of Jacques, so that it may rejoice before the Lord with the saints and angels on high. Amen. Thou that seest this tomb, why dost thou not despise mortal things, since in such a place as this is enclosed all that was a man. What thou art I was; what thou shalt be, I am.'

Lest I become ghoulish—there are more gloomy quotes I could

offer—across the square is the Restaurant du Portalet, where I met my best Banyuls aperitif. I do not know about the hotel side of the place; but in matters of food, the patron was discerning. We showed an interest in regional cooking, wondered if we could have a punctual dinner before going in to Prades for the Festival. 'Laisse-moi faire,' he said. How right we were to trust that man and his pâté and his pilaff with river crayfish and other joys, accompanied by the robust white and red Rousillon wines.

As you ascend, Mont Canigou drops behind our left shoulder. If you stay in this country, which has so much to recommend it, you will find an eastern view of the great mountain with, as a foreground, the superb mirror of a great lake. There is a free sprinkle of ruined castles and fortified villages and, at the other end of the scale, spas, and hydro-electric stations. You reach Fort St. Louis, high on a plateau, another old fortified town on the watch for dead Spaniards. Here you balance between the bleak uplands of the Cerdagne mountains and the uplands of the Capcirs, which are bleak too. You are wonderfully remote, except for the seasonal skier—and I understand this is very good country for the slopes are fine; and in the spring innumerable wild flowers celebrate their fertility rites before the high summer pasture grass grows to support the sheep and goats from the lower valleys. All this in a wonderfully brisk air. From Fort St. Louis your descent to Bourg-Madame and the frontier is an essay in gradualness. But there is one little place just off the road and you should visit it for a moment, even if its name does sound like an hiccough.

Hix has a church of quite unusual form. It is triangular with an apse to each side. Some say it is Moorish by origin; others, pointing to the castle of Puylaurens suggest that it was first a military building later devoted to the church; there are other theories. For curiosity, for emotion (if you admit to it) visit this lorn place, since it is as simple as a child's toy, so simple that the architectural mathematics of it surprise you. The village of Hix is quite small; it offers you its quiet, only jewel.

*　　　*　　　*

We must turn back for another look than a chauffeur's look at Prades and for that trilogy of monasteries, St. Michel de Cuxa, St. Martin de Canigou and Serrabone. And first of all a warning about the second. Do not try to visit it after lunch. Not of course, because you will have done anything low like eating too rich a dish; simply because you will have to climb up two thousand feet of foot-track on a horizontal base of three or four hundred feet, and you will climb every foot of it in full afternoon sun. It is made a little the worse on the first climb, since you always expect the place to be just round the next bend; outcroppings of ruined masonry appear every so often, decoy ducks for the optimistic. They tell you at the bottom on an official notice that it only takes thirty-five minutes. I found the villain who had supplied the information, the local *courrier*.

'But it's true,' he said crossly. 'I do it at least sixteen times a day, and surely I ought to know.'

'What you know may be true for you,' I retorted, 'but not for the *sacré touriste* like me.' But he had vanished, light as a deer on another errand, long before my bolt could get home.

These three 'houses' were Benedictine monasteries in origin, of varyingly ancient foundation, St. Michel being the oldest, the proudest, the richest. Their finest history starts with their second foundation after the defeat of the Moors in the late tenth century, and their great missionary days to restore the spiritual and agricultural life of Rousillon. Like abbeys and monasteries all over England, Scotland and Europe these are ruins. The English ruins lie upon the shoulders of Henry VIII and his grasping advisers; as an Englishman I won't try to apportion blame in Scotland. In Europe the monks without question destroyed themselves. Eighteenth-century thought could not accept any longer these cynically reasonable profiteers from an age of faith. Throughout Europe, first the Jesuits for their endless political interference, and then other orders were steadily evicted. What the kings left the French Revolution swept away, selling their goods, buildings, statuary as '*bons d'état*', state property. These three abbeys became stone quarries for the local mason. As towers rotted and fell through roofs, weather got in; columns tumbled, their carved

capitals were sold in such profusion that of the cloister of St.
Michel you will find more in the Metropolitan Museum of New
York and elsewhere than on the site itself. Do not be discouraged
by these disasters of the past. Enough survives to prove the exist-
ence of an individual school of precious quality. Its origins spread
south of the mountains, even to the east; its influence colours
Elne; there is nothing quite like this group outside this part of
France.

The key lies in the arches one finds in cloister and in naves and
aisles, a horseshoe arch, not so pronounced as at Cordova, but
stemming from the same school of Christian architects who kept
their heads in exchange for their right to exercise their profession
in the Moslem manner. Hence their style is called 'mosarabic'; and
when they came to practise again for a Christian setting, their
designs were still redolent of eastern perfumes. As carvers, they
could not forget the patterns of the eastern textiles on which they
had lain down, in which they had dressed, so that the capitals of
their columns might have an origin in some pattern of confronted
lions or hunting dogs woven in Damascus three hundred years
before. Nor is this my personal fancy. The pressure of scholarship
tends that way and towards the assertion that around the powerful
abbey of St. Michel de Cuxa was assembled in the eleventh and
twelfth century a body of artists who, though drawn both from
Languedoc and from over the Catalan border, worked with an
independent identity.

Not only are the arches and the capitals and columns on which
they rest singular in design. So are the towers. The survivor at
St. Michel is tall and slim, sloped inwards at the base for protection. Six storeys of round-arched windows are grouped vertically
in pairs; and of each pair, the upper is the higher and so gives a
lift to the whole design. The number of windows multiplies the
higher the tower climbs till finally in the tall space over all are
pierced two roundels like watchful eyes below the almost Moorish
battlements. This is a spirited flight to heaven.

The arch leading up to the church is set at the foot of thirteen
steps of old unpolished marble, once white now almost golden, a
transmutation of colour from Peele's line: 'His golden locks

time hath to silver turned'—though the change again happened in the way of service. On the round arch flow a course of hunting animals, sinuous in their grace. In the spandrels apocalyptic eagles are watchful, while cherubim and seraphim cover their feet. Within, the effect of the unpaved floor provoked a lovely illusion of golden dust aetherealising direct vision of the long, high, barrel-vaulted roof with its unfamiliar arches. Beyond this golden mist lies the cross-vaulted chancel; aisles with half-round arches support the great weight of the nave's stone roof. In the Lady Chapel is a sculpture of suffering and death, Christ taken down from the Cross; the Virgin's lips are thin with grief. Of the cloisters just enough is left to make you cry because there is no more; enough is left to let you imagine when once you have seen Serrabone what the glory must have been; the little that is left is enough to make you spit upon the memories of those who by their shortcomings allowed such devastation of beauty to come to pass. But possibly, before acquiring the right to spit, one should have done enough research to name at least three offenders.

These three monasteries are in a way complementary. In its glittering world of bright rock and pine, St. Martin raises a tower much like that of St. Michel, though less subtle. The narrow site determines two levels for the building as we see it now, and the cloister is set on the lower. Good capitals in the local style depict the Seven Deadly Sins in the most discouraging way. On cloister level and below the church is the tiny crypt dating back, it is claimed, to the second foundation of 970, the crypt of Notre Dame de la Souterrance: a miniature cathedral of three aisles with their round arches and square piers on which for capitals are pieces which look like half mill-stones set with the curve undermost but in fact are a recognised mosarabic form. In the church above, started in 1009, you see the same form of capital and that the columns of the nave are set on no base but directly upon the floor—another characteristic of this style. All is of extreme simplicity in finish, rough stone and no decoration. The windows of the little apses which conclude the choir and aisles piously illumine the polychrome fourteenth-century statue

Q

of the founder, St. Goderic, patron of the peasants, a perfect example of the men who were sent out to redeem Rousillon from its sufferings in the Moorish wars.

Secret, remote Serrabone is now the richest architecturally of the three, though the youngest daughter of the Benedictine order in these parts who had no dowry. It was St. Michel de Cuxa who dowered her so richly with sculpture and architecture; for never else could so small a place have afforded such glories. Even today it is not on a road; it is in a field three hundred yards above a road, very easy to miss. I found, too, that it was not easy to get directions from the locals since they did not know the answer either.

Here is the essence of the St. Michel school of eleventh and twelfth artists. It is all very well to say that this or that was derived from Syria or Granada. The real question must always be: How well was it done—forget the origins, interesting though they may be. The conventional animals or birds on the capitals, whether for purposes of design they confront one another, whether their bodies for some lost symbolic purpose are linked to one another, whether you see them in pursuit or in repose the drawing of them is such a miracle as to give confidence to us all. It is so much finer than that of the prehistoric caves, so much more subtle in design and in sense of material that we might say with a happy Victorian sigh 'By A.D. 1100 the world had advanced'. Carved in an age of physical misery and suffering these things must be rated as a great achievement.

Serrabone, St. Michel and St. Martin may be complementary. In one respect Serrabone has something which the others have not got, its narthex. Serrabone explains the cloister which St. Michel has lost; St. Michel explains the idea for St. Martin's tower, while St. Martin by its crypt and different levels keeps a concept which one finds again at Mont St. Michel in Normandy —the interpretation of monastic function by levels rather than by horizontal lay-out. Serrabone, the smallest of the three, always the poorest but perhaps favoured like a youngest daughter by the powers of St. Michel, has preserved the detail which proves the Mosarabic root of these three splendid buildings. For where else in France could you find anything which had taken so deep an impress from Cordova as the clustered columns capped by horseshoe arches, their capitals clacking in the lingua franca of Levant art, as you see at this small rich hidden show place, Serrabone. There is something peculiar (in its exact sense) in those deserted places which have lost their grandeur, such as it was. Outside the scope of this book, perhaps a bare hundred miles west, is the superb ex-cathedral of St. Bertrand de Com-minges, once a town of fourteen thousand inhabitants, housing now four hundred. There, too, in their day as at Serrabone they made an effort of a splendid kind—that it failed is no black mark against the concept.

*   *   *

Prades, at the foot of Canigou, is the largest town in the valley of the Conflent; not a place of any size. Apart from its abbey church, it has no distinguished air of antiquity, old though it is. One would suspect a district capital on an invasion route to be a library of war-like tales and stories of heroic bloodshed. True, there are traces of city walls but only to be found with difficulty, so unobtrusive are they. There is a long, narrow street and a turning down to the main square, where beneath the shade of a plane tree you can contemplate the abbey's plain, old face and its single Romanesque tower. And one would have said that this was not enough to constitute charm. Yet when my mind turns back to Prades, it turns with the same sort of affection which the sight of an old lady brings, whose skin has serenely survived the all or the nothing she has encountered in life and who sits comfortably in the shade talking with an amiable smile.

There is no ostensible reason, therefore, why one should stop at Prades, though it makes a very good centre for excursions. Yet for a fortnight, usually in July when the climate is at its enchanting best—a fine sun tempered by fresh mountain air—Prades becomes a centre of international music, when Pau Casals conducts his festival. Then the whole tempo of the place changes. Visitors have come from all over the world, even from distant

Australia and Japan, and of course quantities from America. Conversation is almost exclusively musical and only touches the weather in so far as it might affect the health and spirits of 'The Master'. Would it be too hot for him? Too thundery? Too windy? Too cold? Every evening the townspeople used to gather in the square outside the abbey church amused by the babel of foreign voices as they watched the crowds assemble. But the set piece of the evening was the arrival of 'Le Maître' in the enormous limousine which the town puts at his disposal during the festival. About a penny-worth of everyone's rates went on the purchase and maintenance of this majestic car. They look at it with the pride of a property-owner.

I was lucky enough to hear the story of the Festival from Casals himself. I saw him in the little house on the left at the end of Prades as you leave for Spain; he lives there in what was the lodge to a great house, surrounded by trees and flowers with a quick, bright stream running through the garden. Because Casals is a Catalan, his house has a Catalan name—Le Cant des Ocels—'The Song of the Birds'. And as you ring the bell at the gate, it responds with a musical chime.

The study was on the first floor, a small room into which seemed to have been compressed the memories of a life time. Books in Spanish, books in French, in English. Sculptures and modern drawings. The signed photographs inevitable in any artiste's room. On a window seat reposed one cello—in the nude, one might say—while two others stood sentry in their boxes on either side. There was still room for a baby-grand piano and ourselves.

He was smiling as he sat and talked to us in his slow, beautifully phrased English. Then suddenly I recognised his old special look, which I remembered from his London recitals with Cortot and Thibault in the 'twenties'. He used to glare at his 'cello as if he dared it not to produce the note and the tone he demanded of it. What I had remembered as something almost fierce, I now saw as pure concentration. An episode came back to me from some book telling how in his young days he was reproved for playing with his eyes shut; the audience took him for blind, he was told, and it made them uncomfortable. So even in his earliest years he had this gift of dying to the world as he played. This intense sincerity is something he has given to the festival as its tradition.

You go, ticket in hand, within the church. The high, late Gothic nave and its rhythm of arches and colour prepares your mind for music. Reddish-brown arches are enlivened with decorations painted in green and gold; shadowy side-chapels glow in a half-light of finely carved and gilt altar-pieces, architectural compositions in wood, mainly of the seventeenth and eighteenth century. One I remember has green leaves and gilded grapes trailing round down the twisting pillars. But the high altar crowns the abbey. In four storeys of architecture and sculpture, it clambers its baroque way to the Gothic roof. The general tone of the background is a darkish fawn; but myriad figures and details of carved landscape gleam with gold as they catch the light. Enthroned centrally is St. Peter as Bishop of Rome, clad in red, in its way certainly as dominant, almost as clashingly barbaric, as the statue of Ste. Foy at Conques. This is the backcloth which will occupy your eyes unconsciously during the period of a concert; and perhaps you may come away, as I did, with the picture of two trumpeting angels, gracefully poised for a flight around the world to blow a fanfare of triumphant news.

When Casals established himself at Prades after he had left Franco's Spain from an undisguised dislike of the regime, at first like Paderewski he had a period of silence, not wishing to play until his people, the Catalans, were set free. He refused golden offers to play in America. One day the intelligent part of America made one of those generous actions of which only they are capable today, and said in effect: 'Very well. If you won't come to play to us, we will come and play with you.' So Alexander Schneider, the violinist, negotiated the first Prades festival of 1950. Since then many of the greatest international names have been on the programme—Schneider of course, Szigeti, Clara Haskil, Myra Hess, Clifford Curzon, and others too many to name. One golden night I was lucky enough to hear Casals playing Schumann's Quartette in E Flat Major with Menuhin, Wallfisch and Horszowski beneath the high arches of the scarce-lighted nave and before the dim glow of the tall great altar.

There is a moving practice at these concerts by which respect for the music, the musicians and the church itself are silently united. There is no applause. As the artist comes in you rise to greet him. When he goes out, you rise again. According to your feelings instinctively you remain standing longer or less long. I swear I found those final moments of soundless homage packed fuller with true emotion than any blast of handclaps and bravos in a concert hall. As the tension dies away, one is once more aware of the golden glow from the side-chapels, of the high vaults of the nave, and perhaps once more of those trumpeting angels.

*   *   *

The concert is over. Perhaps you take a chirping or a sedative glass under the plane trees in the square where the lamps light up the undersides of their well-cut, individual leaves against the last of the July night skies. You listen to conversations in such languages as you can guess at, dissecting, for practice fun, the snob from the intellectual, from the intelligent or trivial comment on what you have heard. We were staying out of Prades and the time came when we must find the car and motor the necessary kilometres to the hotel past the gleaming walls of Villefranche de Conflent, gently snuffing the fresh fragrance of the mountain air, seeing the last of Canigou, ghostly under the moon. Next day you must pack and turn the nose of the car towards the northern stars allowing time, if you can, for a last Sardane in the Rue la Loge at Perpignan, for a few more strictly rhythmical sentences from Madame at the hotel there, time, let us hope, for a last *assiette des fruits de mer* at the restaurant.

'And here,' might have said the chronicler of Renaud of Montauban, 'here leave we to speak of Rousillon and of all those fair lands and valleys and white castles, where so many worthy and valiant knights lie slain in discomforting the paynim. King Charlemagne took counsel with the twelve peers of France and they and the host went their way by the city of Toulouse and thence to Cahors. And so they came to Paris upon Michaelmas, whereupon the King made them a great feast and straitly pledged all men that their prisoners be well entreated until the coming of their ransome.'

Index